W9-BGY-364

LANCE ARMSTRONG
& THE 1999 TOUR DE FRANCE

★ ★ ★

BY JOHN WILCOCKSON

AND CHARLES PELKEY

•••

FEATURING THE TOUR DIARY

OF FRANKIE ANDREU

VELO
press

VELOPRESS • BOULDER, COLORADO

LANCE ARMSTRONG
& THE 1999 TOUR DE FRANCE

Copyright © 1999 Inside Communications

All rights reserved. No part of this book may be reproduced, stored in a retrieval system, or transmitted, in any form or by any means, electronic or photocopy or otherwise without the prior written permission of the publisher.

International Standard Book Number: 1-884737-69-2

Library of Congress Cataloging-in Publication Data applied for.

Printed in the USA

Distributed in the United States and Canada by Publishers Group West.

1830 North 55th Street
Boulder, Colorado 80301-2700 USA
303/440-0601; fax 303/444-6788; e-mail velopress@7dogs.com

To purchase additional copies of this book or other VeloPress books, call 800/234-8356 or visit us on the Web at www.velogear.com.

Photography by Graham Watson
Design by Chas Chamberlin

"We can choose to do one of two things.
We can try and break down…
a Tour de France that's been around forever,
or we can try and repair it.
Unfortunately, there's still some people
that want to see it go away,
want to tear it down.
I'm not one of those people.
I want to be part of the renovation….
My story is what it is…
and I try my best on the bike…
and hopefully
it *is* good for the sport.
I hope *so*."

—Lance Armstrong,
speaking at a Tour de France press conference
in Le Grand Bornand, July 12, 1999.

ACKNOWLEDGMENTS

We owe a debt of gratitude to several people who made this book possible. First, we would like to thank our wives Rivvy Neshama and Diana Denison, who either missed us terribly or at least had the good grace not to mention how much they enjoyed our absences for the month of July.

We would also like to thank Frankie Andreu for his insightful race diaries; Graham Watson for his photographs and great company; John Rezell, whose writing contributions helped us all see that this Tour de France had meaning in places well beyond French borders; Chas Chamberlin for his expert design and indulgence when we tweaked a deadline or two; Bryan Jew for his accounts of Bobby Julich's early-season preparation and of the drug problems at the Giro d'Italia; Rivvy Neshama for her skillful copyediting; Lori Hobkirk for riding herd on everyone involved in this book; and our traveling companions David Walsh of the *Sunday Times* and Rupert Guinness of the *Australian*, for putting up with Charles's driving and John's habit of being the last guy out of the press room every night. Finally, we'd like to thank Lance Armstrong, whose courage carried him through an ordeal so difficult that it made winning the Tour de France seem almost easy.

CONTENTS

PREFACE 3

PART ONE — **THE ROAD TO THE TOUR**

A long and winding road 7

A Tour with an American accent? 29

The other Americans at the Tour 39

Doping dominated after the 1998 scandal 45

The 20 teams and their leaders 63

PART TWO — **THE 86TH TOUR DE FRANCE**

Week 1: Toward a new pinnacle 71

Week 2: In the valley of the shadow 115

Week 3: Paris on the horizon 147

Final results 173

PART THREE — **REFLECTIONS**

Interviews with Tour winner Lance Armstrong 177

Lance Armstrong and the cancer patients 193

Festina fallout 201

Armstrong's winning bikes and components 207

A tale of two people 213

Tour statistics 215

PHOTO SECTION — **THE TOUR**

Through the lens of Graham Watson ....after 146

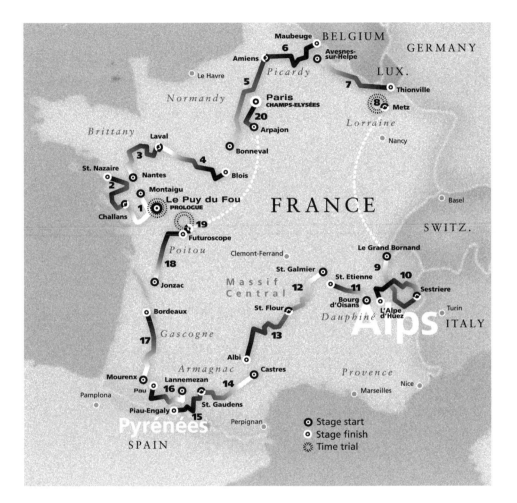

A true American hero

VERY EARLY in the 1999 Tour de France, it became clear that the story of the world's greatest bike race was going to become inextricably entwined with the story of Lance Armstrong. By the finish, after Armstrong had won four stages and taken the Tour by more than seven minutes, the American's victory was hailed as one of the greatest comebacks in sports' history. His dominating success came less than three years after being given little chance to live by the doctors who diagnosed him with an advanced stage of testicular cancer.

This book traces Armstrong's remarkable story from before he contracted cancer, through his recovery and subsequent comeback, to his return to the top of what has been described as the toughest sport in the world. The 1999 Tour was also the one that followed a year of scandal in professional cycling, and all the various doping controversies that dogged the sport are put into perspective in Part I: The Road to the Tour.

In the second part of the book, every stage of the race is reported in analytical detail, with the focus on Armstrong and his remarkable U.S. Postal Service team. Each stage story is complemented by the daily diary entry of U.S. Postal's Frankie Andreu, who was riding his eighth Tour de France. The book includes a 16-page photo section by veteran race photographer Graham Watson, along with maps and stage profiles by *VeloNews* art director Chas Chamberlin.

The book's final part includes two extensive interviews with Armstrong. One examines the difficult and joyous moments he lived through during the Tour itself; the other reveals some of the inner thoughts of the Tour winner, and how he coped with the media hoop-la that followed him all the way to a meeting with the President at the White House. Two other stories, by *VeloNews* senior editor John Rezell, put into perspective the work that Armstrong does in the cancer community. Also in this final part is a detailed look at the drug-related stories that, in the wake of the doping-tainted 1998 Tour, inevitably implicated Tour winner Armstrong—who handled the media's accusations as skillfully as he did his strongest opponents during the Tour's three-week odyssey.

From cancer patient to a true American hero, this is a remarkable story of a young man who has proved an inspiration and role model for thousands, perhaps millions of people around the world.

PART ONE

The Road to the Tour

A long and winding road

OVER THE PAST SIX YEARS, there have been many turning points in the life and cycling career of Lance Armstrong, all of which affected his development as a potential winner of the Tour de France.

Armstrong initially had great enthusiasm for the Tour, winning a stage in his first full pro season at age 21. However, as planned by his then Motorola team, the Texan pulled out of that 1993 Tour at half-distance; and did the same in '94. And by the end of that year, Armstrong wasn't convinced that racing in Europe was what he really wanted to do. He was even saying, "I'm out of here in two years." In other words, after collecting a possible gold medal at the '96 Olympic Games to go with the world championship rainbow jersey he had won in '93, Armstrong planned to quit cycling at the end of '96.

Then came the first turning point in the Texan's journey toward the ultimate goal in cycling. On the first Sunday in April 1995, at that year's Tour of Flanders World Cup classic in Belgium, something clicked inside Armstrong's brain, something that changed his mind. "Now," he said, "I'm in for the long haul."

The Texan's decision was intimately related to the Tour de France, about which he had never previously expressed any strong ambitions, outside of stage wins. But when asked in May '95 what he thought of his future in the Tour, he replied, "I don't know if

I can, but I'd like to contend at some point." Then, in obvious reference to the accomplishments of Greg LeMond, Armstrong added, "I've seen what the Tour has done for American cycling. In fact, that the Tour *is* cycling in America."

Asked about his ambitions for the '95 Tour, he stated, "My goal is to finish the race, and get a Tour de France under my belt. I look at it as an investment for the future."

Armstrong, then 23, was speaking just after winning his third stage at that May's Tour DuPont. "I'd like to do a good Tour this year," he said, "and I'd like to see how I could do with condition like this." He was referring to the way in which he had just scorched the opposition on the DuPont's mountaintop finish at Beech Mountain, North Carolina.

Armstrong realized that climbing is one of the keys to performing well at the Tour, although he believed that the high mountains were never going to be one of his favored terrains. "I'm a big guy," he said. "I'm big-boned…and I can't change that."

The big American had also thought deeply about his climbing style: "I climb a lot out of the saddle, particularly on the steep hills we have at the DuPont. I know the Tour climbs are more gradual…and longer. You have to get in a rhythm." To help develop his climbing style, Armstrong had trained in the mountains of Virginia the week before the Tour DuPont, and he hoped to find time before the Tour to train in the Alps. "I'd like to go and just do climbing," he noted.

The other key to having a good Tour de France is an ability to do well in the time trials. Again, Armstrong had been working hard in this area. Over the 1994-95 winter, he did aerodynamic and power testing with U.S. Cycling Federation coach Chris Carmichael, and he then had a Lotus time-trial bike made to his dimensions. Using this, he placed third at the DuPont prologue, just beating his arch-rival Viatcheslav Ekimov of Russia. He then used his regular low-profile machine to win the DuPont's mountainous time trial in the Roanoke Valley, breaking Ekimov's course record. Other than a very short prologue win at the 1993 Kmart Classic of West Virginia, that was Armstrong's first TT win as a professional.

Looking ahead to the '95 Tour's major time trial in Belgium, the former world champion said, "I'd like to be motivated for that stage. I rode the course the day before Liège-Bastogne-Liège (in mid-April). It's pretty tough, never really flat…and it finishes uphill. It's a strongman's course."

However, the good form that Armstrong enjoyed in April and May of 1995 didn't stay with him through June and July. He *did* finish the Tour de France for the first time— placing 36th overall—but he didn't have the race he wanted. At the Belgian time trial, he finished a disappointing 19th; in the Alps, he made one attack on a downhill, before fading back among the also-rans; and in the stage to Revel, he was beaten to the line by Ukrainian Sergei Uchakov, after a long breakaway. Then, on the first stage in the Pyrénées, Armstrong's Italian teammate Fabio Casartelli died in a horrific crash, which occurred while descending the Port d'Aspet mountain pass. His friend's death deeply affected Armstrong, and three days later, summoning up all his strength, the American scored a solo stage victory at Limoges, to honor Casartelli. On reaching the finish line, Armstrong pointed the index finger of one hand, then both hands toward the heavens. The first words out of his mouth were: "I did it for one person."

Armstrong returned to the Tour de France in 1996, when, sick and out of form, he abandoned the race on a day of torrential rain and cold, less than a week into the Tour. That result was an anomaly in a season when Armstrong, still riding with Motorola, climbed as high as No. 5 in the World Rankings. But changes were ahead. The Motorola team sponsorship folded, and the Texan eventually signed with a new French team, Cofidis, for the following year. He returned to the U.S. in September 1996. His racing season was over, but there was one more official engagement: a media cycling camp, hosted by one of his sponsors, Nike, at Bend, Oregon....

☆　☆　☆　☆　☆

IT WAS THE LAST WEEKEND in September. Blazing sunset maple trees were heralding autumn, but central Oregon was still enjoying a spell of summer heat. Perfect blue skies provided a brilliant backdrop for the nearby Cascade Range and its snow-decked volcanic peaks of Mount Bachelor, Broken Top and the Three Sisters. It was great weather for riding—but what was Armstrong doing here, when his Motorola teammates were laboring at the Vuelta a España, prior to Europe's final flurry of races: Paris-Tours, the world's and the Tour of Lombardy?

The short answer was that Armstrong had been invited by one of his sponsors, Nike, to help introduce a new line of cycling gear. The longer reply would run something like this: "It's been a long year, I was competitive from early February, and I'm now No. 7 in the UCI World Rankings. Motorola doesn't have a new sponsor, and two weeks ago I signed a big contract with Cofidis for 1997. So there's no incentive to carry on training and racing for another six weeks. My season is over...."

Reflecting his off-season mood, Armstrong was relaxed and chatty when he arrived for a Saturday morning ride with a dozen magazine editors, assorted Nike staff and a couple of local racers. He charmed his riding companions on the two-hour loop through the rolling Oregon countryside, and showed a hint of his power on one of the ride's last climbs. Later, while his girlfriend cooled off in the pool at Mount Bachelor Village, Armstrong sat on a condo deck overlooking the Deschutes River gorge, and spoke at length to *VeloNews*.

He first analyzed his 1996 season, which started in February with aggressive performances at the Tours of Majorca and Valencia in Spain; continued in March with a brilliant second place to Laurent Jalabert in Paris-Nice; blossomed in April in the Ardennes hills of Belgium, with a break-through victory at the Flèche Wallonne and second place at Liège-Bastogne-Liège; peaked in May with five stage wins and overall victory at the Tour DuPont; saw sickness in June force him out of the Tour de France; and then revived in July and August with good, but uninspired performances at the Olympics (12th and sixth), fourth places at the World Cup classics in England and Switzerland, and runner-up spots at the Tour of The Netherlands and Eddy Merckx Grand Prix....

VeloNews It's been a pretty tremendous season for you....

Lance Armstrong I would like to think it's been one of my best years. Overall, there were some parts that I was disappointed with—for instance, I was second numerous times. But in terms of consistency, in terms of (UCI) points, it was my best year ever.

VN You said you were going to focus on the spring classics and the Tour DuPont—which turned out to be your best period. On reflection, are you disappointed in quitting the Tour de France when you did?

LA I'm disappointed that happened...that I got sick like I did. I can remember that day I finally stopped. There was nothing I could do. I was physically ill, and I couldn't continue. It's a shame I had to get sick like that, but...it's hard to say how you can control that.

VN What have you learned from that experience?

LA Well, the big mistake was entering the Tour in the condition that I was in—it wasn't bad, but it wasn't good enough, because of the way that the whole season worked...going from February in Majorca to DuPont in May. That's an awfully long time trying to spend at a high level.

I needed a break...and the time between DuPont and (the Tour of) Switzerland was the only time I had. To be out of competition, I lost a lot of fitness. I started back at

Switzerland, and this year it was an extremely hard Tour de Suisse. I felt *good* enough to be competitive, but I was pushing my body above its limit. I just got worn down...and the 10 days between the Tour de Suisse and the Tour de France, I was completely wasted. I started the Tour beat up. Then you had the weather, the extreme conditions...and things only got worse.

VN What do you feel has made you a better time trialist this year?

LA Time trialing takes time, you know. And sometimes I feel old (in this respect). I know I'm not old, but I feel old being on a team with a person like (Kevin) Livingston or Axel (Merckx)—who is younger than I am, and I can see what they feel. In a road race or a hard stage, they're just as competitive as anybody else; but then they get to the time trial, they're four or five minutes behind. I know what that's like. It just takes time...and it's strange because it doesn't seem like it should take time or experience. It's just such a simple and pure event...but the years help. The way I approach time trials now, and the way I approached them before is completely different.

VN How is it different?

LA The comfort level, or the intimidation level. They're fairly intimidating; a lot of times they make or break you. Now I approach them as an event that's good for me, and can benefit me. Especially if it's a harder course. The rhythm of the race changes a lot. And when you get older, you fine-tune your position, fine-tune your cadence. Things like that really help. Then the tactic within the race. If it's a 40km time trial, how do you start? How do you ride the first 10km? Where do you put the emphasis? Back two or three years, I had no idea. My position back then was much different to what it is now. My cadence was different—which would have a lot to do with your power, as well. The more power you have, the bigger gear you can push, and therefore the faster you go.

VN When you're in a time trial, a fairly long one, are you conscious of looking at your heart rate?

LA This year, I never missed a day without a heart-rate monitor. I always wear it, and I always study it—either in the race, or after downloading it. In the time trials, it doesn't necessarily indicate how you're riding. The nicest thing to have in time trials is your splits relative to the others. You can look at speed, you can look at heart rate, but you don't really know where you are until you hear how your peers are doing. That to me is the biggest factor. It can be both good and bad. Say you get the first split and you're a minute down after 10km...that's a little demoralizing. But if they say you're 30 seconds up on somebody, it's like fueling the fire. You go even faster.

VN Has the equipment you've been using helped you go faster?

LA The (Litespeed-titanium-tubed) Blade I used this year I thought was a much nicer bicycle than the Lotus I rode for a good part of last year. In the wind tunnel, it (probably) wouldn't compare to a Lotus, but for me—on the road, riding the bike, accelerating the bike, putting force into the bicycle—it was a much better bike. For me, it was super-stiff, handled well, very clean...aero'...still traditional, still had all the tubes there, nothing too fancy. But stiff. I like that stiff ride.

VN Do you study other riders' styles—like Chris Boardman's?

LA Everybody studies Boardman. He's such a perfectionist with the event of time trialing and his position. People say, "Why don't you get in a position like him?" Well, it doesn't quite work like that. My back doesn't quite bend over that far, and my back has that hump that his doesn't have. And my shoulders are a little wider, and a little bigger than his.... You can't compare. But you can look at everybody's position, take a little something from it.

VN Moving on to teams, at what point in the season did you feel that you really had to look for another team?

LA We started talking in April, just to have a start with some teams...because most of the deals are done in the summer. First of all, I never thought that this team [Motorola] would not have a sponsor. In talking with my agent, I said, "You know, let's talk to some teams, just so we have something there." But, of course, I'd never thought that we'd need to go to a foreign team. To me, it's mind-boggling that Jim Ochowicz doesn't have a team.

VN At first, it looked as if you were going with Festina. What happened?

LA A couple of different things happened. They were pretty aggressive in the beginning. They were the first team to really step up and make a good offer. And they were certainly the first team that I was very interested in going to. I think our timing was just off. I was gonna give Jim Ochowicz at least until the end of August. These guys gave me an offer in June and wanted a decision in July. That was a good six weeks before I was ready to make a decision. Then the fact that they had a super Tour de France meant I was expendable. I took it hard, because that was the team that I was most interested in.... I was amazed when my agent called and said that they had dropped their offer.

VN When did Cyrille Guimard and the Cofidis team first come into the picture?

LA The first time I heard about Guimard having a team, and that the rider he was most interested in was me, I read in *VeloNews*. I thought, "Hmm, Guimard? I don't know...." That was probably at the time when I just assumed I was going to Festina, and, if not, Jim was going to find something else. So I didn't take (Guimard) too seriously. Then Festina withdrew their offer, and Och' wasn't finding anything, and then Guimard was there and still very interested. So we began to talk seriously. And that was around the time of the Olympics.

VN Was there any problem when you asked to bring some teammates with you?

LA No problem. From day one, I said Livingston is coming with me. And later on, when I wanted to bring Frankie (Andreu), it really wasn't a problem...although the second guy is always a little harder. But they'll be pleased with Frankie...and Kevin.

VN What are Kevin's qualities?

LA I think his best quality is probably his head. The kid is so down to earth. His morale is always good. It's amazing. You can be in the nastiest hotel, staying in the worst city in the world, and Kevin is there at the dinner table, goofing off. Here I am ready to strangle someone, and Kevin's there rolling up a bread bullet and throwing it at somebody. The kid is always up. That's important for me, to have somebody who keeps up my morale, and the morale of the team.

Physically, I think he's gonna be a damn good rider. The second half of this year, he already started to show it. We raced on the national team together; he always had talent in the climbs, looked good on the bike. Then, at the end of '95, when I asked him to move to Austin, he came down and set up shop, and we trained all winter.

VN Is Guimard wanting you to change anything in the way you train, prepare yourself?

LA We haven't talked that deeply. I got measured up, and he looked at the position. My position will change a little bit. We haven't talked much about training or planning the season, yet. Of course, they've already said that the Tour is the No. 1 goal...which is fine. Guimard runs a program completely different from what I've been used to, and I understand that going in. So I'm trying to prepare myself for that. I really am motivated to learn French and be part of this program. They expect me to be a leader, and part of that is communicating. Just approach it like that and I think everything will work out.

VN What does Guimard expect from you at the Tour?

LA He doesn't expect me to win. Guimard's a smart man. He thinks that I could win (the Tour) someday. I don't even know if *I* think that. This year, he expects me to be very good, to get results....

VN In terms of stage wins, or top 10, or what?

LA He wants me to play a key role in the Tour de France, whether that comes from being very aggressive in stages, or being conservative and riding to a sixth-place finish. I don't know. I think it's better to be a little more aggressive and try and win stages. If you can win a stage or two, that's much better than being sixth or seventh in the overall.

Again, it's not easy to be top 10 in the Tour de France.

VN Have the unexpected things at the '96 Tour given you a different perspective on your own chances in the Tour? Winner Bjarne Riis, for instance, five years ago was a domestique with Guimard....

LA Look at the whole Tour, all the way down from (Richard) Virenque to (Laurent) Dufaux.... These guys are good riders, but are they Miguel Induráins, or Greg LeMonds? I don't think so. All year, you're competitive with them, and the only difference is that your seasons are arranged a little differently. But you know you can be competitive with them. And look at the Tour of Spain, you see the caliber of rider that's achieving a certain result, and in my mind that could be me. So that gives you something to think about. Not only in the Tour....

If I took my DuPont form, or my Ardennes form, and put it into, say, the Tour de France, this year, where would I be? I can ask myself that. I'd probably be pretty good, I think. With the time-trialing legs I had, and the climbing legs I had, I think things would have been fairly successful. But that wasn't how things were arranged. I just have to move those legs from May to July. And in July, the weather is much better suited to me....

VN People would say to that, "July may be a better season for you, but the Tour de France has 20km climbs, which DuPont doesn't."

LA I'm right with 'em. I'll second that. I have no idea. Not only do they have one 20km climb, they've got three in one day, for three days in a row. Listen: That's a big question mark. I'm a big rider. I'm a big guy, in terms of weight....

VN Has your weight changed much in your four years as a pro?

LA It's gone like this (*indicating up*), then down, and then back up again. And this year, towards August, it started to come down again. I started this season heavier than ever, with a lot of muscle. I was at least 80 kilos (176 pounds), but still very competitive. I did more power training this winter than ever. Now I've learned that my body reacts very quickly to any sort of power training. For instance, if I did a month's worth of swimming workouts, my upper body would be twice as big as it is now. And it's already too big for cycling. So I have to be a little more careful with my power training.

VN What do you call power training?

LA Weightlifting. And some fixed-gear stuff. I was doing a lot of fixed-gear training this winter. And in and around Austin, fixed gear can be.... If you talk about a 42x15 on some of those climbs that we have in the Hill Country, you're barely getting 40 rpm— that's just power training. In the big mountains, I think weight is a big issue.

VN Have you thought about changing your diet?

LA The diet is the first thing that comes to mind, of course. It comes down to mathematics. If you're gonna ride an hour, you're gonna need X amount of calories. Any more, and you're putting on weight. Any less, and you're taking off weight. I understand all of that. I have no problem being serious with training, to ride, say, seven hours, seven days a week. But if you told me I can only eat a 100 grams of pasta, and one piece of bread, and you can't have a glass of wine with your dinner—that would just kill me. But that's what it takes, I know.

I think that's something this new program will help me with. I know the French are fanatical about weight. When Laurent Fignon was on that program, they would hide food from him, because they thought he was too heavy. That's the reason why I think Riis won the Tour this year—his weight. Last year, he was third, and he was super-skinny already. And I've heard estimates of him losing as much as five kilos (11 pounds) from last year to this year. That's mind-boggling. I was talking to Riis at Leeds (in August), and we got to talking about weight and kilos, and he told me: For a 10km climb, one kilo is one minute, roughly. In his case, on a 20km climb, that's 10 minutes!

☆   ☆   ☆   ☆   ☆

THREE DAYS AFTER this interview, in which he was talking about what it would take to win the Tour de France, Lance Armstrong's world suddenly narrowed. It was October 2, 1996. That morning at his home in Austin, Texas, the 1993 world champion coughed up a lot of blood into the sink. He was scared, rang his doctor, and made an immediate appointment. To help the doctor make a diagnosis, Armstrong told him that he was also experiencing some soreness in one of his testicles. He thought nothing of the fact that for as long as he could remember one testicle was bigger than the other. Like thousands of other men, he believed that was "normal." And maybe it was. The doctor said that Armstrong's soreness was "most likely an infection."

As a precaution, the doctor sent his patient to the radiology department of St. David's Hospital for some ultrasound tests. "Then they did X-rays on some other parts of my body, which struck me as odd," Armstrong said. "They told me to go immediately back to the doctor's office. This was after closing hours. He showed me the ultrasound and told me we had a problem. I was in complete denial. I thought, 'It can't be. I'm only 25. Why should I have cancer?' After two or three minutes, I asked. 'What do we do? When do we start?' I checked into the hospital the next day."

Armstrong successfully underwent surgery to remove the malignant testicle, but a CT-scan showed that the cancer had spread into the abdomen; also, there were spots of the cancer on his lungs. [It was later revealed that the "spots" were a dozen golf-ball-size tumors.] It is unlikely that the reason for one testicle being enlarged for several years was a tumor. The disease is fast-growing—but if it had been diagnosed earlier, the chances of a complete recovery were almost 100 percent. Although Armstrong had been examined hundreds of times in the previous 10 years, he said he hadn't had his testicles checked since eighth grade. However, with the cancer now in an "advanced" stage, Armstrong's oncologist Dr. J. Dudley Youman, from the Southwest Regional Cancer Center in Austin, told him that the cure rate was "between 65 percent and 85 percent."

Five days later, on revealing his condition to the world, Armstrong said in a press conference, "As strong as I feel, there are moments when I cry all the time. Days are up and down." The day before the October 8 press conference, Armstrong underwent four hours of "very aggressive" chemotherapy, the first session in a course of treatment that would continue until Christmas '96.

"I have been assured that there is no reason that I cannot make a full and complete recovery." Armstrong said. At his side during the press conference were his mother Linda Walling, who raised Lance as a single parent; his then girlfriend Lisa Shiels, an undergraduate at the University of Texas in Austin; and his agent, Austin lawyer Bill Stapleton, who moderated the press conference. Stapleton said, "Lance has been unbelievable these last few days," referring to Armstrong's very upbeat attitude through what had been the darkest week of his life.

"I don't want to sound too confident," Armstrong said, "(but) I intend to beat this disease, and further, I intend to ride again as a professional cyclist."

When asked about the causes of his cancer, Armstrong did not want to speculate. "Nobody knows," he said. "All we know is that we can fix it."

However, Armstrong did speak about the rigors of his chosen profession. "What athletes do may not be that healthy, the way we push our bodies completely over the edge to degrees that are not human," he said. "I've said all along I will not live as long as the average person. The Tour de France is not a 'human' event, but it doesn't give you cancer at 25."

Despite all that, Armstrong went on to say, "I'll be out on the bike next week. The doctors have said I can do 50 miles at a time." This positive attitude was a strong reason for believing that Armstrong would be back as a world-class athlete, maybe as soon as the following year, when he was due to lead the new French-based team, Cofidis.

The Cofidis directeur sportif, Cyrille Guimard, joined the Austin press conference by telephone to say that he, the team sponsor and the riders "are all with you, Lance, in this latest competition." The same sentiments were expressed by Armstrong's Motorola team boss, Jim Ochowicz, who also passed on wishes for his speedy recovery from Eddy and Axel Merckx.

Indeed, there was unmitigated support for Armstrong from the media throughout Europe. Journalists have a high regard for the Texan and just wanted to see him back in the peloton, bringing the kind of excitement to the sport that few others can provide.

Testicular cancer, which Armstrong was fighting, is one of the less-publicized forms of cancer. It is the leading type of cancer for males ages 15-34, with an estimated 7200 cases per year in the United States, about 4.9 percent of them fatal.

Armstrong's first oncologist, Dr. Youman, said, "Armstrong is in an advanced stage. Twenty-five years ago, the disease was almost universally fatal. But today we have a better than 90-percent cure rate, unless it has spread to the lungs. That's why he is at 65-85 percent."

Everyone was optimistic, but the prognosis would become much darker....

$$\star \quad \star \quad \star \quad \star \quad \star$$

'AT FIRST, THE CHEMO' WAS EASY ... but the news was getting worse," Armstrong recalled, during an interview in early December, two months after the initial shocking news that he had testicular cancer. He said that the worst day came when the doctors told him he had two lesions on the brain that required surgery.

"I sat there in the office with my mother and my girlfriend," Armstrong said. "When they came in and told me they had bad news, that it was in my brain, I started bawling...but you know, every step along the way, even when the news was bad, there was still a positive side to it. That day they said the two spots were small and easy to get to. So, I said, 'Let's get them.'

"Every time they give me news, they tell me what the chances are. And you know what? I don't care what they are, as long as I have a chance. I can't imagine what it's like for those patients who have to hear the doctor say there's no chance. I can't imagine it. I don't care if I have a 50-percent chance of recovery, or 40 percent or 10 percent or 5 percent. Just give me a chance to live, that's all I want. Just give me a chance...."

During this interview with *VeloNews* senior editor John Rezell, the telephone rang just about every five minutes, with an irritating fake urgency echoing throughout Armstrong's spacious Mediterranean-flavored villa on the shores of Lake Austin. Life bustled within the elegant walls, and there was no time for constant interruptions. So the phone rang on and on, slowly fading from consciousness.

Armstrong had just returned home from a shopping spree with close friend Dan Osipow and his wife Claudine. They were greeted by the thumping bass from the stereo in Armstrong's mammoth home-entertainment center, the controls at the hands of Cofidis teammate Frankie Andreu, who sat sprawled across the spongy sofa recovering from his early-December training ride under the warm Texas sun.

Soon, Armstrong's girlfriend Shiels arrived. Shortly afterward, a neighbor, Ann, from down the cobbled street of this gated community, popped in to help Shiels select which shoes to wear for the upcoming Korbel Night of Champions featuring the *VeloNews* Awards—where Armstrong would receive the North American Cyclist of the Year award.

Aside from his chalky, pale complexion and the horseshoe-shaped scar atop his shining chrome-like dome, few signs showed that Armstrong had spent the previous two months battling for his life. His handshake remained firm, his spirits bubbled and his voice boomed with confident strength—although his always intense blue eyes appeared to probe deeper than ever. "I feel great," Armstrong said, as he settled into the chair at his desk.

Despite all the comforting distractions of everyday life, though, the battle at hand never strayed far from Armstrong's thoughts. It was the first week of December, and in four days the champion would face his final scheduled round of chemotherapy at University Hospital in Indianapolis. The first two of the four rounds were like child's play, so much so that Armstrong found time to sneak out of the hospital for dinner a time or two. But the reality of the fight hit hard in the third round, when his reaction to the chemotherapy was violent enough to prompt doctors to sedate him. On his return to Austin for two weeks of recovery, the man who had been so open to the media with his personal war canceled all interviews but one. Although all the tests proved that Armstrong was winning his fight and was recovering rapidly, there was no telling what the final week of chemotherapy would be like.

"I've never felt the cancer," Armstrong said, his face quickly drawn to a whiter shade of pale, while his eyes dropped to concentrate on a paper clip dancing between his fingers and the desktop. "But I've felt the chemo'. And it's hard. It's *real* hard."

In the blink of an eye, it became apparent what Armstrong and others with cancer mean when they say cancer is something that will be with them forever. It changes a person at the core, no matter how well the physical impact can be hidden.

"It's kind of hard for me to understand how sick he is, because every time I see him he's so upbeat and so healthy," Andreu said. "It's like he's just setting the world record for curing cancer. But we've talked, and Lance has really made me aware of a lot of things in life we take for granted."

An eight-foot-tall cardboard get-well card smothered with signatures of well-wishers leaned against the wall in the foyer. Meanwhile, back at his agent's office in downtown Austin, four boxes stacked four feet high sat near secretary Stacy Pounds's desk. They contained most of the letters sent to Armstrong—all but those from Armstrong's cancer-inflicted brethren. Armstrong kept those at home never far from his reach.

"There are dark days," Armstrong said, "dark moments that aren't easy. But I read those letters and I walk out of this room motivated to continue the fight."

On this day, a stack of some 30 e-mail messages arrived. The outpouring of support had been moving and enlightening. What immediately captured attention was the common theme throughout the messages of those who have been touched by Armstrong's career. It's a theme Armstrong never understood before.

"Ninety-nine percent of those start off with, 'You inspired me...'" Armstrong said. "I mean, I knew people knew about me, some say they've seen me race, or seen me on TV, or read about me, or a friend has told them about me...but I've never realized that I inspired people. That's not something I think about when I'm racing. But now I know I have the ability to inspire people, and even if I never race my bike again, I just want to keep on inspiring people. I know I can do that, and that's a big reason to live. There are a lot of reasons to live."

And throughout the day, Armstrong recited the reasons to live, all aspects of life that had passed by him as unnoticed as the wonderful French countryside during a frantic stage of the Tour...until that day in October when doctors told him he had testicular cancer.

"Yesterday was a good day," Armstrong said, despite the fact that rain drenched central Texas under cold, cloudy skies the day before this interview.

"There *are* no bad days," he explained. "Some days are better than others, but there aren't any bad days."

After Armstrong's final scheduled chemotherapy, doctors planned to tell him the next step. It could be more chemotherapy, or radiation treatment, or surgery. Or, as Armstrong hoped, a clean bill of health. With pleasure, he noted that there is a scale from 1 to 100 that doctors use to rate a patient's chemotherapy. "Most people score around 30 to 40," Armstrong said. "My doctor said I'm as close to 100 as he has ever seen."

The doctors in Indianapolis raved that they had never had a cancer patient begin a fight in such fine physical condition. Armstrong hesitated to give that aspect too much credit. "I was doing some incredible things late in the year," he said, "and I had the cancer in my lungs at that time. It's something you just aren't aware of. That's the scary part of it."

Many argue that mental attitude is a major key to fighting cancer. Armstrong agreed: "I always raced 90-percent physical, 10-percent mental. This is closer to 50-50. And that extra 40 percent is a lot of work. It's very hard."

Still, every step of the way, in the face of challenging revelations, Armstrong's positive attitude had shone through. "Now, the chemo' is getting harder, but the news is getting better," he said.

Once again, Armstrong's mind wandered off to a place that so many thousands of cancer patients know.

"I feel changed, yeah, certainly," he said. "The letters from cancer patients, a lot of them say that we're the lucky ones and everyone else isn't. We get to see how precious life is. I don't know if I buy that, but I understand it. You know, the sun setting on Lake Austin. That's a reason to live. Getting up each morning. That's a reason to live. Starting a family someday. That's a reason to live."

So each day, no matter how up or down Armstrong felt, he would ride his bicycle. Just a few months before, he did so totally for one reason: It was his job. He admitted freely then that he wouldn't ride if he didn't have to. That had changed. He was loving his bicycle, loving riding, even if it was the hardest part of his battle.

"Wow," Armstrong said, as he autographed a photograph for charity, taken during the Olympic road race in July. "Look at how buff I was. Look at those muscles. That's all gone."

On this day, during his daily 90 minutes on the bicycle, Armstrong, Andreu and teammate Kevin Livingston rolled up to a woman cyclist. "She was in her 40s and looked like she just started to ride recently," Armstrong said. "The second we got to a hill, she dropped me. That's hard. That's frustrating.... It's frustrating, because every time I'm on my bike, I suffer. And I don't usually suffer."

It was part of the battle and one of the areas in which Armstrong hoped to make a difference, as he forged into the public arena to bring about cancer awareness.

"I know how easy it would be to just give up, and a lot of cancer patients do that—because the treatment is so hard," Armstrong said. "It takes so much from you, much more than you can imagine. And it would be easy to just sit back and wait for the next round. But exercise is so critical and helps you get through the treatment. And that's what I want others to know, that you have to fight with everything you have. Every day."

The man who could mount a battle on his bicycle worthy of any heavyweight title bout now had a new arena; and he had learned from the people in those ranks.

"A lot of people don't like going to the Regional Cancer Center down in Austin, because the people in there don't look so good. They look like people who are dying. It's a pretty rough scene," Armstrong said solemnly, before his eyes began to sparkle and a smile crept across his face. "But I *love* going there. I *love* seeing all those people and they love seeing me. Man, those people are fighting for their lives. Talk about fighters. Talk about heroes...."

Then slowly, the impact of his battle crept to the forefront again. Armstrong stared out the window of his office, to the sunset lighting up the forest-green hills and the wind gently ruffling the leaves of the palm trees lining his driveway, which leads to the garage. Inside the garage, a shiny black Porsche and a sparkling Harley-Davidson motorcycle sat as testament to his success as a bicycle racer, just as the luxurious home did. Armstrong cringed and bit his lip.

"You know," he said, "the house, the car, the money, the fame...I'd give it all away in a second to be cancer-free. I really would. I'd be homeless if I had to. It all really doesn't mean anything unless you have your health. That's everything."

Then, more of the perspective that escapes most 25-year-olds just rolled from the young Texan like the fresh, sparkling current of a mountain stream: "I know I'm going to still make mistakes in the future. I'll still do stupid things from time to time, and they may hurt some people. But I know I'm going to try not to. I'm going to try to be the best person I can and make the most out of every day—and always look at the positive side of things. Always."

★ ★ ★ ★ ★

INTO 1997, THE POSITIVE NEWS regarding Armstrong's cancer continued. The intense chemotherapy had worked. The cancer was in remission, and the 25-year-old cyclist could start thinking again about the rest of his life. Asked about the thoughts that were going through his mind in those early months of recovery, Armstrong said in an October 1998 interview, "When I first learned I was sick, my first thought was that I can't race again, which looking back was a silly thought. I should have thought, hey, I won't live again. Now it's reversed. If they tell me I'm sick again, if I relapsed, I wouldn't think about the sport at all. I'd forget it immediately. I'd only think about my life. It's a change for me. I love the bike, the sport. But if I have to give it up again, that's all right, too. Life is more important."

It took great strength, both physical and mental, to come back from cancer and to again set his sights on cycling....

"I had a lot of support," Armstrong continued. "Not only did I get e-mails or cards or phone calls...I got a lot of books. I can't say that I read all of them, and I can't say that's what—learning something from a book—got me through my dilemma. The well-wishers and the cards and the messages helped a lot; I was very motivated by that.

"But at the same time I think the desire I had on the bike before—to be a champion, to try and win races, or work hard—is the same desire that helped me when I was sick: 'This is something I want. I want to get better.' And you can't be taught that...necessarily. Maybe you can be pushed in a certain direction, but it's a unique quality that you have to be born with.

"I think the training, both physically and mentally, helped me tremendously. When I was diagnosed (with cancer), physically I was in great shape. And mentally, having been a professional cyclist—which I consider to be a hard life—the *grind* of a cyclist helped. I was able to set goals for myself with cancer like I had in the past. The doctors also set objectives for me, for my progression."

Recovering from cancer wasn't enough for Armstrong; he wanted to help others achieve the same goal, by whatever means it took. The result was the setting up in the spring of 1997 of the Lance Armstrong Foundation.

"Most people think it's a charity for testicular cancer," Armstrong said. "Which it *is*;

but we thought from the beginning that we needed to be a little broader than that, because it accounts for so few cancers…less than 4 percent of all cancers, all of them in young men. We wanted to broaden it, so we went with urological cancers, which is testicular, prostate, renal and bladder. We focus on educational awareness and research. With the awareness alone, if you look at cancer now and cancer 10 years ago, there's been a lot of progress. A lot of that progress hasn't been so much in science, but a lot in awareness. If someone is diagnosed even a month or two months earlier, then their chances of survival sometimes go from 50 percent to 90 percent."

The setting up of the foundation gave rise to another positive turn in Armstrong's life: At the kick-off promotional event, he met a tall, willowy blonde named Kristin Richard; within a year they would marry. "The foundation was trying to do their first event," she explained, "and they needed a sponsor. And my client—I was working for an advertising and public-relations firm—was looking to sponsor an event in Austin. So I heard about his foundation, and sold the idea to my client.

"And then I met him at the press conference that kicked off the event and the relationship with my client. He had no hair, he was as cute as a devil…. I knew nothing about cycling. I had no idea who Lance was. I had no idea about anything. Nothing."

It didn't take long before Richard learned more about pro cycling and the role played in it by her new boyfriend. Armstrong took her with him to Europe that July, where they paid a short visit to the 1997 Tour de France.

"Yes, that was funny," she remembered. "We came to the Tour de France, when we did our trip to Europe, and we got out of the car in the *village*—Cofidis was Lance's sponsor at the time—and we get out, and he is completely bombarded by photographers and microphones and everything, and I thought, why are they so interested in him? And then I started to learn a little bit more. It was very amusing, as I had no idea of any of his accomplishments, and nothing about cycling."

It was a few weeks after that trip that Armstrong stepped up his training with Carmichael—now an independent coach—and together they decided that early 1998 would see his return to the European peloton. But, first, he needed a team. Cofidis had got cold feet regarding Armstrong's future, and wanted to make a big deduction in his reported $1 million a year salary.

"Back at the end of '97, we really started to look around September time, because the deal with Cofidis was not going to be worked out," Armstrong said. "It was better that I left, with everything that transpired there. There were a few interested teams: Telekom was moderately interested; TVM had a definitive offer, and that was on the table;

Mercatone Uno was a pretty serious consideration.... Of course, all of these were for basically no money. They said we'll take you on the team, so they were at least offers to get going again. And the Postal offer was there as well, which I accepted."

So, it was in a U.S. Postal Service team jersey that Armstrong made his big comeback in February 1998, in the south of Spain. Asked what it felt like to finally be back in a race, Armstrong replied, "I didn't like it. I was uncomfortable in the Ruta del Sol. I'd been away from the sport for 18 months, except for attending a few races as a spectator, so there was a lot of attention and a lot of pressure that I was uncomfortable with. I was very glad when the first day was over...I felt a huge sense of relief."

Armstrong was back racing a bike, but did he think that perhaps for that first, five-day race, his expectations were too great? "Yeah, yeah, probably were," he said. "It was a confusing time. It was hectic to come back, with the coverage. But in hindsight, I should never have put any pressure on myself then."

In Spain, Armstrong pushed himself to ride with the best on a mountaintop finish, and managed to finish an unexpected 15th overall. The next race up for him was the eight-day Paris-Nice in France. Again, he had high expectations, but came in only 23rd in the Paris prologue. The next day, in bitterly cold, wet conditions, he came to another turning point in his career. This time, he decided to quit. It looked like cycling was not for him.

"When I stepped off the bike in Paris-Nice, the people that were there agreed with me that that would be the last time I would race a bike in Europe ever again," Armstrong stated. "I was pretty convinced of that, as was Frankie (Andreu), who has probably been my closest friend over the years, and been around me the most. When he saw me, he said, 'I think I've seen you do your last race.' It wasn't a sad moment, and I think he was happy for me at the time. He wanted what was best for me. If that was racing bikes, great. If it wasn't, that's great also.

"Again, I was confused. But I was relieved in a sense...because it was cold. But I felt a certain sense of relief that night, flying home (to Nice)."

What was the first thing he did after leaving the race? "I called Kristin and said, 'I'm coming home.' I didn't have time to explain, so she was confused—didn't know whether I'd crashed or what."

"He called me when I was in the supermarket in France," Kristin recalled. " But I didn't know if he was hurt, or something had happened in our family and he had to come tell me directly.... And then when he came back, I had known his sense of confusion.... He just wasn't sure that was what he really wanted to do with his life. So I think that was just a moment where the confusion just culminated, and he needed to step back and take a break. He thought he maybe needed to retire, but he just needed some time, to adjust and think."

The couple returned to Texas, with Kristin knowing she had to prepare for their early May wedding. A week later would come the Lance Armstrong Foundation's annual charity weekend, which included a Friday night criterium, and a 100-mile mass ride, the Ride for the Roses. But for several weeks after quitting Paris-Nice, Armstrong was uncertain about his future in cycling.

"I knew we had the Ride for the Roses in Austin," he said. "There was a race, and I knew I had to train for the race—and *that* I had to do. So at some point I knew I had to unpack my bike. I eventually unpacked it, stopped playing so much golf, stopped drinking too much beer, and then started to *slowly* train, just for fun, just with friends, for two hours a day at the most.

"And then we got this idea of doing a training camp in Boone, North Carolina, with Chris (Carmichael) and Bob Roll. [A former Tour de France rider with Ochowicz's 7-Eleven team, Roll was then competing mainly in mountain biking.] And that for me was the turnaround, I think. To be there, in that environment, with terrible weather—and when I say terrible weather, I mean in the 40s and raining, for eight days. We never had a break from the rain. Terrible conditions that I never would have ridden in in the past…but I was there, I said we're going for a training camp, I'm going to train and see if we can get going again. To see if I want to do it, to see if I have fun, to see if I love the bike.

"And I think I discovered there that I *do* love the bike. And that I can get through conditions that are just terrible. It didn't hurt to have Bob there. He was keeping me entertained the whole time. I left there a different person. And at that point I decided to race in Atlanta, and that was sort of the beginning of it all…."

Armstrong had taken another turn. He raced in the Grand Prix at Atlanta, working as a team rider for his Postal Service teammates. He then traveled to Southern California for his marriage, and even trained on his wedding day, preparing for the race in Austin.

"It was not a huge race, and I suffered bad in that format. I hadn't done a criterium in years, and I'd never done one at nighttime. I really suffered," Armstrong recalled. Nonetheless, he did win the 56km race, cheered on by thousands of frenzied Austinites. "That was the first time that I felt that 'rush' from winning, I hadn't felt since the Tour DuPont in '96. So it was a long time [two years]. That helped…."

With that boost, Armstrong returned to Europe in June, with a vow not to quit another race. That was his attitude going into the four-day Tour of Luxembourg. It worked out even better than expected….

"When I called Kristin after I won the first stage in Luxembourg, she said you don't sound very happy," Armstrong said.

"I, of course, was screaming and dancing around the house," his wife interjected.

Armstrong explained, "Winning is not the same as it used to be. But I think it's a good thing, in that before I would win, and I would be so, so high, and then I would come to be too low. And it was difficult for me to be consistent. Whereas now when I win, it's great and all, but I know that the sport can forget so quickly, and you're only as good as your last race. And you have to race again the next day. You have to defend the jersey, and in Luxembourg I had to defend the jersey, so there was no point…. I guess it was nice to win, and win against a professional field in Europe, but I knew it was a stage race, so…."

Armstrong went on to win the Luxembourg race; and right after that he won another stage race, the Rheinland-Pfalz tour in Germany. Those successes convinced him that he wanted to continue racing as a pro cyclist. He had just a one-year contract with the Postal Service, at a fairly low base salary. So he entertained offers from some European teams.

"After I had won in Luxembourg and in Germany, I started to look for offers and options, speak with a couple of teams. And still, they're not interested. The director of the Rabobank team, Theo De Rooy, said, 'Yes, we want you on our team, but first we have to talk to Rabobank.' And the sponsor says, 'We can't have him. If he gets sick again, it's bad publicity.' So I said, okay. Same thing with Mapei. The director (Patrick) Lefévère says, 'We want him on our team.' Dr. Squinzi, the Mapei boss, says, 'No, he's bad publicity if he gets sick again.'

"What do I have to do?

"The best one, though, was (Roger) Legeay at Crédit Agricole. He was very interested, I have to give him that. And we started talking, and he said, 'Well, what do you want?' And I told him the money, and he says, 'But that's the money of a *big* rider.' And I said, 'I realize that.' So I said, okay, you're right. And obviously it didn't work out. So, it's been interesting.

"I think if I had not signed with Postal, I think I would have found a place somewhere. But it's amazing this sport, when you've proved you're competitive again, you've proved you're strong, proved you're healthy, they either think you want too much money, or you're bad publicity if you get sick again. And at a time when the sport has just been beat up beyond anybody's wildest of dreams (by the Festina Affair at the 1998 Tour), I like to think that I represent what's good in the sport. At least a good story. Somebody that has come back from near-death that is incredibly healthy…I think that the story is good for the sport. And they want to talk about *bad* publicity. Maybe I missed something along the way...."

What the European teams did not understand was that Lance Armstrong was just developing his capabilities in 1996, when cancer put his career on hold. And if they had bothered to open their eyes, they would have seen that the 1998 Armstrong had even more to offer. Speaking in October '98, he explained. "I'm a lot lighter than I was in '96, but in '96 I was the heaviest I'd ever been. Not so much fat, but just bulky.... I won Flèche Wallonne at about 79 kilos (174 pounds), and now I'm about 72 kilos (158 pounds), so it's about 15 pounds difference. When you talk about climbing, and numerous climbs, that's all the difference right there."

Those skeptical teams must have been regretting their words, when they saw the lighter, more determined Armstrong come in fourth at the '98 Vuelta a España, after matching the best climbers in the high mountains. Was it the 15 fewer pounds that made the difference?

"That probably helped," Armstrong answered, "but again, people haven't stopped asking, 'How did you climb like that?' But in the past I've never tried to climb like that. When the team says, okay, you do the classics...and then do DuPont in the middle of May, it's difficult to come back to be in top form in July. But for chrissakes, I won Flèche Wallonne. I've been there every year in Liège, I've won the world championships and DuPont, I've climbed (well) in Paris-Nice. It's not as if I came off the flatlands of Holland, never seen an overpass...."

He was then asked whether having cancer had made a difference to the way he looked after himself, particularly in terms of what food he ate.

"No. I wish I could say yes," the Texan replied. "I eat healthy because of the weight issue. My main motivation for eating well is not because I had cancer. It's because I don't want to be fat and get dropped on the climbs. That might sound funny, but they help each other, I suppose. If there's evidence that eating poorly causes cancer—which I'm sure it does some of the time—in my situation I don't think testicular cancer is related to hamburgers and margaritas. I don't know to what it's due. It's certainly not occupational or diet-related."

In concluding this interview, which was conducted a couple of days before Armstrong raced to a brilliant fourth place in the 1998 world road championship, he was asked if he thought a pro cyclist's lifestyle was healthy. He replied, "It definitely doesn't add years to your life. I'm almost certain that 10 years as a pro, doing the Tour de France and big events like that, takes years off your life...but is that compared to a life of smoking and drinking, which takes 20 years off your life? It's a question of what you choose to do. I don't think much about it. I'm very protective of the years that I have left—I don't know how many I have, but I don't want to lose any of them. It's a job, and it's what I've chosen to do."

☆ ☆ ☆ ☆ ☆

AND SO ARMSTRONG TRAVELED a long, involved, often treacherous journey from his early days as a talented, but unfocused pro cyclist to the summer of 1999, when he stood on the brink of a serious assault on the Tour de France. On the way, he lost a friend in a terrifying race accident; he fought and survived a near-fatal cancer; he met and married his perfect match; he overcame a long period of self-doubt about returning to a career in cycling, before making a second comeback; he set up and fostered a successful cancer-awareness foundation; he coped with the skepticism and dishonesty of certain team sponsors; and through it all he had to summon up the strength to train harder than ever before, to be ready for his sport's ultimate challenge.

The Tour de France is 23 days long. Every day except two, the 180 selected riders from 20 teams race for up to seven hours. Three of the days are devoted to individual time trials, an event called the Race of Truth, because each competitor has to race against the clock entirely alone. Doing well in the time trials is a make-or-break for a potential Tour winner. Equally as important is the ability to climb the high mountain passes of the Alps and Pyrénées, where the less-talented riders can lose tens of minutes each day to the true mountain goats. Then there are the fast, flat stages, on which a contender needs the help of a strong team to control the many attacks. The Tour is a daunting athletic venture. It's one that Lance Armstrong felt ready to conquer in 1999.

A Tour with an American accent?

ONE YEAR AFTER SOME of its darkest secrets were aired to a shocked worldwide audience, professional cycling had a chance to display its brighter side when the 86th Tour de France started at Le Puy-du-Fou on July 3. And leading the way in the "good news" department looked likely to be the top American prospects, Lance Armstrong and Bobby Julich.

The race organizers dubbed this the Tour of Redemption, in the hope that no more drug-related scandals would sully the Tour's high-profile reputation. Toward that end, the Société du Tour de France announced at a June 16 press conference that one complete team (TVM-Farm Frites) and five individuals (including Richard Virenque), all of them tainted by doping-related investigations, would not be invited to the race. Another team (the Vini Caldirola-Sidermec squad of Francesco Casagrande) had its invitation revoked the next day.

As if this self-inflicted expiation weren't enough, fate also stepped in with a few of its own body blows. On June 20, the 1997 Tour champion, Jan Ullrich, announced he would not start, after the right knee he injured in a spectacular fall at May's Tour of Germany forced him to quit the Tour of Switzerland. And Ullrich's announcement came two days after his Danish teammate, 1996 Tour winner Bjarne Riis, crashed and broke his arm in the Swiss tour, and a week after Marco Pantani, humiliated by his blood-test expulsion from the Giro d'Italia, let it be known that, for certain, he would not defend his Tour title.

Not since 1956—when three-time defending champion Louison Bobet pulled out before the start—had the Tour begun without a past winner on the start line. Back in '56, that situation allowed a French regional rider, Roger Walkowiak, to score the biggest upset win of the past 50 years.

In 1999, only two of the 180 starters had ever stood on a Tour podium: Julich (third in 1998) and Swiss Alex Zülle (second in 1995). Of these two, it seemed that Zülle had yet to recover from the seven-month suspension that resulted from his part in the Festina Affair, and his admission that he knowingly used performance-enhancing drugs, including EPO. Julich, however, said he was ready for the challenge. Although he had been hindered by injuries and allergies, the Cofidis team leader showed in June that his form was ascending. He would start the Tour as a favorite to step up from third to the top place on the Paris podium.

Challenging the 27-year-old Coloradan were a dozen other potential winners, headed by two former Giro d'Italia champions, Mapei-Quick Step's Pavel Tonkov of Russia and Polti's Ivan Gotti of Italy, and two former Vuelta a España winners, ONCE-Deutsche Bank's Abraham Olano of Spain and Banesto's Zülle. The others who looked set to challenge for the yellow jersey were Armstrong (U.S. Postal Service), Dutchman Michael Boogerd (Rabobank), Swiss Laurent Dufaux (Saeco-Cannondale), Spaniard Fernando Escartin (Kelme-Costa Blanca), Italians Stefano Garzelli (Mercatone Uno-Bianchi) and Giuseppe Guerini (Telekom), and Kazakh Alex Vinokourov (Casino).

I N A MODERN TOUR, all-around team strength plays a huge part in determining the eventual outcome, and as the countdown to the prologue began it was looking more and more that the U.S. Postal Service squad might be the strongest of all. Why, the American team? Well, just look at its June results....

At the Dauphiné Libéré, the Postal men (without their "classics" riders Frankie Andreu, George Hincapie, Marty Jemison and Christian Vande Velde) battled to the end of the eight-day stage race with the Casino team of eventual winner, Vinokourov. After Armstrong won the prologue, his teammate Jonathan Vaughters went with the key breakaway on stage 2, then took the lead from Vinokourov by dominating the demanding Mont Ventoux time trial (with Armstrong, Kevin Livingston and Tyler

Hamilton also placing in the top 10). After defending Vaughters's yellow jersey for the next two days, the Postals just came up short on the last mountain stage, with Vaughters cracking on the very last climb, but still finishing second overall.

Then, at the four-day Route du Sud, the Postal team was even stronger. First, Hamilton and Armstrong placed second and fourth in the short time trial; then Vaughters again went with the race's key 19-man stage 2 break; and when Armstrong and Vaughters finished one-two on the last day's mountaintop finish, Vaughters ran out the easy overall winner from Rabobank's Dutch-Aussie, Patrick Jonker.

Meanwhile, at Spain's Tour of Catalonia, Hincapie came in third, third, second and third in four mass-sprint finishes.

Putting together the two halves of the Postal team—the classics men and the climbers—looked like making a winning combination for the Tour. Its first-year directeur sportif Johan Bruyneel finally chose a team aimed at winning the yellow jersey—seven Americans, Armstrong, Andreu, Hamilton, Hincapie, Livingston, Vande Velde and Vaughters, along with their strong Danish teammate Peter Meinert-Nielsen, and Frenchman Pascal Deramé. The one surprise was the non-selection of Jemison, especially as the Utah rider had just taken the stars-and-stripes jersey at the USPRO Championship in Philadelphia. His absence was explained by team manager Mark Gorski: "Marty isn't always a team player. And we can't start the Tour with anything less than 100-percent commitment to the team."

With or without Jemison, it seemed certain that the Postals would have the best team of climbers in the race, at least judged on their performance in the final stage of France's Route du Sud. That stage finished atop the 16km-long Plateau de Beille climb, where Pantani dropped everyone in the 1998 Tour.

Speaking shortly after his stage win from Vaughters on June 22, Armstrong told *VeloNews*, "Our attack was planned, but we didn't know what Jonker and the other guys (from the stage 2 break) would do. Tyler set a hard tempo at the bottom (of the climb), then Kevin made *very* hard tempo. Only five of us were left: Kevin, Jonathan, me, Jonker and Gilles Bouvard. Then, Jonathan and I attacked, and rode the rest of the way together. We probably went a bit too early...about 10k from the top."

Looking ahead to the Tour, Armstrong said, "I'll try and do a good prologue, then stay out of trouble for the first week—try to avoid crashes and mechanicals. Then comes the Metz time trial (on July 11); that's the big objective. I looked at the course the day before the Amstel Gold Race (in late April). I rode two laps of the course. In my head, I've divided it into three sections. The second part has a 3- to 4-

kilometer climb that's pretty hard, out the saddle. And all three parts have fast technical downhills. It's definitely a strongman's course."

Looking ahead, it seemed that Armstrong and Julich would be two of those strongmen. To prepare themselves for the challenge, the two Americans—who are both based in Nice on France's Mediterranean coast—had very different journeys through the spring....

RMSTRONG'S FOCUS on the 1999 Tour really started in September 1998, when he not only came in fourth overall at the Vuelta a España, behind Spaniards Abraham Olano, Fernando Escartin and José Maria Jiménez, but in doing so he matched Europe's very best climbers. Looking back at that race, Armstrong told *VeloNews* in March. "Last year's Vuelta came as a complete surprise to me." Surprise or not, it gave Armstrong—inspired by his team's new directeur sportif Johan Bruyneel—a goal for 1999: The Tour de France.

With the Tour his season's focus, Armstrong didn't plan on getting any big results early in the year—neither did he plan on a run of bad luck. The Texan dislocated his collarbone in the first stage of February's Tour of Valencia; and shortly after, he collided with a car while on a training ride in Nice.

He slowly got back into shape and managed to ride Paris-Nice in mid-March, but only as a training exercise. Discussing that period in his preparation, Armstrong said, "I didn't have big ambitions, so it wasn't especially frustrating. The bad luck with the crashes and stuff, *that* was frustrating."

Looking ahead to the Tour, Armstrong said, "It's a whole new challenge.... I mean, the Tour de France, whew. I'll give it a shot. I don't want to make any predictions overall, but I'd like to win a stage again and factor in the overall. Top 5 or 10, I don't know....

"You have to be careful with a beast like that. Make no mistake about it. I'll be very motivated when it starts, but until then...."

Following Paris-Nice, Armstrong would normally ride the spring classics, in which he has done so well in the past. Instead, his focus was on training for the Tour; but he was going so well at mid-April's Circuit de la Sarthe stage race in France—winning the time trial and only losing the race overall because of an untimely puncture—that he decided to compete in one World Cup race. This was the Dutch one-day classic, the Amstel Gold Race. Here, Armstrong showed his best aggressive strength, making the key breakaway and, after being foiled by Rabobank's team tactics, finishing second in a very close sprint to Dutch champion Boogerd.

In early May, Armstrong was back in training at his Nice, France, home…which wasn't what he really wanted to be doing. "I'm feeling good for the moment, and would have liked to have been racing," the U.S. Postal Service leader said, "but the team's calendar of events in May—Four Days of Dunkirk and Tour de l'Oise—isn't that appealing."

Since his second place in the Amstel Gold Race in late April, Armstrong had raced just once, at the German classic Rund um den Henninger Turm, at Frankfurt on May 1. "The race was pretty negative, as Telekom controlled everything for (Erik) Zabel," Armstrong noted. "I didn't feel that great, anyhow…."

Speaking from France on May 8, the Texan said, "I am training hard, and getting ready for our alpine training camp in a week or so." It had been three long, eventful years since Armstrong last competed at the Tour de France. And four years since he raced through the Alps. He got a reminder of what to expect when he and his U.S. Postal Service teammates Hamilton and Livingston spent five days in mid-May riding the first few mountain stages of the Tour.

"We did the two Alps stages, to Sestriere and L'Alpe d'Huez," reported team director Johan Bruyneel, who followed the three riders on their long road trip. "Everyone looked good. The idea was to reacquaint the riders with the long mountain climbs. It was a good thing we could combine the training with riding the stages."

Besides the long, tough alpine stages, the Postal trio also rode the last part of the stage to St. Etienne, and then the six-climb stage through the Massif Central from St. Galmier to St. Flour. Bruyneel said that the weather wasn't great for the trip, but he was "satisfied" with the outcome. "Now, they know what to expect," Bruyneel added.

The weather was also wet in the Pyrénées the following week, where Armstrong covered the six-climb stage from St. Gaudens to Piau-Engaly on his own, in the rain, in a seven-hour session. The information he gathered from these road trips would probably prove invaluable when he was in the Tour itself…

Armstrong flew back from Europe to Texas on May 25, where he attended the charity banquet for the Lance Armstrong Foundation in Austin, rode the BMC Software Downtown Criterium the next night (he finished second), and the Ride for the Roses charity ride on May 30. "The ride weekend was a great success from a fund-raising point of view," Armstrong said. "We raised $1.1 million, which is considerably bigger than last year."

After that whirlwind visit to Texas, Armstrong and wife Kristin flew back to Nice on Memorial Day. With the Tour de France only a month away, Armstrong would now focus on his climbing strength even more than he had been. To measure his form, Armstrong and training partner Livingston had been making regular visits to the 12km Col de la Madone, near their Nice base, to do all-out time trials. Two weeks before the late-April Amstel Gold Race, Armstrong conquered the Madone climb, in terms of time and power output, very close to what he recorded shortly after coming in fourth at the 1998 Vuelta a España. Then, on his training ride May 8, Armstrong managed to increase his power output by 2.3 percent over his pre-Amstel ride. And by late May, before the trip to Texas, he increased his power output by another 4.8 percent, coming within a minute of the unofficial hill record set by Tony Rominger in 1994, when the Swiss twice broke the world hour record.

On returning from Texas, Armstrong and Livingston did five- and four-hour training rides in the hills behind Nice, before they left for the eight-day Dauphiné Libéré race. There, Armstrong would win the prologue time trial, finish fifth in the Mont Ventoux time trial, second on the final stage, and eighth overall. That was quite a performance after going into the Dauphiné with virtually no racing in the previous five weeks. He admitted that. "Just training for most of the month before, plus my trip to the States, threw me off. But I rode into it...."

By the end of the Dauphiné, the Texan was more like his old belligerent self—particularly on the final stage, the day after teammate Jonathan Vaughters lost the race lead to Casino's Alex Vinokourov. "The stage started uphill," Armstrong said, "and we were a little pissed when Casino rode a hard tempo...a little too hard. Everyone was mad."

Armstrong's reaction? Yes, he went on the attack, being joined by two climbers: third-placed Italian Wladimir Belli of Festina and Spaniard Joseba Beloki of Euskaltel-Euskadi. Casino, apparently aided by the Lotto-Mobistar team, had to work hard to bring them back.

Then, after La Française des Jeux's Christophe Bassons had won the stage in a long, solo break, Armstrong convincingly took the field sprint for second.

Armstrong's Dauphiné was all the more significant in that he acted as a team rider for four days, devoting his efforts to helping Vaughters keep the race lead he won on the Ventoux. Such selfless work would no doubt be reciprocated by his teammates at the Tour.

After the Dauphiné came the four-day Route du Sud in the Pyrénées—where

Armstrong would take the final stage and help Vaughters win the overall. This would be followed by a week of training with Livingston at Nice—riding long hours, and not very intensively.

"I don't need the intensity," Armstrong said. "My engine is good, and I'm ready to go!"

As if to conform those words, Armstrong did his Madone hill-climb test just before leaving for the Tour. The result was more than encouraging: He broke Rominger's record by 43 seconds, and developed a power output of 490 watts—right up there with five-time Tour winner Miguel Induráin.

Armstrong was ready for the Tour.

JULICH, TOO, HAD A VERY QUIET START to the season, and by mid-April, he had chalked up only nine days of racing. To put that into perspective, most European pros at that point in the year had chalked up between 30 and 40 days of competition. It wasn't planned that way, though.

In his first race of 1999, Spain's Ruta del Sol in February, Julich suffered a freak ankle injury, and it would turn his spring schedule upside down. But typical of the Cofidis rider, he turned the negative into a positive, and emerged from the early season with a new training program, and a sharpened focus on the Tour.

Julich was anything but focused when he returned to Europe from Philadelphia in January, after a winter when he married his long-time companion Angela Morgan, and bought a new house just outside their adopted hometown of Philadelphia.

Speaking to *VeloNews* in the hushed lobby of the elegant Hotel Bedford in Liège, Belgium, during the spring classics, Julich said, "We settled on the house on the seventh of January, moved in on the eighth, and I left to come here on the 13th, so you can imagine how flustered I was...just so much stuff to do.

"When I came over, I don't think that I was really ready yet. It seemed like the Tour de France was too far away...too far away to start making the major commitment that it's gonna take to win the Tour."

That was before the Ruta del Sol. During the first stage, Julich dropped his chain while shifting from his big chainring to the small, and when his left foot jerked down from the top of the pedal stroke to the bottom, Julich injured his ankle by doing "an action like pointing your toe really hard, and the two bones in the back of the ankle kind of clacked together." The result? An overstretched muscle and a hematoma.

His injury was originally misdiagnosed by an MRI technician, but when Julich finally saw a specialist in Monaco, he was ordered off the bike for two weeks, followed by several more weeks of rehabilitation.

"He [the specialist] told me that I'd have two weeks off my bike and I'd probably have pain for five weeks.... I wound up having pain for six weeks," Julich recounted between sips of strong Belgian coffee. "But that allowed me to refocus and have a lot of time when I wasn't riding my bike to really think about what it's going to take for me to win the Tour de France this year."

The biggest adjustment that he made? "I bought an SRM system, which allows you to look at your watts [power output] as well as your cadence and heart rate," said Julich. "The training that I've done with that system since my injury has been a huge benefit, because I'm concentrating more on the watts, which I think is where I lost the Tour last year."

Julich was visibly excited, while talking about the new focus of his training: generating more power. "I really enjoy my training now," he said. "I'm motivated. It's a great, great idea.

"So, hopefully, my heart rate will be lower and I'll be more comfortable in a bigger gear," he explained. "If I can put on 15, 20, 30 more watts at my threshold, even if I am spinning, still that's going to be much more of a benefit than just trying to do the same old thing that I've done in the past. I realize that what I've done in the past wasn't so bad, because I got third in the Tour de France; but I've looked at my weaknesses and I really determined what it is going to take for me to win the Tour."

Whatever it takes, a confident, more powerful Bobby Julich seemed to be ready to tackle the Tour—thanks to a minor injury. "I'm totally convinced that this is a positive thing that happened," he said, "and with my career, it always seems that setbacks turn into more of a blessing in disguise."

So instead of his season starting in February, Julich didn't really start racing until early April, while Italy's Giro del Trentino in late April and Switzerland's Tour de Romandie in early May represented the real launching point for his slow build-up to the Tour. And as others used these short stage races as a final tune-up before the Giro d'Italia, Julich placed a quiet 30th (4:37 back) at Trentino and 27th (12:00 back) in Romandie.

Julich thought that his light early-season racing schedule would work out to his benefit. But a difficult May ended with a disappointing performance at the Bicicletta Vasca in Spain, May 26-30. On the first stage, Julich was one of several top riders to miss a split in the field, finishing more than 14 minutes behind the leaders. On the second day, he lost another six minutes, and finally quit the race on day three.

Prior to the Spanish race, Julich had been troubled by a sore throat and swollen glands. "It was definitely confirmed as an allergy problem," he told *VeloNews* on June 3. That day, Julich was in Como, Italy, seeing his chiropractor to help treat the problem.

And so with just a month remaining before the start of the Tour, Julich was confident that his preparation was back on track, as he headed into the Dauphiné Libéré, starting June 6. His results at the eight-day French race were only a little better, but as the Tour drew closer, Julich told *VeloNews*, "I feel great. I feel like I've been coming along well the whole time."

He was confident despite his lack of results. Fortunately, he dealt with similar setbacks in the 1998 season. "Plans are just a guideline to keep you on track," he said. "But you've got to be able to go with what's dealt to you, and go with any situation."

Indeed, his situation started to look better during the Route du Sud, less than two weeks before the Tour. Julich was strong enough to go with what turned out to be the race's key break on day two, and he did well enough on that familiar climb to the Plateau de Beille to place 10th overall in the four-day race.

It was then back home to Nice to rest up and complete his last-minute training before the start of the Tour—which he would start as one of the prerace favorites. "This is what I've been thinking about since the '98 Tour finished," he said. "It'll be a relief to finally get it underway."

What he didn't reckon with was arriving back home fatigued—due to, Julich believed, his allergies coinciding with his biggest block of racing and training. "I was extremely tired," Julich said, "so I knew I had to rest." That would mean his starting the Tour somewhat below his high level of 1998.

SO THE 1999 TOUR WAS SHAPING UP to being not only the most open race in years, but also one of the most exciting. It brought to mind the '87 Tour, which started without defending champion Greg LeMond (recovering from gunshot wounds) and developed into a nail-biting contest between Frenchman Jean-François Bernard, Spaniard Pedro Delgado and, the ultimate winner, Irishman Stephen Roche. The 1999 Tour looked like it would be just as gripping, and this time a new generation of Americans held center stage....

The other Americans at the Tour

AFTER BOBBY JULICH'S THIRD-PLACE finish at the 1998 Tour de France and Lance Armstrong's fourth place at the Vuelta a España, it was a given that these two would be the American focus of attention at the 1999 Tour. But what about the other half-dozen U.S. riders who would toe the start line on July 3? What were their ambitions and goals, and how would they fit into the big picture? To find out, we spoke to the Yanks who would ride in the shadows—but also could have their place in the spotlight.

FRANKIE ANDREU: The helper

WHEN ASKED WHAT WERE HIS GOALS FOR THE 1999 TOUR, the first words out of the mouth of U.S. Postal Service veteran Frankie Andreu were: "I figure I've ridden seven tours, each with 21 days, so that's 147 opportunities to win a stage. I have no Tour wins, so I need to change my track record." Over the years, Andreu, 31, has come close to stage wins, but his main duties always have been to protect his team leader and help lead out their top sprinter.

And when he has been in position to bid for a stage win, the tall Michigan man often has acted unselfishly—like in the long Tour stage to Autun in 1998, when Andreu sat back as French teammate Pascal Deramé attacked from the 13-strong break they were both with. Andreu chased down all the counterattacks, giving Deramé the chance to bid for victory—which eventually eluded him.

So Andreu is realistic about his chance of a first stage win. "There are bigger fish to fry," he said. "With Lance (Armstrong), Kevin (Livingston), Tyler (Hamilton) all going for the overall, it will take a lot of sacrifice to keep them fresh and in the front during the Tour."

The same goes for most of the flatter stages that could be "winnable" for Andreu: "As much as I have personal goals to win, my job will be to do leadouts for George (Hincapie), and keep our G.C. guys in contention. You can't do well without help, and I am the helper."

TYLER HAMILTON: Into the unknown

ALTHOUGH THE FRIENDLY NEW ENGLANDER IS ALREADY 27, and this would be his third Tour, Tyler Hamilton is very much like the new kid on the block. He didn't start cycling until he was in college, and 1997 was his first full season of racing in Europe. And after he placed second to Jan Ullrich at the major time trial of the 1998 Tour, he knew that bigger things awaited him. "I'm excited," he said, about the upcoming Tour. "For the first time I have form and feel 100 percent. I didn't have that in previous years."

Hamilton—short in stature but high in ambition—was speaking in April, before a final build-up to the Tour that would include a week's training with Armstrong and Livingston in the Alps, another few days alone riding the climbs in the Pyrénées, along with stage races like the Dauphiné Libéré and Route du Sud. But despite his personal ambitions, Hamilton was realistic about the U.S. Postal Service team's major goal.

"Lance is the No. 1 guy going into the Tour, and I'm ready to sacrifice for him without a doubt," he said. "But we need to have two or three guys going into the Tour with chances for the G.C.

"I still have to see what I'm capable of…. I want to say I'll be climbing in the front group; I think a top 15 is possible. But, for me, climbing takes a little longer to grasp than time trialing."

Hamilton *has* shown good climbing skills, such as in the 1998 Tour of Catalonia, but at the immediately following Tour de France, sickness prevented him showing his true climbing strengths. He felt that his intestinal problems were conquered, and he said he is now much more health conscious. "You have to be careful what you're eating and drinking," he stated. "So I now make sure that I always wash fruit, for example, before eating it."

His sensational 1998 time-trial performance would make Hamilton a rider to watch at Metz on stage 8; but the stage he was really looking forward to was the one a couple of days later that finished on L'Alpe d'Huez. "When I rode Alpe d'Huez in '97," he remembered, "the crowds were just totally crazy; I never imagined anything like that. I didn't even feel my legs…it was such an adrenaline rush."

GEORGE HINCAPIE: Ready and willing

BETWEEN APRIL 1998 AND APRIL '99, George Hincapie's capabilities grew exponentially. It began with his outright victory at the First Union USPRO Championship in Philadelphia; continued with his challenge for the yellow jersey in the first week of the 1998 Tour; and climaxed with his fourth-place finishes at spring 1999's Paris-Roubaix and Ghent-Wevelgem classics.

So what could the North Carolina-based New Yorker realistically expect from the 1999 Tour? "I'd like to win a stage," he said with his customary modesty, "and maybe go for the yellow jersey for a day—but there are lots of factors."

One of those factors was Hincapie's duty as a team rider. "We have three leaders this year," he said, referring to Armstrong, Hamilton and Livingston. "And I'll be taking care of one of them." That means sheltering his charge from the wind, say, on the early parts of mountain stages.

But Hincapie himself would be protected during the first week, and expected to win a stage. In the past, he would equate a stage win with a field sprint; but the "new" Hincapie is not only more confident, he's more savvy. "My chances are better sprinting from a small group," he said.

Hincapie said that he was happier with his form than in 1998, even though his efforts in the spring classics had made him more tired. He was enjoying a recovery break at home until mid-May, when he'd use Britain's Prutour as a build-up to defending his USPRO title; while, again the same as last year, he would race the Tours of Luxembourg and Catalonia before the Tour de France.

Given his newfound confidence, Hincapie, who'd be 26 a few days before the Tour, would be ready for the ride of his life the first week of July.

KEVIN LIVINGSTON: Morale booster

IN MORE WAYS THAN ONE, the U.S. Postal Service's Kevin Livingston is following in the footsteps of his former Cofidis teammate Bobby Julich. They both rode for Motorola in their European team debuts, and both rode the Tour de France for the first time in 1997. Julich—18 months older than Livingston—came in 17th, while Livingston was 35th. in 1998, it was Livingston's turn to be 17th, while riding exclusively for team leader Julich in the mountains.

Now with the Postal Service, hired to be the team's top climber, Livingston could again be riding as a support rider—this time for Lance Armstrong, who a few years ago persuaded Livingston to move to Austin, Texas. They often train together in the winter, and in the summer, they both live in Nice, France. As their lead-up to the Tour, they planned to spend a lot of time together. Along with teammate Tyler Hamilton, Livingston and Armstrong were due to spend a week training in the Alps, followed by two tough French stage races: the Dauphiné Libéré and Route du Sud.

If all went according to plan, the happy-go-lucky Livingston would be riding alongside the best climbers at the Tour. He now has a different master, but the Missouri native could again improve his Tour finish. Maybe not the 17th-to-third leap achieved by Julich, as Livingston still needs to improve his time trialing, but what was certain was that Livingston's cheerful demeanor would be a factor in helping Armstrong's morale in the quest for the yellow jersey.

CHRISTIAN VANDE VELDE: The young talent

ONLY 22, MIDWESTERNER CHRISTIAN VANDE VELDE is on the fast track to fame. With a long family pedigree in cycling, and his own strong background in track racing, Vande Velde now has his sights set on the grand tours.

Without pressure from his Postal Service team, he comfortably finished 90th in September 1998's ultra-mountainous Vuelta a España, and he was now on target to ride his first Tour. He said that his big test would come at June's Tour of Catalonia—"If I'm good (there), I'm sure I'll be going to the Tour."

The prospect of tackling the world's toughest and most-publicized bike race didn't faze this tall, confident young man. "If I'm given the opportunity (to ride), I won't turn it down. And I'm not going to be bummed if I don't do it (this year). I'd just be proud to be on the team."

If he did make the team, Vande Velde was confident that he'd be ready. "I don't know if I'll have to do the whole Tour," he said, "but I would be very pleased to finish, and get in a good time trial at the end."

And given Vande Velde's position as a world-class pursuiter—he was planning to ride the World Cup track meet in Texas in late May—perhaps the Tour's 7km prologue time trial would be a goal. But, he said, "I've not thought about that."

He *had* thought about the mountains, though. "My climbing has come 'round two-fold since (the Vuelta), and my weight's down four pounds compared with the same time last year. I didn't eat huge meals in the winter."

Part of the inspiration to lose weight came at the end of last year's Vuelta, when, Vande Velde remembered, "I was five pounds lighter than I'd ever been in my life, and the team doctor says, 'You're still fat!'"

So, if his chance did come to ride the Tour, the youngest member of the Postal Service team could be expected to be not only lean, but ready to surprise the world with his great talent.

JONATHAN VAUGHTERS: On the way up

IT SEEMS THAT JONATHAN VAUGHTERS HAS BEEN AROUND FOREVER—but he wouldn't be 26 until just before the Tour. He was a brilliant junior racer, often out-climbing the seniors, in the early '90s; had three seasons of trying to make it in Europe with a minor Spanish pro squad; and then enjoyed a win-filled 1997 season at home with Comptel-Nutra-Fig that saw him end the year on top of the National Racing Calendar rankings. And 1998 should have seen him riding his first Tour de France....

Then, just before *La Grande Boucle*, Vaughters badly gashed his left leg at a stage race in Germany, preventing him starting the Tour. "I didn't come around until the world's," said the bean-thin Coloradan, referring to his excellent seventh place in the world time trial championship in October.

So 1999 seemed destined to be the year when he made a real breakthrough in the European ranks. He was riding well at Spain's Semana Catalana—"I attacked with (Peter) Luttenberger on the second-last day, and I was going to miss the last day so I could be ready for the Critérium International the day after," he revealed. "Then, that night, I came down with the flu."

So Vaughters, who was hoping to shine in the Critérium, had to miss the two-day race put on by the Tour de France organizers. A few weeks later, he returned to Colorado the day after figuring in the long, opening breakaway at Liège-Bastogne-Liège, to have a wisdom tooth extracted.

The "tooth thing," as he called it, had probably weakened his immune system. With that now behind him, along with four weeks of power training from his high-altitude

Denver home, Vaughters would then tackle his two major objectives for the season: the eight-day Dauphiné Libéré and the four-day Route du Sud in France. And as a past winner of the world's highest hill climb—up the 14,264-foot Mount Evans in the Rockies—Vaughters had targeted the Dauphiné's time trial to the top of Mont Ventoux.

If he did well there [he won!], he would be expected to ride the Tour. And what would he do there? "I'll play more of a worker role for Mr. Big Shot," he said, referring to Armstrong. "The first week will be a struggle for me ... then I can do what I'm good at [climbing]. I hope I'd be one of the guys entrusted to help (Lance) in the later stages of the mountains."

Doping dominated the year after the 1998 Tour scandal

I T IS NO EXAGGERATION TO SAY that the 1998 Tour de France was defined not by competition but by scandal. That scandal, triggered by a seemingly routine early-morning police inspection of a team car driven by Festina team soigneur Willy Voet, showed the extent of cycling's long-rumored drug problem. The police discovery of more than 400 vials of Epogen, human growth hormone, testosterone, and an assortment of other drugs triggered a slew of arrests, confessions and lengthy ongoing investigations. The so-called "Festina Affair" also marked the beginning of a concerted effort by cycling to "clean up the image" of the sport. But the 12 months following the '98 Tour showed that the problems of cycling transcended a mere question of "image," a point underscored by the end of the 1999 Giro d'Italia, when Marco Pantani, the man widely credited with rescuing the 1998 Tour de France in its darkest hour, was himself implicated in scandal.

A ROUTINE STOP?

The problem of doping in cycling—indeed in most sport—is not new. Bicycle racing in particular, with its intense aerobic demands, seems a natural candidate for those promising to give athletes an edge over the opposition. With time, the varieties of drugs became more and more sophisticated: amphetamines in the 1950s, '60s and '70s; steroids in the '80s and, perhaps the most frightening development, EPO. This is a pharmaceutical form of recombinant Erythropoietin, a naturally occurring protein produced by the human kidney that, in turn, triggers the production of red blood cells by bone marrow. Manufactured by the American pharmaceutical giant Amgen under the brand name Epogen, recombinant Erythropoietin has provided near miraculous benefits to patients suffering from extreme anemia—a red-blood-cell count lower than 29 percent of total blood volume. But in a healthy adult—with a normal hematocrit level of between 37 and 46—a boost in the number of red blood cells can provide a noticeable jump in aerobic performance. Too much of a boost can also pose a serious threat to health as the viscosity of blood rises, making it increasingly difficult for even a healthy heart to pump this artificially thickened sludge through the vascular system. Indeed, in the late 1980s and early '90s, the drug was implicated as—though never proven to be—a factor in the deaths of several apparently healthy cyclists.

With a history of doping behind it, the sport attracted the attention of France's Minister of Youth and Sport, Marie-George Buffet. Buffet had specifically mentioned cycling when urging French legislators to more than double her budget for anti-doping efforts. On the heels of France's widely celebrated 1998 World Cup soccer victory, the country was ready for the beginning of another sporting ritual, the Tour de France. On July 8, just three days before the scheduled start of the '98 Tour, Voet's official Tour de France Fiat sedan was pulled over by police near Lille. The stop, on a quiet back road away from the major thoroughfare, *appeared* to be a normal, quite routine, check by customs officials intent on controlling smuggling at the Franco-Belgian border. But later reports suggested that Voet, Festina and the Tour itself were the focus of an ongoing investigation. What the police search did do was bring the problem to public attention and trigger a new round of police efforts.

In Reims, just to the east of Paris, authorities immediately reopened a case that involved a strikingly similar traffic stop four months' earlier. At the time, police said they had too many other "important matters" on their hands to worry about suspected performance-enhancing drugs. The vials, however, were confiscated and placed in a police evidence locker.

"I don't know how it got in the car," Priem asserted when police reported that the confiscated items included 104 vials of EPO. "Our car stops often in the course of a day. That gives anyone the opportunity to place anything they want in the car. I know that we stop often." Authorities didn't buy the claim, and Priem as well as team doctor

Andrei Mikhailov were hauled off to police detention in Reims.

The TVM case was re-opened only after the Festina drug bust became public. And the subsequent revelation of the Festina team's organized doping program seemed almost an accident...but was it? In September 1998, as the fall-out from the Festina Affair continued, French sports authorities revealed the existence of a high-level anti-doping working group, overseeing a program that had been established in April 1998. The decision to stop Voet, it seemed, came well before July 8. Voet, the French newspaper *France-Soir* reported, had been tracked for more than a day by officials already certain of the contents of the Festina Fiat. While the original TVM stop may have been an incidental discovery, the *France-Soir* report suggested that the search of Voet's car was not.

"Customs did not come across Festina by chance," the paper quoted an unnamed official as saying. "As part of an effort by a combination of (government) officials and several ministries, customs was given very specific instructions to act."

Planned or not, the French police did more in a single three-week period to reveal the extent of doping in cycling than had years of testing, controls and public pronouncements by the UCI.

The investigation of the Festina Affair would continue for more than a year—well beyond the 1999 Tour. In Lille, investigating magistrate Patrick Keil spent months questioning riders, team officials, doctors and finally those he said might be guilty of "turning a blind eye" to the doping concerns.

Festina's directeur sportif Bruno Roussel and team doctor Erik Rijckaert were expelled from the Tour, arrested, and taken to Lille. The three were jailed and questioned separately.

Rijckaert maintained his innocence, the other two confessed and acknowledged the existence of a carefully monitored, organized doping program. Indeed, upon his release, Voet told of the existence of 30 years' worth of very specific diaries, specific records that outlined the doping programs of each of the teams he had worked on.

The riders, too, were detained and most—with the exception of Richard Virenque and Neil Stephens—acknowledged their knowing participation in the team's doping program.

Virenque, the four-time winner of the Tour's best-climber's jersey, vehemently denied ever having received doping products of any sort. Stephens, an amiable Australian domestique with a reputation as a selfless hard worker, simply denied knowing the specific nature of the injections he had received from Rijckaert.

In the ensuing months, the 35-year-old Stephens would quietly retire, a decision he said had nothing to do with the Festina controversy. Meanwhile, Voet and Virenque began a very public debate over that rider's continued denial of doping allegations.

"Once I was in prison," Voet told the French newspaper *L'Équipe*, "I saw that on television he [Virenque] was describing me as some sort of dealer, a trafficker in drugs, and that I supplied other teams as well. All I can say is, never."

Voet repeated his charge that Virenque was one of the Festina squad's heaviest drug users. It was a charge the French rider would continue to deny—through his departure from Festina; through his temporary retirement from the sport in December; and through his return to cycling a few weeks later, when he signed on with the Italian squad, Polti. Indeed, Virenque strenuously maintained his innocence all the way to the 1999 Tour de France.

By New Year's, Keil had directly charged eight individuals of involvement in the use and distribution of performance-enhancing drugs. In addition to Voet, Roussel and Rijckaert, Keil charged Festina's logistics manager Joël Chabiron with dealing drugs, along with La Française des Jeux soigneur Jef d'Hont, Casino rider Rodolfo Massi, ONCE team doctor Nicolas Terrados, and a pair of pharmacists, Eric and Christine Paranier. On March 30, 1999, Virenque was named as a suspect of an investigation into his alleged violation of France's anti-doping laws.

Keil also turned his attention on the officials purportedly in charge of the sport. By spring, the magistrate had summoned Tour race director Jean-Marie Leblanc, UCI president Hein Verbruggen and French Cycling Federation president Daniel Baal to his Lille courthouse. None of the three was officially charged, but Keil reportedly made each explain in detail how the sport could be so riddled with drugs without their knowledge.

"I believe he understands the nature of our efforts to control doping," Verbruggen later said. "We had a very cordial conversation and I explained just what cycling is doing."

NEW CONTROLS

Part of what cycling was doing involved the establishment of new "longitudinal" doping controls. The UCI's chief medical officer, Dutch physician, Leon Schattenberg, even before the 1998 scandal erupted, had advocated stricter medical controls for the sport. Indeed, cycling was only the second major sport—cross-country skiing being the first—to require its athletes to submit to blood testing as a means of controlling the use of EPO. But Schattenberg wanted to expand the UCI's two-year-old blood control program to include a requirement that riders submit quarterly medical reports that provide a complete blood count, measuring hematocrit and hormone levels. The idea was to provide long-term medical data for each rider, so allowing authorities to flag anyone who's report indicated a sudden or dramatic shift in any of those levels.

After the '98 Tour, the French Federation, under Baal's direction, took an even more aggressive stance, requiring that riders also willingly submit to random out-of-competition testing, to confirm the quarterly numbers submitted by team physicians. The conflicting policies also signaled the beginning of a growing rift between Verbruggen and Baal, also a UCI vice president and once considered the Dutchman's apparent heir to the UCI's top post.

A PROBLEM OF OLYMPIC PROPORTION

While the Tour de France is indeed cycling's premier showcase event, the sport and its governing body are a part of the Olympics, and as such the troubles at the Tour begged for a response from the head of the Olympic movement. However, the response from International Olympic Committee president Juan Antonio Samaranch wasn't exactly what the world had been expecting. Rather than condemning the use of performance-enhancing drugs, Samaranch seemed to imply that doping involved vast gray areas of unanswerable questions.

"Doping is everything that, firstly, is harmful to an athlete's health and, secondly, artificially augments his performance," Samaranch told an interviewer near the end of the 1998 Tour. "If it is the second case, for me that is not doping. If it is the first case, it is."

The response was immediate and quite negative. Some suggested that the aging Samaranch should consider resigning. Samaranch later said his comments were "misconstrued" and called an emergency summit on the subject of doping to be held the first week of February 1999. The result, he suggested, would produce a unified and coordinated campaign by all Olympic members in the effort "to rid sport of the scourge of doping and the suspicion that infects all aspects of competition."

LET'S CALL A CONFERENCE

Three days of speeches, three days of arguments, three days of competing press conferences...and that was supposed to solve the problem.

In the closing moments of the International Olympic Committee's "World Conference on Doping in Sport," the IOC president held up the two-page "Lausanne Declaration," acknowledged the "reservations" expressed by many of the more than 600 assembled delegates, but nonetheless asked for consensus. "Can we agree?"

Samaranch asked. The room responded with a round of applause and the three-day conference was concluded. Samaranch later declared the February 2-4 meeting at IOC headquarters in Switzerland to be "a great victory in the fight against doping," and then everyone went home.

But despite the president's declaration of victory and a pledge of $25 million to establish an anti-doping agency, many characterized the IOC's stance as "weak," "diluted" and with penalties that have "a loophole big enough to drive a truck through." To underscore that point, soon after Samaranch's declaration of success, the 15-member European Union rejected the IOC's strategy as ineffective. Indeed, its failure to develop an effective anti-doping strategy may ultimately leave the IOC on the sidelines, as governments around Europe have already initiated their own, considerably harsher, means of dealing with the problem.

Conceived soon after the Tour scandal, the Lausanne summit was supposed to be a showcase of IOC unity, in the face of doping in sport, producing an IOC-coordinated response to the problem.

But it is important to recall that the conference was conceived at a time when doping was the biggest scandal facing the IOC. In the following months, however, a series of increasingly embarrassing allegations of bribery connected with the awarding of Olympic venues, made the doping conference suddenly seem secondary. In fact, a majority of the 480 assembled journalists were at the Lausanne conference simply because they had stayed over after the IOC's emergency conference on the bribery scandal ended a few days earlier. ("I'm not covering drugs; I'm just on a Samaranch death watch," joked one American reporter.)

INDEPENDENT AGENCY

When the IOC drugs summit was in its early planning stages, its goals were outlined in a pre-conference agreement that was endorsed by a majority of governing bodies affiliated with the Olympic movement. At the center of the proposal were two tenets: the establishment of an "independent anti-doping agency;" and the imposition of a mandatory minimum two-year suspension for any and all drug violations by athletes.

In Lausanne, the independence of the proposed agency was immediately called into question, after Samaranch suggested that it be headed by the man already in charge of the IOC anti-doping effort, Belgium's Prince Alexandre de Merode.

In an opening-day speech, U.S. Olympic Committee executive director Dick Schultz suggested that any agency headed by anyone from the IOC would simply lack credibility. Another U.S. delegate, White House drug policy advisor General Barry McCaffrey, pointed to events of the preceding weeks and said that the organization lacked the legitimacy to oversee the anti-doping effort.

Schultz called for the establishment of a "truly independent" agency, one without ties to the Olympic movement. His suggestion was rejected by members of the IOC, but garnered support among athletes and government representatives. Verbruggen was among several IOC members who said Americans had little or no business questioning the ethics of the Olympic movement, since the U.S.'s own system of professional sports is "almost exempt from scrutiny, except for those two weeks every four years when they participate in the Olympics."

"You Americans," Verbruggen said, pointing his finger toward the one American journalist he recognized in the crowd of reporters surrounding him, "you Americans have the nerve to name a man, who would be banned for life under Olympic rules, Sportsman of the Year...and then come here to preach to us about the ethics of sport, and then suggest that the Olympic movement isn't capable of regulating itself."

Verbruggen correctly pointed out that American sports hero Mark McGwire—*Sports Illustrated*'s 1998 Sportsman of the Year—had publicly acknowledged using Androstenedione, a supplement legal in baseball, but banned under the rules of most other sports.

"I am disappointed in a great number of politicians, and especially the Americans," Verbruggen offered. "I mean, I don't know if you heard Dick Schultz giving lessons to the IOC that the president of that (doping) agency cannot be, for objective reasons, a member of the IOC. He can say that with dry eyes without saying that perhaps this agency should also go and control professional sports in America? Jesus. The Americans here have set new standards as far as hypocrisy is concerned."

Ultimately, however, Samaranch, de Merode and other IOC leaders conceded that the independent agency probably will not be headed by a member of the Olympic committee; though it is still likely to be based in Lausanne. The IOC's vice president, Dick Pound of Canada, said that he expected governments to take an active role in the agency, "and we also expect them to make at least as much of a financial commitment as we've made."

TWO YEARS—MAYBE

If arguments over the supposed independence of the anti-doping agency caused discord, debate over the establishment of a mandatory minimum sentence at times threatened to divide the Olympic movement.

Soon after the pre-conference agreements were released in the fall of 1998, Verbruggen and the Swiss president of FIFA, soccer's governing body, Joseph Blatter, refused to endorse a proposed mandatory minimum two-year suspension for doping violations, saying that the proposal was both unfair and unrealistic. At the time, some IOC members threatened to pull both sports from the Olympics, if they continued to insist on suspensions of less than two years. But the UCI and FIFA held their ground and emerged with what some say was the biggest concession of the anti-doping summit.

The congress did adopt a "mandatory minimum sentence," but Verbruggen and Blatter succeeded in having one sentence included that all but nullified that standard.

The compromise language states: "However, based on specific, exceptional circumstances to be evaluated in the first instance by the competent (international federation) bodies, there may be a provision for a possible modification of the two-year sanction."

That phrase, said the International Triathlon Union's Mark Sisson, "is a concession to cycling, soccer and, more importantly, any attorney who wants to argue against a penalty applied to their client. This leaves a loophole big enough to drive a truck through."

But it is legal concerns, said Verbruggen, that drove his opposition to the mandatory minimum in the first place. "What happens to a federation if we impose such a penalty and then the suspension is lifted?" Verbruggen asked. "Who then pays an athlete's lost wages?"

According to Verbruggen, the potential impact on an athlete's earning power is a valid "exceptional circumstance" under the definition. And UCI attorney Philippe Verbiest echoed that position.

"The punishment has to fit the crime and consider the concept of proportionality," Verbiest said. "One has to take into account that for a top professional, a two-year ban might be, or probably will be, the end of his career. So, in effect, it amounts to a lifetime ban, and that, certainly in Europe, is a sanction which will not be upheld by any single court. So, it's better to have realistic sanctions that have no chance of being challenged than to have strong sanctions that will simply lead to litigation and ultimately be reduced to less than acceptable. I think it's entirely realistic to take into account the outcome of the proceedings, not just the public relations value of making a statement when the real result will be quashed in court."

If there are to be extenuating circumstances considered, Sisson suggested, "those should be established by the Court of Arbitration for Sport (in Lausanne). If we mention it in this document, it ensures that no one will ever have that sanction enforced. Period."

As the summit wound to a close, Verbruggen characterized the resulting position paper as "acceptable," while Sisson expressed disappointment. "It's a start, I guess," said Sisson. "Maybe that's all you can hope for from one of these things."

"No, the best you can hope for from one of these things," Verbruggen later said, "is to take an honest and realistic view of the problem. What good is a two-year suspension when the biggest problems in sport are undetectable products? Claiming that a two-year suspension does any good when none of them are willing to even do blood testing is just public relations, now isn't it?"

DOPED TO DEATH

While the IOC's top officials were hunkered down in Lausanne and Verbruggen was touting the UCI's success, the French newspaper *Libération* began a series of articles written by Philippe Rochet and Jean-Louis Le Touzet outlining the preliminary results of the new French Federation's longitudinal medical studies. The results were alarming.

In "Doped to Death," the two reporters suggested that more than one half of the French peloton showed signs of biological disorders, rooted medical authorities said, in the use of performance-enhancing drugs, especially EPO.

Gérard Dine, a hematologist at the Biotechnical Institute at Troyes, said 60 percent of those tested "showed serious anomalies in iron metabolism," with blood iron levels sometimes five to 20 times greater than those of a normal population. Of those exhibiting heightened iron levels, 40 percent showed signs of pancreatic and/or liver damage.

Dine implied that the elevated iron levels were the result of iron injections that are "commonly associated with the repeated use of Erythropoietin (EPO)."

IN CHARGE OF THE HEN HOUSE

While French police seized the headlines during the summer of '98 for their raids on the Tour de France, investigations into doping in sport heated up in Italy at the end of October 1998, when well-known sports doctors Professor Francisco Conconi and Dr. Michele Ferrari were formally placed under investigation by police in Ferrara in northeast Italy.

Conconi, Ferrari and former Italian Olympic Committee president Mario Pescante were suspected of violating laws that cover "improper acts against sport," and "the administration of medicines which could endanger health." As part of the investigations, their homes and laboratories were searched. Documents and computer files covering the last 16 years were seized.

Police are trying to discover if research funding from the Italian Olympic Committee (CONI)—which should have been used for research into discovering new anti-doping techniques—was instead used to improve doping in sports such as swimming, cycling, athletics and cross-country skiing. In the 1980s, Conconi was accused of using blood-boosting techniques. In the previous few years, he had unsuccessfully worked on techniques for detecting Erythropoietin in urine tests.

Speaking to the Italian press after his home was searched, Conconi denied any wrongdoing and said he hoped the police investigation would end the rumors of his involvement in doping. "I'm pleased that the police have come to control things, because then they will show that research is not doping," he said. Dr. Ferrari—also under investigation by police in Bologna for links with a pharmacy suspected as a source of EPO—refused to make any comment.

The Conconi and Ferrari case brought new attention to another group of the world's top riders. Several of Ferrari's current and former clients—including super sprinter Mario Cipollini, Claudio Chiappucci, Gianni Faresin and former world cyclo-cross champion Daniele Pontoni—were hauled into court in March '99 for questioning by the judge in that case, Giovanni Spinosa.

By June—when Italian cycling was struck by another major blow—authorities had stepped up the pressure, searching the homes of top riders and expanding their investigation.

APRIL FOOLISHNESS

In one of the most bizarre "doping" tales to emerge in the year after the Tour scandal, the entire peloton was stopped by police just 3 kilometers after the start of the penultimate stage of Belgium's Three Days of De Panne. Just before 9 a.m. on April 1, Belgian police chased down the race with sirens and lights blazing, and stopped the race in its tracks. The entire Mapei-Quick Step team—including overall race leader Tom Steels—was taken into custody, and driven away in police vans with a motorcycle escort.

Authorities in Courtrai had been alerted to the discovery three days earlier of five flasks of amphetamines, packed in a video cassette box and destined for Italy. Despite knowing of the package for three days, the police made a point of waiting for this most public of venues to make their arrests...and their point. But after questioning the Mapei riders and staff, Belgian prosecutor Louis Denecker announced that he had narrowed his investigation to a single individual. Not a rider, the focus was on the team's Italian soigneur Tiziano Morassut, who was arrested the following day.

Within hours of their arrest, the Mapei riders were exonerated and released, but team and Italian officials were livid. Mapei team director Patrick Lefévère said he was amazed by the audacity of the police. "When I first heard about it, I thought it was a cruel April Fool's joke."

But extreme as it was, the Mapei incident was no joke. Authorities all over Europe seemed intent on demonstrating their enthusiasm for uncovering both real and imagined cycling scandals and doing it in the most public manner possible.

A NEW CASE IN FRANCE

In May 1999, a new French scandal erupted. As the investigation continued in Keil's Lille courthouse, French police unveiled a new and potentially widespread drug investigation that again touched some of the world's top riders.

Police raids on May 6 and 7 appeared to be the culmination of an ongoing investigation into distribution channels used to divert illicit performance-enhancing substances—including EPO and what authorities called "masking agents"—from their originally legitimate sources. The late-night and early-morning raids resulted in the detention of 14 people, including Belgium's UCI World Cup leader Frank Vandenbroucke, who was taken into custody at the Amiens home of Cofidis teammate Philippe Gaumont— one of the original targets of the investigation. Also detained in the original police sweep were Raphael Martinez, cousin of world under-23 cross-country champion Miguel Martinez, and Lionel Virenque, the brother of Richard Virenque, one of the early victims of last year's "Festina Affair" at the Tour de France. But by the end of the weekend, Michele Colin, the magistrate in charge of this latest investigation had released without charges all but five of the detainees.

Formal drug-trafficking charges were filed against lawyer Bertrand Lavelot—who has served as Richard Virenque's and several other cyclists' attorney—and Bernard Sainz, variously described by the French media as either a "homeopathic doctor" or a "horse breeder."

Three riders—Gaumont, Yvon Ledanois (of La Française des Jeux) and former GAN team pro Pascal Peyramaure—were questioned and then released, charged with using, but not trafficking in, illegal drugs. Vandenbroucke, Martinez and Virenque were among those released without charges being filed against them.

WRONG PLACE, WRONG TIME

The arrest of Vandenbroucke, who had abandoned the Four Days of Dunkirk stage race the previous day, appears to have been an incidental consequence of his being at the home of Gaumont when police arrived. Similarly, Raphael Martinez, a 27-year-old former road racer who now races for Diamondback, said he was simply at the wrong place at the wrong time. His troubles began when he called on Saiz for what he said were "homeopathic" treatments.

"I have used this doctor before a few years ago, when I was road racing. I had nothing in my legs," Martinez said. "I stopped seeing him when the problems went away. I called him just this week when my results so far have been poor. I haven't seen him in more than one year and now I see him the week they want to arrest him."

Martinez was taken by the police soon after leaving the Sainz home. "All I had with me was a list of food he said I should eat and some drops that he gave me to help create glucose," said Martinez, who was released less than 24 hours later.

Through his attorney, Gaumont offered a similar defense, saying that his only connection to Sainz was that he had "used substances prepared and supplied by him and which were presented as being of a homeopathic nature."

PRESUMED INNOCENT...

While Gaumont and Martinez loudly proclaimed their innocence, and Vandenbroucke was released without being charged, the team managements at Diamondback and Cofidis immediately distanced themselves from the detained riders.

Martinez was told that he would not be allowed to compete at the Diesel-UCI mountain-bike World Cup event in St. Wendel, Germany on May 9. And on May 10, Cofidis team officials summoned their two riders for a "discussion" of the case with manager Alain Bondue at the team headquarters in Wasquehal in northern France. Bondue told Vandenbroucke and Gaumont that they were to be suspended, with pay, until the case was resolved in their favor. In a press release issued that afternoon, Cofidis officials emphasized that the two should be presumed innocent until proven otherwise. The release also emphasized the Cofidis team policy, that if a rider is found to have taken or distributed illegal substances, he will be immediately fired from the team. The policy was applied in that fashion in 1998 when then-Cofidis rider Francesco Casagrande, was first suspended and then fired when it was shown that he had twice tested for abnormally high levels of testosterone.

In the Netherlands, the Dutch team, TVM-Farm Frites—which also was touched by the 1998 drug scandal—announced that it had ended its relationship with the Paris lawyer, Lavelot, who had on occasion served as legal counsel for the squad. And in France, the already besieged Tour de France director Jean-Marie Leblanc felt compelled to reassure the public that the 1999 event would, indeed, take place.

Leblanc added that he did not "want the Tour to be a victim of these suppliers. We must intervene. The Tour must not submit to the trouble linked to accusations against teams, riders or personnel for doping offenses. I emphasize the word trouble, and we will remain vigilant."

PANTANI'S DISGRACE

For three weeks at the Giro d'Italia, Italy belonged to Marco Pantani. At each day's start, as soon as the yellow Mercatone Uno camper van pulled into sight, the fans would come running. They would push up against the metal fencing separating them from their hero, and shrill shrieks of "Pantani, Pantani" would rise up from the crowd the very moment he emerged. On the high mountain climbs, teenagers and middle-aged men alike wore bright yellow 'do rags and *Il Pirata* T-shirts. And at the finishes, they would serenade him each time he put on the pink jersey. Oooooh, oooooh ... Maaar-cooo ... Pan-tan-ee!

And then, it all came crashing down. When Pantani's morning blood test on June 5, before the start of stage 21, revealed a 52-percent hematocrit level, the Giro was thrown into a frenzy of a different kind.

The morning of the test, on Italian television, Pantani expressed surprise at the result. "I can't understand it," he said. "I've already had two tests done, wearing the pink jersey, and my hematocrit was at 46 percent."

He then hinted that he might be through with the sport. "I've come back several times in the past, but it will be difficult this time," he told a crowd of reporters. "I've touched the bottom. It's too much. I'll say good-bye to cycling."

With a hematocrit level two percentage points above the UCI's 50-percent limit, Pantani was declared "unfit to race." The UCI's blood tests are labeled "health checks," and while Pantani's result was not a positive test for any controlled substance, an elevated hematocrit level is a possible indicator of the use of EPO.

Pantani faced a 15-day mandatory "rest period," after which he could be re-tested in Lausanne, Switzerland, and would be allowed to return to racing if the result was under 50 percent.

But the damage to the image of Pantani—and the sport—had already been done. "It is traumatic not only for the Giro, but also for cycling," said Verbruggen. "Pantani and [Frank] Vandenbroucke are two riders we hoped would relaunch cycling. Instead, they're involved in this bad story."

"There's two problems with cycling," Verbruggen continued. "It's the hardest sport there is, and it's very commercialized. These two facts create big pressure, so obviously there's more doping in cycling than other sports. But if there's a culture of doping, there's also a culture of anti-doping."

Pantani's expulsion from the Giro also attracted the attention of judicial authorities already investigating allegations of drug use in the Italian peloton. Not only was Pantani ordered to appear in court in June, but so were the doctors who attended him following a traumatic 1995 accident that resulted in a severely shattered leg. The doctors told the court that blood tests immediately following the accident showed the Italian rider had a hematocrit level well over 56 percent. Pantani pointed out that his accident happened just after his return from three weeks at high altitude, competing at the world championships in Colombia.

SCHATTENBERG: PROOF THAT THE TEST WORKS

It was with a mixture of surprise, disappointment and even a bit of satisfaction, that the UCI's chief medical officer learned that the Giro d'Italia's overall leader was to be ejected from the race. "This cannot be seen as a good thing," said Leon Schattenberg, "It is very sad." But Schattenberg said he could take solace in the fact that the action taken by UCI officials at the Giro also underscored the integrity of the organization's testing program.

That said, Schattenberg noted that his first response was one of simple surprise. Surprise not from the allegation that one of cycling's best had been using EPO, but rather that Pantani's doctor had allowed the rider's hematocrit to drift above the UCI's maximum level.

Ironically, Pantani had been one of the most vocal supporters of the UCI's testing program, advocating the international body's testing methods over those of CONI, the Italian Olympic Committee. Pantani had even threatened to leave the race in the event that he and other riders would be forced to undergo testing by both agencies.

"I was surprised," Schattenberg said from his home in the Netherlands. "Yes, I was disappointed, but I was also very surprised that at this point that, after two years of testing, we would see such a result from the leader of the Giro."

While Schattenberg was a driving force behind the UCI's 1996 adoption of an upper hematocrit standard, the Dutch physician had repeatedly acknowledged that the current hematocrit protocols have done little to stop the use of EPO.

"At this point, it is impossible to detect," Schattenberg said during the 1998 Tour de

France. "The best we can hope to do is to control it until we develop tests to detect it."

It was at a late-1996 meeting of UCI officials, team directors, riders' representatives and cycling doctors that the upper limit of 50 percent was adopted. That figure was not an arbitrary target, but was based on a set of blood tests taken from riders in the mid-1980s—presumably data not affected by the later introduction of Amgen's Epogen. The data showed that riders then had an average hematocrit level of 43. That meant that 43 percent of an average rider's blood consisted of oxygen-carrying red blood cells.

Schattenberg and others initially proposed that the upper limit be established at 53, a number equal to the mean of 43 plus three times the standard statistical deviation from that mean. It was a figure adopted earlier by the International Ski Federation for cross-country skiers, and should apply to about 99.5 percent of the population. But it was riders and team directors who suggested a lower figure of 50—the mean plus only two times the standard deviation—applicable to about 95 percent of the population.

The hematocrit level of healthy adult males can vary widely. For example, according to Mercury team physician Prentice Steffen, the team's David Clinger has an average hematocrit of just 39.

Riders with naturally high hematocrit levels have the option of applying for special dispensation from the rules, if they can provide evidence supporting that claim. Since 1997, 15 riders had received such exceptions. Assuming that Pantani was not using artificial means to boost his hematocrit, his doctor should have made such an application, said Schattenberg.

"Pantani's own doctor controlled for hematocrit the night before and even he said that the level was 49.7," Schattenberg said. "They have never asked for an exception. They have never supplied a record of tests to show that his level is higher than most. The doctor's defense—altitude, dehydration—is, I think, not a good one. They had the opportunity to rehydrate by the morning."

Schattenberg freely admitted that the establishment of any upper limit has simply provided sophisticated users with a range within which they can work. Since unannounced hematocrit tests were first adopted in 1997, the UCI has carried out about 850 tests. The average hematocrit level of those tests is now two points higher than the presumably "clean" samples taken in the mid-1980s.

"We expect, in the near future, to make things more difficult for anyone trying to manipulate hematocrit within acceptable limits," he said. Schattenberg predicted that within the "near future" the UCI's testing protocol would include analysis of reticulocyte—new red blood cells—levels within a rider's sample.

Red blood cells have a given life expectancy of about five to six weeks. New cells, reticulocytes, are visibly different than their older counterparts and it is a relatively simple matter, noted Steffen, to classify those cells in their respective age groups.

"There should," said Steffen, "be a fairly even distribution of new, middle-aged and old cells. If there is a spike in one age group, that should trigger questions."

Schattenberg said that the UCI's biggest challenge is to establish a range within which normal external factors, such as a sudden change in altitude, can be accounted for, while still spotting the unusual external factor, such as the use of EPO.

"We can't stop it," he said, "but we can try to make it much more difficult until there is an effective test."

AND OTHER TROUBLES

The Lille case, the Italian investigation and the Pantani matter were by no means the only doping-related events that occurred in the months following the '98 Tour. Danish television reported in January '99 that medical records indicated that when he was with the Italian team, Gewiss, in 1995—before the UCI's blood tests began—1996 Tour winner Bjarne Riis of Telekom had competed with a hematocrit level of 58 percent. It was a charge Riis quickly denied. The 35-year-old rider, now a significant shareholder in a company that sponsors the Danish pro squad Home-Jack & Jones, was asked by the company's board of directors to appear and present his side of the story. Riis, incensed by the board's request, sold his shares and resigned his spot on the board.

Months later, the German magazine, *Der Spiegel*, printed an article alleging that the entire Telekom team engaged in an organized and structured doping program similar in nature to that of the pre-1999 Festina team. Telekom, and its 1997 Tour winner Jan Ullrich in particular, immediately threatened court action. German courts had not yet acted on the case, but did issue a preliminary injunction barring the German magazine from publishing more of the story and ordering *Der Spiegel* to print a letter from Telekom, refuting the charges made in the original article.

PRELUDE TO THE TOUR

It was in this environment that Tour director Leblanc and the sport of cycling neared the 1999 Tour de France. As is traditional, on June 16, Leblanc and the Société du Tour de France made their final team selections for the upcoming event—those teams whose UCI world ranking did not earn them an automatic selection to the Tour, including Lance Armstrong's U.S. Postal Service squad. But the June announcement also had one very untraditional element to it. Leblanc used the opportunity to dis-invite teams, riders and other individuals whose participation the Tour director and the organization said would be counter to the spirit of the "Tour of Redemption." Topping the list was the entire TVM-Farm Frites team—a squad embroiled in its own drug scandal during the '98 Tour—and Virenque, who had moved from Festina to the Italian team, Polti, and a rider who continued to maintain his innocence of drug charges. Also on the list was ONCE-Deutsche Bank team director Manolo Saiz, who spoke critically of the Tour, the organization and French police before withdrawing his team in protest in 1998. The following day, Leblanc revoked an invitation extended to the Italian team, Vini Caldirola-Sidermec, after its strongest rider, Sergei Gontchar, was excluded from the Tour of Switzerland for an elevated hematocrit level. It appeared that the roster was set.

TVM representatives immediately threatened legal action, while Saiz and Virenque's team owner Franco Polti followed-up with appeals directly to the UCI. It was that latter approach that proved successful.

Polti's attorneys argued that UCI rules require a race organizer who intends to exclude a rider or other participants from an event must notify the affected parties at least 30 days in advance. On June 27, the UCI concurred, saying that the June 16 exclusions by the Société were therefore unfair and should be nullified. The following day, Leblanc conceded defeat, re-issuing an invitation to both Saiz and to Virenque, adding that if Virenque did win this year's Tour it would be "an insult" to the other riders and teams participating in the race. Interestingly, the UCI decision was not applied to the TVM squad. The difference, said Verbruggen, was simply that Virenque and Saiz had appealed the decision to the UCI, and the Dutch team had not. The following day, a TVM spokesman said the team was also abandoning its decision to pursue the case in the courts.

So almost a year after the Festina Affair nearly ruined the 1998 Tour, many of the team's original members were ready and able to ride the 1999 edition: Polti's Virenque, Banesto's Alex Zülle, Saeco-Cannondale's Laurent Dufaux and Armin Meier, as well as Christophe Moreau and Laurent Brochard, riders who had confessed to doping, but now committed to riding clean and, therefore, invited to remain on the restructured Festina team.

A Tour of Redemption? Of complete redemption? Probably not, but most certainly 1999 should be considered a Tour of Transition.

The 20 teams and their leaders

BANESTO (Spain)

After winning the Tour five times in succession with Miguel Induráin, Banesto had since struggled. In 1999, with climber José Maria Jiménez reserved for the Vuelta, the pressure was on its ex-Festina leader **Alex Zülle**, who was struggling to find form after his seven-month suspension. Also struggling was its Polish hope Dariusz Baranowski, so Banesto's top man could likely be its most reliable climbing domestique, Manuel Beltran.

BIGMAT-AUBER 93 (France)

Chosen as a wild-card team, BigMat was the only Division 2 squad in the race. As such, it had no chance of contending for the overall, especially since its leader Pascal Lino was serving a team suspension for drug irregularities. With nothing to lose, BigMat was expected to put riders in as many breaks as possible. Among the names to look for were Russian **Alexei Sivakov**; French veterans Thierry Gouvenou and Thierry Bourgignon; and Aussie sprinter Jay Sweet.

CANTINA TOLLO-ALEXIA (Italy)

Not originally selected, Cantina Tollo would start because Vini Caldirola lost its wild-card slot when its Ukrainian Sergei Gontchar tested over the 50-percent hematocrit level at the Tour of Switzerland. Few of the Cantina riders had ridden the Tour, so its main hopes lay with Danish leader **Bo Hamburger** (15th overall in 1998) and Italian sprinter Nicola Minali (a stage winner in 1994 and '97).

CASINO (France)

The Casino team cut its budget big time in 1999, and most of its stars left, too. Luckily, its home-grown talent came through, with its Kazakh all-arounder **Alex Vinokourov** (who was discovered in French amateur racing) and French climber Benoît Salmon winning, respectively, the Dauphiné Libéré and Midi-Libre stage races. This would be the Tour debut for Vinokourov, 25, who could find the high mountains too big an obstacle to hope for more than a top-10 placing.

COFIDIS (France)

Bobby Julich was thrilled to finish on the podium in 1998, but not even the American expected to come to the start line a year later as the prerace favorite. Signs were that his form and fitness would come good for the Tour, but there were question marks against his team riders, particularly 1998's King of the Mountains, Christophe Rinero. Julich's most valued team helpers would be Swiss Roland Meier and Belgian Peter Farazijn.

CRÉDIT AGRICOLE (France)

With Chris Boardman lacking the form that earned him the yellow jersey in the prologue for the previous two years, his Crédit Agricole team would probably focus on stage wins rather than the G.C. It's best bets for the overall were **Jens Voigt** and Cédric Vasseur, while Swede Magnus Bäckstedt and Aussies Stuart O'Grady and Henk Vogels were possible stage winners.

FESTINA (France)

Despite ridding itself of its pre-drug investigation stars, and halving its budget, the "new" Festina squad had several successes in the spring—mainly from Italian climber-time trialist **Wladimir Belli**, and time trialist Christophe Moreau. At least one of these could win a stage at the Tour, but they weren't likely to be at the top of the G.C. sheets.

KELME-COSTA BLANCA (Spain)

Spaniard **Fernando Escartin**, 31, has been knocking on the door of the Tour podium for several years. Now he had a chance of success, if his best climbing teammates, such as José Castelblanco, also had good form. Escartin's weakness is his time trialing ability, although that had shown strong signs of improvement in the past two editions of the Vuelta a España.

LA FRANÇAISE DES JEUX (France)

Frenchmen Jean-Cyril Robin and **Stéphane Heulot** would both be shooting for top-10 finishes; but the team's best hope for publicity was in stage wins for the likes of Anglo-Italian Max Sciandri and Frenchman Emmanuel Magnien.

LAMPRE-DAIKIN (Italy)

With team leader Oskar Camenzind never scheduled for the Tour, Lampre's focus would be on stage wins for Czech sprinter Jan Svorada or Belgian Ludo Dierckxsens. Also worth keep an eye on was 26-year-old Italian **Marco Serpellini,** who was a potential stage winner *and* G.C. contender.

LOTTO-MOBISTAR (Belgium)

Lotto could be expected to be the animators of the 1999 Tour. It had no G.C. contender, while it had no true sprinter. The squad's best players could be its younger Belgian climbers—Mario Aerts, **Kurt Van de Wouwer** and Rik Verbrugghe—while veterans Jacky Durand would be looking for a stage win.

MAPEI-QUICK STEP (Italy)

Whenever **Pavel Tonkov** had ridden the Giro d'Italia, he had been a contender (with one win, two seconds, a fourth, a fifth, a sixth and a seventh in his seven participations). But he had started the Tour twice, and twice he pulled out. In 1999, he passed up the Giro in favor of the Tour, and with strong climbers like Gianni Faresin, Manuel Fernandez Gines, Axel Merckx and Tobias Steinhauser to help him, Tonkov could be a No. 1 contender. Sprinter Tom Steels did not have the same support as he had in 1998, so he would have to work harder to win stages.

MERCATONE UNO-BIANCHI (Italy)

With Marco Pantani not starting, Tour neophyte **Stefano Garzelli**—winner of the 1998 Tour of Switzerland—was Mercatone Uno's likely leader. If the young Italian did not perform, the team could be expected to ride for the experienced Enrico Zaina, or shoot for stage victories with Dmitri Konyshev or Fabio Fontanelli.

ONCE-DEUTSCHE BANK (Spain)

Abraham Olano may have won his native Vuelta a España the previous September, but only after struggling on the mountaintop finishes—aided by his then Banesto teammates José Maria Jiménez and Manuel Beltran. With ONCE, Olano could rely upon fellow Spaniards David

Etxebarria, Marcos Serrano and Marcelino Garcia to help him in the mountains. But Olano's erratic time-trial strength would probably prevent him from shooting for the yellow jersey.

POLTI (Italy)

After unexpectedly winning the Giro d'Italia, Ivan Gotti was hoping to carry his renewed confidence and form into the Tour. That plan changed when French teammate **Richard Virenque** was allowed to start the Tour, in the hope of taking the polka-dot jersey for a fifth time.

RABOBANK (Netherlands)

The Dutch haven't had a real Tour contender since Steven Rooks and Gert-Jan Theunisse thrilled the fans on L'Alpe d'Huez a decade ago. Now they had **Michael Boogerd**, fifth in 1998, and winner in 1999 of Paris-Nice and the Amstel Gold Race. Boogerd's main weakness is the time trial, but he seemed to have great support for the mountains in Swiss teammates Niki Aebersold and Beat Zberg, Dutch-Aussie Patrick Jonker and fellow Dutchman Maarten Den Bakker. Meanwhile, Aussie sprinter Robbie McEwen looked capable finally make his Tour breakthrough and take a stage.

SAECO-CANNONDALE (Italy)

As usual, Saeco's first goal would be to increase the stage-win tally of Mario Cipollini; but the Italian squad could make even bigger headlines with its two G.C. contenders, Paolo Savoldelli of Italy and **Laurent Dufaux** of Switzerland. Savoldelli was Pantani's main rival at the Giro until his expulsion, while Dufaux had been slowly improving his form since ending his suspension May 1 for his part in the Festina Affair. Dufaux took fourth at the 1996 Tour, but his lack of race miles would probably catch up with him by the end of the Tour.

TELEKOM (Germany)

No Ullrich. No Riis. No Heppner. And probably, no Aldag. All four were on the injured list. To make up for their absence, the German team would focus all of its initial energy on engineering stage wins for Erik Zabel. Once the mountains arrived, Zabel would probably scale back to building points for a fourth green jersey; while Telekom's best climbers—German Jörg Jaksche, and Italians **Giuseppe Guerini** (third in the '98 Giro) and Alberto Elli — could make the most of Ullrich's absence.

U.S. POSTAL SERVICE (USA)

As its team directors promised, the U.S. Postal riders were all approaching their top form for the Tour, headed by potential Tour winner **Lance Armstrong**. The team had a plethora of riches, with Jonathan Vaughters, Kevin Livingston and Tyler Hamilton all racing well in the mountains and time trials. Added to this quartet's excellence would be the sprinting prowess of George Hincapie, the continued reliability of team workers Frankie Andreu, Pascal Deramé and Peter Meinert-Nielsen, and perhaps the blossoming talent of Christian Vande Velde.

VITALICIO SEGUROS (Spain)

This second-year team would be hoping for a top-10 finish by either of its top Spanish hope, **Angel Casero**; and potential stage wins by Colombian climber Hernan Buenahora.

PART TWO

The 86TH Tour de France

WEEK

1

Toward a new pinnacle

FOR EIGHT YEARS Americans had waited for Greg LeMond to be joined by a second compatriot in wearing the yellow jersey at the Tour de France. That wait came to an end late on a sunny evening July 3, when a smiling, resplendent Lance Armstrong stepped onto the Tour podium after winning the prologue at Le Puy du Fou in western France. It was an emotional moment for the 27-year-old Texan, and for those American cycling fans who saw their hero slip on the hallowed golden garment. Friends and teammates fought back tears, and thought back through the past two years and nine months since Armstrong was diagnosed with testicular cancer—and then fought back to health so bravely.

Now he is a shining beacon to all cancer patients, and in his once-again powerful hands he not only held the key to winning the 1999 Tour de France, but the very future of pro cycling. When, right after his prologue victory, he was asked about his feelings at the end of cycling's blackest year, Armstrong said, "Remarks are made assuming we're all doped. That's bullshit. I'm here, and I hope the other 179 riders are here, to see cycling reassert itself and to reassure people that we are champions."

Since his last appearance at the Tour, Armstrong was more than 15 pounds lighter—due to the debilitating chemotherapy treatment he received in 1996 and '97, and also his subsequent change in routine and a healthier lifestyle. The lower body weight had helped Armstrong become a different type of cyclist. As he said in Le Puy du Fou, "I think I'm a better rider than I was before...certainly I'm a better person."

Winning the prologue, of course, didn't insure final victory in Paris on July 25, but given Armstrong's winning mindset, his newly acquired climbing skills in the high mountains and his U.S. Postal Service team's all-around excellence, the task ahead looked more than possible.

Through the first week, Armstrong was the top contender for victory in most observers' eyes. On general classification, only the time-bonus-talking sprinters had jumped ahead of him—while prerace favorites Michael Boogerd, Alex Zülle and Ivan Gotti slid out of contention after a dramatic stage 2 to St. Nazaire, with each of them losing more than six minutes.

On the downside, Armstrong lost climber Jonathan Vaughters to a scary crash on the same stage, and that meant that the team's other mountain goats, Kevin Livingston and Tyler Hamilton would have added responsibilities in the Alps and Pyrénées, in the Tour's second and third weeks.

Besides Armstrong—who remained a handful of seconds behind race leader Jaan Kirsipuu of Casino and Estonia, going into the time trial at Metz—the other likely contenders for the vacant Tour title appeared to be Spaniard Abraham Olano of ONCE-Deutsche Bank, Russian Pavel Tonkov of Mapei-Quick Step, Italian Paolo Savoldelli of Saeco-Cannondale and Spaniard Fernando Escartin of Kelme-Costa Blanca. But none of these riders seemed to have the leadership qualities, the ambition or the charisma that had carried Armstrong to the edge of a new pinnacle.

PROLOGUE TT
Le Puy du Fou • July 3

A new level for Lance

IN HIS SEVEN YEARS AS A PROFESSIONAL CYCLIST, Lance Armstrong has shocked, thrilled, confounded and dazzled. His achievements are legion. Pre-cancer, he collected world and national championships, two stages of the Tour, and a couple of European classics. Since making his return to European racing in early 1998, Armstrong had accomplished new feats: He won a national tour (Luxembourg), finished fourth in another (Spain), and took a mountaintop stage win (at the Route du Sud). But what he achieved in this Tour de France prologue took him to a whole new level.

The Armstrong who won the 6.8km Le Puy du Fou time trial—beating runner-up Alex

Zülle by a massive seven seconds—was reminiscent of Miguel Induráin and Bernard Hinault. On similarly tough Tour de France prologue courses, Hinault obliterated the field at Basel, Switzerland, in 1982; and Induráin did the same here at Le Puy du Fou in 1993. Both champions, of course, went on to win those Tours—each taking another of their five victories.

It was too early to say whether Armstrong, too, would go on to win the 1999 Tour, but the manner in which the American won at Le Puy du Fou led to comparisons with those past great champions. And the 27-year-old also showed champion qualities in the meticulous way he readied himself for the prologue, on this humid day in the Vendée.

Armstrong had already ridden the course several times the previous day, learning the best lines to take through the several tight turns, and the gear ratios he needed on the constant changes in grade. This was *not* a straightforward, city-street prologue, like the ones taken by specialist Chris Boardman in three of the previous five years. This one was entirely on country roads, most of which had been resurfaced since Induráin won the '93 prologue—which marked Armstrong's debut in the Tour de France. The course's main feature was a half-mile-long, 187-foot climb called the Côte de Fossé, which averages a grade of 7 percent, with a short section of 14-percent grade immediately following the turn onto the hill. This is where Armstrong experienced his only moments of doubt in an otherwise faultless, 50.788-kph ride. "At the last minute," he said, "I changed to the small ring [44], but I couldn't get it back to the big ring (when the grade softened)."

To help him decide on that big ring-versus-small ring dilemma, Armstrong had quizzed each of his teammates after they completed their rides; and he even did a lap in the team car, wanting to see how the course looked at true racing speeds, by following teammate Tyler Hamilton, 90 minutes before his own start.

Hamilton used the small chainring on the climb for his 18th-place, 8:29 ride. That was the same time obtained by Jonathan Vaughters, who never shifted from his big ring, a 54. George Hincapie also rode the hill in the big ring, to take 15th place in 8:28; while Tour rookie Christian Vande Velde, 14th in 8:27, shifted into his 44x19 for the climb. With such conflicting evidence, it was probably inevitable that Armstrong would make that last-minute decision change.

Besides such in-depth technical considerations, Armstrong also handled the physical and mental challenges like a champion. When his start was less than an hour away, he began warming up, using his race bike on a wind-trainer. At times, three Postal riders would be on the wind-trainers, which were set up beneath a canopy strung between the team's two rented camper-vans.

After the fast warm-up, Armstrong went back into one of the vans to dry off. Then, in

FRANKIE'S DIARY ◎ July 1 ◎ Le Puy du Fou

Tests and travelers' tales

I was wondering what today would be like. For eight years, I have done the token medical tests that the Tour gives its riders each year. They consisted of a two-minute EKG, weight, height, fat, blood pressure, pulse, and lung-capacity test. That was it; the whole procedure had the riders in and out in under 10 minutes. But this year, because of all the past doping problems and the French crackdown on doping, I was expecting something different. I was wrong. It was the same test as usual—only quicker.

George did get into a bit of trouble at the medical testing though, when he took off his shirt for the EKG testing. Our director Johan jumped out of his seat saying, " George what the hell have you been doing?" He saw that George had no tan lines. You're supposed to be *training* before the Tour, not hanging out at the beach.

There are always a few hiccups while traveling to the start of the Tour. The Gerona boys—George, Christian, Tyler and Jonathan—had a delayed flight leaving Barcelona, so they missed their connection in Nice. They were supposed to arrive in Nantes at the team hotel around 5 p.m. Instead, they didn't show up till 11:30 p.m. Another hiccup happened when Mark Gorski and his crew arrived at Paris-Orly from America. I will know more details tomorrow, but they were delayed about three or four hours in customs. They were bringing some T-shirts for the team, but a problem arose with customs because the shirts had the Tour logo on them. I think it was some kind of trademark infringement thing.

The morning training consisted of the usual tinkering and adjusting of our new team bikes. Some guys changed handlebars, while others changed the cleats on their shoes. Its funny how some guys hop on the bike and go, while others sit outside for hours measuring every piece on the bike that can be measured. Some guys even changed their shoes. Everyone has a different idea about what can be tinkered with before a big race and what is completely off limits.

The team Fiat cars were waiting for us at the airport. Because the Tour is sponsored by Fiat, we are not allowed to use our team Volkswagens. The staff flew in a couple of days early, and went to Paris to pick up the cars. The cars come already equipped with radios and televisions in them. The TV is placed in the rear of the car, to help cut down on unnecessary accidents. In the past, directors would be so busy watching TV that they would slam into the cars in front of them. Of course, every director thinks this only happens to other guys.

That's why we have already jimmy-rigged our car to have a TV in the back of the car *and* in the front.... Instead of having to fly to Paris to pick the cars up, a team can arrange for their team Fiat's to be delivered to their team hotel at a certain date. But if you did this, you wouldn't have time to fine-tune your cars.

When we got on the plane in Nice, Kevin started bragging to Lance and me about how he had packed everything under the sun to bring to the race. He said he could live out of his suitcase for a *year*, if he wanted to. When we landed, we discovered that Kevin might have packed everything under the sun, but he forgot to pack his team tennis shoes. Lance got these shoes for everyone for one reason—the team presentation.

Luckily, the team had a spare pair of shoes in the truck. Even better luck was that they were exactly Kevin's size.

a long-sleeved skinsuit, he returned to the wind-trainer about 15 minutes before his 7:07 p.m. start. He looked nervous, slowly turning the pedals, chatting to team boss Mark Gorski, adjusting his rear brake cable, and then listening to Hincapie's comments on his ride. By now, the evening sun had broken through the all-day cloud cover. Armstrong then donned his helmet, climbed aboard his time-trial machine, and bumped his way across the grass toward the start area....

At the same time, about 100 feet from where Armstrong had been warming up, Bobby Julich—the final starter, two minutes after Armstrong—was making *his* final preparations. Unlike the Texan, Julich chose to do his fast, wind-trainer warm-up at the end. He was wearing just a sleeveless T-shirt and rolled-down bib shorts, and was sweating profusely until he dismounted, drank a gel-pack and some water, and went to dry off in his Cofidis team van, exactly 15 minutes before starting. Then, after his mechanic had removed, cleaned and refitted the wheels on his race bike—carrying it across the grass to the start—Julich pedaled his road bike the short distance to the road.

Once there, like stalking cats, he and Armstrong slowly pedaled their titanium race machines around a small barricaded-off section, awaiting their start call. Julich was straight-mouthed, his eyes expressionless, as he focused internally on the enormous task ahead. Armstrong's face was more lined, reflecting the huge pressure that had been on him for months, to be totally prepared for this moment. But he looked confident, and gave a split-second wink of recognition, as a reporter gave him a thumbs-up. Armstrong then climbed the steps of the start house, just as Crédit Agricole's Boardman sprinted away down the ramp.

Armstrong was next...followed by world time trial champion Abraham Olano of ONCE-Deutsche Bank...and then Julich.

As Armstrong set off, the controversial Richard Virenque—given a last-minute reprieve to ride the Tour by the Union Cycliste Internationale—was about to finish his prologue. There were boos among the cheers coming from the tens of thousands behind the course's continuous line of metal barriers, as the Frenchman finished with a very ordinary 8:53.

The fastest time was still the 8:20 set almost three hours earlier by eighth starter Rik Verbrugghe of Lotto-Mobistar—one of Belgium's promising young bloods. But a couple of riders behind Virenque came one of his former teammates, Christophe Moreau, still with Festina after a six-month drug-related suspension, who blazed home in 8:17.

Another rider caught up in the Festina affair, Zülle, seemed to have the prologue sewn up when he arrived four minutes later, storming up the slight rise to the finish, to record an 8:09—three seconds faster than Induráin's course record. Zülle's ride looked all the more impressive when Boardman arrived next, with a time one second slower than Moreau's.

Meanwhile, Olano and Armstrong were waging a fierce battle out on the course. The Spaniard—looking immaculate in his white, rainbow-striped world's jersey, and fresh from 400km of solo training in the Pyrénées—hurtled through the first 3.7km at more than 56 kph. His intermediate time of 3:56 was five seconds faster than the previous best, just set by Boardman, and eight seconds faster than Zülle.

This opening section was mainly downhill, including a couple of long curves, with a tight right turn through a roundabout onto a short hill, before leveling off and reaching the sharp right at the start of the Fossé climb.

Armstrong reached the checkpoint second best, just three seconds slower than Olano, and ready to launch himself over the very difficult 3.1km finale. "My teammates agreed that the race would be won on the last half of the hill to the finish," Armstrong said later.

By the top of the climb, angling across a grassy hillside, the American had taken command, three seconds faster than Zülle, with Olano in third, another three seconds back.

Armstrong kept up the pressure on the next mostly downhill 2km, smoothly negotiating three fast curves, before neatly rounding a slow-speed U-turn 400 meters from the line. By the finish, he had added four more seconds to his winning margin on Zülle, and another five seconds on Olano.

Lance's crash and the yellow book

Last night we were debating how to solve a problem. We were trying to avoid driving for four hours, going back and forth to the course. Our hotel is situated 70km from the prologue course and from where the team presentation takes place. We wanted to see the course in the morning—a two-hour round-trip drive—and then we would have to go to the 9 p.m. team presentation, another two-hour drive. Sitting in the car for several hours wouldn't exactly keep the legs fresh, the day before the start of the Tour.

By morning, we decided to drive to the course and ride home. Lance and George decided to stay and ride the circuits, and then drive home. My ride for the day was 100km, and when I got back to the hotel, everyone asked if I had heard about Lance. Juan, our mechanic, picked up a wheel that was all twisted and told me Lance was hit by a car on the prologue circuit. George said he was following Lance as they passed a bunch of cars that were stopped at the bottom of a hill. The exact moment when Lance looked down to see what gear he was in, a car started to pull out.

Lance swerved to avoid it, but the mirror caught him on the hip and sent him over. The driver was the third director of Telekom. He lost it—no, not Lance, the driver. He couldn't believe he had hit a rider and kept apologizing and saying, "God, I hope nothing's broken." Well, Lance was fine. He had a few words with the director, then hopped back on his bike and rode for another hour before making the drive back to the hotel. At lunch, Lance still seemed fine, so I suppose no harm done.

We received our yellow Tour books today.
We call it the "race bible." This book is what you look at every night and every morning to get an idea of what the day will be like. It also can provide sleepless nights. The "bible" lists and shows everything, including the start area, degree of difficulty of the mountains, how long the transfers are for the staff, the finish area, and where the medical and press areas are. Pretty much anything you can think of you will find in the bible. We get a mini version of the "bible" to carry in our pockets, to look at during each stage.

This information is put on laminated cards that we carry with us, and it provides us with the course profiles and location of feed zones each day. Right now, I have 21 cards sitting in my bag, I already look forward to when they are gone.

Along with the "bible," we also receive a small book detailing all the rules and regulations. It describes the procedure for the feed zones, the time bonuses for each stage, prize money, how to protest and other technical stuff. I only keep this book for one reason: It contains the percentages for the time cuts in the mountain stages. That's the most important rule: You have to finish within the time limit in order to keep going.

Also included in this Tour package is a book on the history of the Tour. It contains names of all the mountains raced in the Tour, finish cities, winners, losers, and anyone who has ever won a

GEORGE HINCAPIE

Tour stage. It can have lots of useful or useless information, depending on who you are.

On top of all of this, we get a book that lists each team and where their hotels are for the entire three weeks. This includes little maps to help find the mom-and-pop places, and gives their telephone and fax numbers. It is not very difficult to track and locate a rider during the Tour. In fact, you can send a letter to any rider you want during the Tour. You just address an envelope with "DYNAPOST-LE TOUR," and under it you put which team and which rider or staff person it should go to. Intermittently, throughout the Tour, they deliver the mail to the teams. It was crazy the amount of mail a French rider like Jean-Cyril Robin— who was on our team last year— would receive. The mail guy would show up and pass out one for George, one for Tyler and 30 to Jean-Cyril. J.C. would then have to sign his postcards and write each person back. Most of the time that's what people want, an autographed card.

Tonight is the team presentation. We are scheduled for a 9 p.m. showing, but knowing how these things work, it will probably be an hour late. Since we have an hour's drive home after the presentation, we won't get back to the hotel till probably after 11. Before the presentation we have a meeting. Surprise! Today, the Tour announced a mandatory meeting between all teams, riders, staff and doctors. Pretty much anybody working in the Tour has to attend this meeting. Because I will get back to the hotel past my bedtime, and because I'm not a night owl, I'll tell you about the meeting and team presentation tomorrow. And I'll also be talking about the prologue, the first day of the 1999 Tour.

FRANKIE'S DIARY ◎ July 3 ◎ Le Puy du Fou

Meetings—and the yellow jersey!

As I wrote yesterday, last night we had to attend a mandatory Tour de France meeting, and after that do the Tour team presentation. The meeting was a closed meeting with no press allowed inside. They didn't *have* to be inside: The microphone was so loud that with the windows open in the back, you could have been a block away and heard what was going on. The first to speak was Jean-Claude Killy, boss of the Société du Tour. He gave a little pep talk about how it's everybody's dream to do the Tour and how all the little kids look up to us. It was pretty tame.

Next was race director-general Jean-Marie Leblanc. He told us how the Tour was in jeopardy and how our jobs were also in jeopardy, if the same mess as last year happened. His talk was a little more stern. Next was UCI president Hein Verbruggen, who was nowhere last year when the shit hit the fan. His talk was to the point, saying that the UCI has rules and you have to follow them. The police have rules and you have to follow them. His stance was no tolerance for anything. His talk was direct and forceful.

The meeting started at 7 p.m. When we entered the building we were given headphones to wear, so we could hear the translation in English. There were three channels—Spanish, Italian and English. Looking around, it felt like I was at a United Nations meeting, seeing everyone wearing the headphones. Ironically, guess which two teams were late to arrive to the meeting? Festina arrived 10 minutes late; and Polti, with Virenque, arrived more than 35 minutes late.

Nothing like making a good first impression.

The team presentation was outside in a theme park of medieval times. Each team was introduced with their directors for a few minutes in front of the 15,000 crowd sitting in the stands. All in all, it was pretty quick. ONCE was the team in front of us. When they announced Manolo Saiz, the director of ONCE, the crowd started to boo and whistle. I think they were upset that he was allowed to come and participate in the Tour.

LANCE ARMSTRONG

That afternoon, driving to the team presentation, we had a small accident. We lost one of the team bikes off the car rack. Kevin saw the whole thing. The bike just lifted up and landed in the middle of the freeway on its handlebars and saddle. When it happened, Kevin told the others in the car, "Man, whoever's bike that is he's going to be pissed." When they got out of the car, they found out that the bike was Kevin's.

Saw a small highlight on Eurosport news the other day. They showed Virenque going to the medical control. On his way out, a spectator tried to kick him, and he may have made contact. Anyway, Virenque freaked and started chasing the guy trying to hit him. This is while all the film crews and photographers were there. They were tripping all over each other in all the chaos....

The first part of today's diary wouldn't have started the way it did if I knew then what I know now. Lance is in the yellow jersey, after winning today's prologue. This will be my second time defending the yellow jersey in the Tour. My first time was when Sean Yates took the yellow in 1994. Kevin defended the yellow jersey last year when Laurent Desbiens had it for three or four days. The prologue course was tailor-made for Lance, an 8-kilometer time trial with a steep 700-meter-long climb. It was a course for the powerful and strong. I felt good at the start and decided to attempt the hill in the big ring, so Lance would get a feel if maybe the small ring was better. This had been an ongoing debate for two days: big ring or small ring. I discovered the big ring was the right way to lose the race. I completely blew at the top of the hill and never recovered until after the finish line. It was an experiment that was pure hell for me, but maybe it helped Lance in the long run. With the form Lance had shown in the previous races, we all knew it was possible for him to take the prologue. You could tell Lance knew he could do it, too, because he was nervous. Normally, he is not like that.

Tomorrow, there are three time bonuses, and along with the finish bonus there is a total of 50 seconds the sprinters can take back on the leaders. I don't think anyone will take that much time tomorrow, but by the next day, the jersey could change hands. If we were really on the ball, then maybe George could get the time bonuses from the other sprinters and take the yellow jersey from Lance. We can only dream.... Then again, one of our dreams has already come true.

Behind, Julich was not having such a good time. He later said, "In order to hit the prologue right on, you have to be not only really fresh, but also very prepared...to find the rhythm. I felt like I had the form, but not the rhythm."

As a result, from reaching the first checkpoint in eighth only six seconds slower than Armstrong, the Cofidis leader lost another 18 seconds on the hill, and ended up in 22nd place, 28 seconds behind a champion named Armstrong.

STAGE 1
Montaigu–Challans • July 4

Going about their business

ON THE HIGH ROAD RUNNING ALONG a ridge grandly named Mont Mercure, you almost feel as if you *are* with Mercury, the god of travelers. The ridge's elevation is less than 1000 feet, but it's the highest point of the Vendée, overlooking a countryside of wooded knolls, cow pastures and cornfields that roll down to a coastal plain stretching west to marshes, sand dunes and beaches on the Atlantic Ocean. The views were particularly evocative on a rain-filled afternoon, with banks of leaden clouds hanging over a chlorophyll-colored landscape.

There wasn't much wind to disperse the clouds on this opening road stage of the 86th Tour de France, and frequent heavy rain showers looked likely to make the day a nervous one for the 180 riders, as they headed out of tiny Montaigu on a meandering journey to the market town of Challans.

The most nervous of all, it seemed, was the man wearing the first *maillot jaune* of his storied career: Armstrong. On this Fourth of July, the American was mobbed by the media before the start, and once on the road, he knew that the responsibility of controlling the race lay with him and his devoted Postal Service teammates.

They performed their task impeccably. On the up-and-down opening section, including the gentle 4km rise to Mont Mercure, the team averaged 39 kph. Then, heading down to the plains, they didn't chase when solo-breakaway specialist Thierry Gouvenou of BigMat-Auber 93 headed off into the rain.

The 30-year-old French rider later said that he hoped Armstrong's team would let him not only pursue his break, but also win the stage. And within 10km, racing through the region's historic former capital, Fontenay-le-Comte, Gouvenou already had a four-minute lead. But Armstrong and his men weren't prepared to let him get away that easily.

It was the job of Tour veteran Frankie Andreu and Danish teammate Peter Meinert-Nielsen to take care of these situations…and they did.

The two powerful Postal workers towed the peloton for the next 80km, restricting Gouvenou to a maximum lead

---

FRANKIE'S DIARY © July 4

America's big day

It's the Fourth of July. Kind of cool having an American in the yellow jersey today. And it's the first time for an American on an American *team* to have the yellow [although the 7-Eleven team did have the yellow jersey in the '80s with Canadians Alex Stieda and Steve Bauer].

From day one, the team plan was to be at top form for the Tour. This was specifically pointed at Lance, Kevin and Tyler, and all of them have met that challenge. After a tranquil spring, these riders—and Jonathan—put their noses to the grindstone to prepare for the Tour. They had two different camps—one in the Pyrénées and one in the Alps—to look at the Tour's mountain stages. Each camp was about one-week long and included several back-to-back seven-hour days in the mountains. After that, they went to race in the Classique des Alpes, Dauphiné and Route du Sud. And the results from these races proved that the team's plan was working. The hard part now is taking this early success of wearing the yellow jersey and continuing it through the next three weeks.

We woke up to rain and finished in the rain. It was a 208km-long wet day. Our main objectives were to keep Lance out of trouble and to let George go for some of the time-bonus sprints. Before the stage, we had the usual sign-on; but today, we also had a team presentation because we were leading the team G.C. At the presentation, each rider gets one of the Crédit Lyonnais lions. For some reason, they had only eight today, and I got flicked. I told the guy that tomorrow I wanted *two* lions, to make up for the one I missed today.

When Lance arrived at the start area, it was pure chaos. He might as well have been a rock star. There were cameras and journalists everywhere, trying to get at him. Even Lance said it was crazy: "It's nice to get on the bike and get away from all that."

As the race began, everyone was seeing how they felt. Eventually, a rider from BigMat, Thierry Gouvenou, got away by himself. Peter and I then rode on the front for about 100km, keeping the time gained on the peloton in check. We let him stay around four or five minutes, until the sprinter teams could take over for the finish. We have to keep the time close; otherwise, the sprinter teams won't show interest in putting in an effort to go for the stage. In the final sprint, Kirsipuu (Casino) won in front of Steels (Mapei). George got pinned along the barriers and waited for a gap to open, but it never happened. Because of the bonus sprints on the road and the finish bonus, Kirsipuu is now around 16 seconds from Lance, and O'Grady (Crédit Agricole) is 20 seconds back.

In the races, there are two ways to tell if one of us on the team is riding a spare Trek bike. The first clue is that the spare bikes have yellow tires on them. The tires on the spare bikes are clinchers, while our race wheels that are Rolf's have tubulars. The second dead giveaway is the color of the water-bottle cages. Our race bikes have black cages, while all the spares have red ones. This makes it easy for the mechanics to keep the bikes separate and know which bikes have to go on which cars for the race.

I saw Jeff Pierce today. One year, Jeff won the final stage of the Tour on the Champs in Paris. He broke away solo and, more impressive, he stayed away—something that never happens nowadays. He mentioned that the last time he had been to Europe was nine years ago. He is here with Lotto and GT bicycles. GT became the bike sponsor of the team when Lotto became very unhappy with Vitus, its old supplier. Jeff said they finalized the deal in the first week of June, and now the entire team is on GTs. To be able to outfit a Tour team that quickly is incredible.

A quick run-down of teams that have had drug problems this year:
• Mercatone Uno: Pantani's high hematocrit level in the Giro
• Festina: car stopped at border with steroids, and soigneur driving the car was fired
• Lampre: bag full of syringes and drugs found during Tour of Switzerland
• Saeco: high hematocrit for one rider at the Tour of Switzerland
• Polti: the whole Virenque thing
• Cofidis: Vandenbroucke, who is now cleared of everything, and Gaumont, who's under official investigation
• TVM: nothing this year, just they can't do the Tour
• Casino: Roux positive at the Flèche Wallonne
• Telekom: speculation of drug use from *Der Spiegel* magazine, which, I think, is like the *National Enquirer*
• BigMat: team suspended Pascal Lino for using corticoids without informing his team doctor
• Kelme: high hematocrit for one rider in Giro
• Vini Caldirola: Gontchar with high hematocrit in Switzerland; made selection for the Tour, then eliminated
• Mapei: soigneur busted for sending amphetamines in the mail to Italy…yeah, this is stretching it
• Amore & Vita (did not qualify for the Tour): the team that publishes its riders' hematocrit for everyone to see on its Web page. The team says it has nothing to hide. It has had three riders this year suspended for having high hematocrit levels. One rider tested high early in the year, and the last two were discovered during the first day of the Giro. All were fired immediately from the team. When the last two were fired on the first day of the Giro, the team hired back the first rider who was fired in the spring. This is a good system. With the team's track record, I would have thought you would have seen at least a couple of 52s published on its Web site.

of 6:40, and pulling the pack within 3:30 by La Roche-sur-Yon, the region's modern capital. Here, the Postal riders made a clever move to snaffle some bonus seconds at the city's intermediate sprint: Shielded by Postal teammates leading the pack, Vande Velde accelerated with Hincapie on his wheel, to take the four- and two-second bonuses before the other sprinters realized what had happened.

The stage was now within 45km of the finish, close enough for Andreu and Meinert-Nielsen to ease back and allow the sprinters' teams to take up the tempo. A strong, but steady pace was enough for Gouvenou to be caught 16km from Challans. Immediately, Lampre-Daikin's Ludo Dierckxsens counterattacked. The 34-year-old Belgian had won his national championship in a solo break the previous week, and his move here came after riding patiently near to the front for the previous 20km. Dierckxsens, showing commendable speed, moved 23 seconds ahead after 8km of effort; but that was as much as he was allowed, and he was caught just inside 4km to go.

Mario Cipollini's Saeco-Cannondale team did most of the tempo on the run-in, but this wasn't the famous red train seen at the Giro d'Italia. Instead, on narrow roads coming into the small town, the mix at the front also included Mapei-Quick Step (for Tom Steels), Telekom's Erik Zabel, La Française des Jeux (for neo-pro sprinter Jimmy Casper), Crédit Agricole (for Stuart O'Grady)…and even BigMat (for Frenchman Christophe Capelle and Aussie Jay Sweet).

The result was what Casino's Kirsipuu—the winningest pro racer of the early season—called "a sprint not controlled at all." Kirsipuu, 30, had been trying to win a Tour stage for five years; so when teammate Pascal Chanteur gave him a beautiful lead-out around the last turn, 350 meters from the line, the squat, thick-thighed Estonian made the most of it. He first followed BigMat's Carlos De Cruz, before unleashing a vigorous sprint that gave him a clear victory over a late-charging Steels, with a disappointing Zabel in third.

The tally? An Estonian had won a Tour stage for the first time; the rain had stopped; and Armstrong was still in the yellow jersey. Even Mercury had done his job: Only one rider was slightly hurt in a pileup 25km from the finish.

STAGE 2

Challans–St. Nazaire • July 5

Major operation

TO WIN A TOUR DE FRANCE AS OPEN AS THIS ONE, a rider and his team have to be on the alert every minute of every stage. In the first week, in particular, you have to ride intelligently, staying close to the front to avoid the crashes that inevitably occur, and ready to take the initiative whenever an opportunity to make time presents itself. It's just as important to study the details of every stage beforehand—none more so than this 176km stage 2 between Challans and St. Nazaire.

Always within sniffing distance of the ocean, the completely flat course never ceased changing direction—a particularly challenging prospect on a day when 30-mph winds were blowing from the sea. Halfway through the stage came a challenge that wouldn't look out of place at Paris-Roubaix: the Passage du Gois.

This narrow 4km-long causeway was originally built with rocks and paving stones 200 years ago to link the island of Noirmoutier with the mainland. Five sections of paving stones, some of them cracked, still remain, while concrete and bitumen have been used in this century to replace parts that had sunk. The causeway is underwater for most of the day, and can only be crossed at low tide. On this day, it was still covered with seawater less than two hours before the race arrived, which would leave some stretches still wet, with barnacles growing on each side, and wet mud beyond the edges.

The Gois has been included in only one previous Tour, in 1993, when it was crossed early in a much longer stage, and was completely dry. Even then, the crosswind caused the peloton to be temporarily split. This year, there was much more significant damage—caused by both the speed set at the front, and a mass pileup 1 kilometer into the crossing.

But it was with another pileup, exactly an hour earlier, that the story of this stage really began. About 30 riders were involved in this first crash, which happened just where the course turned onto the coast road, 34km into the stage. Among those who went down were pre-race favorites, Rabobank's Michael Boogerd and Banesto's Manuel Beltran, along with the Postal team's Hamilton.

Boogerd fell awkwardly and his front teeth bit though his lower lip, which he couldn't release until helped by one of the race doctors. Hamilton hit his head and was dazed; and he needed a spare bike because the crash bent his forks and broke both wheels.

With the main group riding at more than 45 kph, it took the delayed riders up to 25km of chasing before making it back, so the field was together when it reached the modern, 100-foot-high bridge onto Noirmoutier Island, 7km before reaching the Gois causeway.

Boogerd later said that he knew it was important to be near the front, but made the decision to stay toward the middle of the pack.

Unfortunately for him, the Postal riders set a ferocious pace on the climb over the bridge, causing several riders to be dropped. They continued their effort on the flat, dune-lined road on the island, knowing that a kilometer before the causeway was a sharp right turn—from the wide main road to the narrow Gois approach road.

Hincapie took up the story, saying, "The guys all did a lot of work to get Lance near the front. Then, about 2k before the right corner, I took Lance to the front. I really put myself in the red there, so I was just basically hanging on for dear life (when we reached the causeway). I realized that there were only about 15 of us left.... We were going *so* hard, and there was no shelter at all, that we pretty much assumed there wouldn't be many guys left (with us)."

Hincapie said he was turning a 54x13 as hard as he could go, which meant a speed of probably 55 kph when they hit the causeway, especially after the right turn gave them a tail wind for about a kilometer. Then, the back road swung left to the first section of paved causeway, still wet from earlier rain and the receding tide. "It was dangerous, really dangerous," Armstrong commented.

With Armstrong and Hincapie in the front group were overall contenders Vinokourov (and Casino teammates Kirsipuu and Chanteur), Stefano Garzelli of Mercatone Uno, Paolo Savoldelli (and Saeco teammates Laurent Dufaux and Mario Cipollini), Stéphane Heulot of La Française des Jeux, and Axel Merckx of Mapei. Also there were Crédit Agricole's Henk Vogels and Magnus Bäckstedt, Telekom's Steffen Wesemann and BigMat's Lylian Lebreton.

The causeway and the cat

It's amazing how the day's objectives can change so quickly. This morning we were thinking about how to keep the yellow jersey without expending too much energy. The main difficulty in this completely flat stage would be a 4-kilometer causeway that crosses the sea. It's passable during the day with low tide, and flooded during high tide. You can imagine that the causeway would be a little slick and wet by the time we arrived.

The race was calm till the first bonus sprint of the day at 30km. After that, the attacks opened up, and the battle for good position for the causeway was already starting—even though there were still 50km till we arrived there. To make matters worse, it was windy; and I'm sure every team told their riders to be first into the causeway. The battle was furious, trying to keep Lance in good position to get across this causeway safely. Looking back, it was a good thing we did. After the entrance to this 4-kilometer causeway, there was a huge crash. Guys went down everywhere. You could see riders trying to brake, but they hit the ground instantaneously. Going across the causeway was very, very scary. It was wet, slippery and windy. It felt like a risk to even turn your wheel to change directions. I was scared to ride on the edge of the road; it was too slick.

Coming out of the causeway, the group had split—partly because we went fast, and partly because of the huge crash. There was a front group of about 40, and ONCE immediately started riding. It took us a few kilometers to figure out why. We didn't know there was a crash at the time, and that in the rear group there were a few favorites. Right away, Johan told us to go to the front and help ONCE. The reason was that in the second group were Gotti, Belli, Zülle, Boogerd, Robin, and some other favorites in the overall. In the second group, Banesto started to chase immediately. They came within 30 seconds of catching us, but we were in time-trial mode in the first group, with about 10 guys.

It became an 80km team time trial, trying to increase the gap between the second group and us. We had five ONCE riders, two Casino, two Cofidis, and Christian and I, riding full tilt all the way to the finish. We put over six minutes on the guys behind.

Lance lost the jersey today to Kirsipuu who

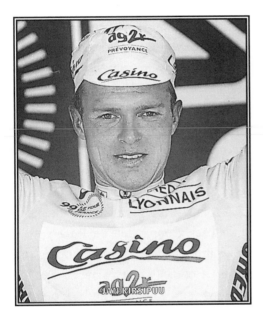

JAN KIRSIPUU

won every bonus sprint; but Lance did manage to eliminate some very strong riders for the *classement*....

Lance is not bummed that he lost the jersey, but he *is* bummed that he will lose some of the perks that come with the jersey. For example, each jersey leader—points, yellow and mountain—gets their own private camper at the finish. It has a fully stocked fridge and a television, and all the press are kept out. It was ideal for winding down from the race and changing into some fresh clothes.

In the race today, the Spanish guys had a new nickname for Jonathan. They call him "El Gato," the cat. This is because yesterday he flew

into a crash and went flying, but somehow landed on his feet and without a scratch on his body. The bad news is that today Jonathan lost his nickname. He was one of the unlucky ones to get caught in the crash on the causeway. He crashed bad, cutting his chin wide-open. He got back up and continued riding, while the medical staff bandaged him. But after 10 or 15km, some of his other injuries became evident, and it was necessary for him to stop. It truly is bad luck, because Jonathan's form in the mountains would have provided some very big surprises.

Also involved in two crashes today were Tyler and Pascal. Tyler has a sore knee, and both of these guys are a little beat up, but they should be able to continue tomorrow.

One of the official sponsors of the prologue was Carnac cycling shoes. They issued about 300,000 pamphlets to pass around the course, and the cover featured George—highlighting, of course, his Carnacs. We both received some new yellow riding shoes, but I can't change shoes in one day, George can and he did.

A little trivia information for you:
• The average weight of a Tour rider this year is 70 kilograms (154 pounds)
• The average resting pulse is 53 beats per minute
• The tallest rider is Mario Scirea (Saeco) at 195cm (6 feet 4 ¾ inches) Usually, Eros Poli is the tallest, but he didn't get selected to do the Tour this year. He is on a French team and the director had to take some French guys to the Tour, so Eros was left out. The other Crédit Agricole riders were not happy about this.
• The lightest rider is Pellicioli at 52kg (114 pounds)
• The heaviest rider is Bäckstedt at 95kg (209 pounds). That should give you a new appreciation for suffering in the mountains.
• The biggest lung capacity was Morin's at 7.83 liters
• The lowest cardiac resting pulse was Demarbaix at 33 beats per minute.

One other rider, Heulot's teammate Christophe Bassons, had also been in the group, but flatted halfway across the causeway, leaving 15 riders ahead, now riding with a three-quarter tail wind.

Behind them, the pack had split into five or six groups before even reaching the Gois crossing, where thousands of fans were watching from boats, safety towers and the mud flats. Then, on the first right curve, about a kilometer out across the causeway, several riders fell, blocking the roadway for the back groups. It was here that Postal's Vaughters crashed heavily, head first, cutting open his chin and soon causing him to quit. Rabobank's Marc Wauters also crashed hard, bounced onto the mud on the right, and clambered back on to the causeway before abandoning. And Hamilton, who said he was riding alongside Boogerd and his team, "hoping to be safe," was among the dozens who were delayed.

When a head count was taken back on the mainland, the 15 leaders were 30 seconds ahead of a chase group of 40, with the next group, 20-strong, at 45 seconds. These three groups soon came together and set off at blitzkrieg speed across the flats toward Machecoul, with a 37-second gap on another group of 50. In this chase group were top Tour favorites Zülle, Boogerd and Polti's Ivan Gotti. They and the teammates with them now faced what looked likely to be a long, possibly desperate pursuit....

At first, the gap came down—to as small as 25 seconds, with 83km still to race. But with only Rabobank, Polti and Banesto working for the back group, while the leaders were being pulled by ONCE (with six riders), Postal (with Vande Velde and Andreu doing the work, while Armstrong, Livingston and Hincapie sat in), Cofidis (with two men riding for Julich, Casino (for Vinokourov), Casino (for Vinokourov and Kirsipuu) and Mapei (for Tonkov), the gap inevitably started to grow again. It took 20km to grow from 25 seconds to a minute...and it then grew exponentially, to reach 6:05 by the finish.

There, after covering the last two hours at a phenomenal average speed of 54.67 kph (!), the 74 riders in front contested a rather normal-looking field sprint—even if the sprinters and their lead-out men were stiff and tired from the frenetic pace. Lars Michaelson led out for French upstart Casper, but the La Française des Jeux sprinter was helpless as Steels took command in the final 50 meters, to win from Kirsipuu and Cipollini.

Hincapie, in sixth, finished very fast, but, as he said, "the last 50 meters, I've got so much speed, so I just need to be like two or three guys forward. But it's hard (to contest the sprints), because we're all helping Lance...."

On this day—even though Vaughters crashed out—Armstrong took a big step forward in his quest to win this Tour. Eliminating Zülle, Boogerd and Gotti from the yellow jersey race was the result of intelligent planning, hard work and tactical excellence.

STAGE 3

Nantes–Laval • July 6

Turns of the dice

A THIRD MASS SPRINT, A SECOND STRAIGHT WIN FOR TOM STEELS. It all seemed so simple for the big Belgian. But behind the final result were a host of happenstances that took others out of contention before they had a chance to make their own claims for success.

Take the case of the U.S. Postal Service's George Hincapie. The previous day, he had finished sixth on the sensational second stage from Challans to St. Nazaire—even after doing a huge amount of work for team leader Armstrong. There would be less work for him on this stage 3 from Nantes to Laval, because Armstrong had conceded the yellow jersey to sprinter Jaan Kirsipuu, whose Casino team now had the responsibility to lead the pack.

So it was an easier day for Hincapie, who sensed that his sprinting form was good enough by now to contend for the stage win. That was the theory...until a compact peloton reached a roundabout inside the final 5 kilometers. "Suddenly, everyone put on their brakes and I had to stop, clip out of my pedals," Hincapie said. "So the last three kilometers I had to sprint (on my own) down the hill (into Laval)...then with 2k to go, just as I got back into the top 20, I got completely pinned.... From then on, I moved up one rider at a time, and so when I got to the sprint I was already at the limit."

Hincapie still came in fifth...but what if?

Despite his bad luck, the American at least was still able to make a play for victory. That wasn't the case with Jacky Durand of Lotto-Mobistar. Ever since the 1999 Tour route was announced last October, Durand had been talking about the Tour stage finishing in his hometown, where he is the region's main sports hero. On the way into Laval there were banners proclaiming Durand's fans loyalty and enthusiasm for him; and his name was painted on the black, rolling roads though the rural landscape of wheat fields and meadows. The fans, of course, were hoping that Durand would at least figure in one of his patented long-distance breaks, if not win the stage.

Again, that was the theory. But from early in the stage, the former French champion was struggling at the back of the pack, along with others nursing injuries from the previous day's crashes. Durand had fallen in the pileup on the Gois causeway, and needed to get a replacement bike. When he restarted, he found that the brakes were not working too well on the spare bike. So on seeing his team car stopped on the roadside as he caught back, he attempted to stop, but skidded onto the car door, and fell into the road. Not seeing him,

FRANKIE'S DIARY ◎ July 6 ◎ Laval

Sprinting, and time to move

It's two for Steels and it looks easier for him each time. After winning yesterday, Tom took today's race in a massive, very fast bunch sprint. In the weeks prior to the Tour, I wouldn't have said that Tom would win a stage this year—based solely on his performance. But based on his past history and how Tom seems to always find a new level of fitness for the Tour, I would have guaranteed a stage win. In the races leading up to the Tour, Tom gets up there every day for the challenge of the sprint, yet he remains cautious and careful. He knows the risks and he's not ready to take them till he has to. He doesn't kill everyone by lengths, and sometimes he's unable to come around the first rider for the win. He must have been waiting for the Tour, because now he is a whole different rider—with a support team that any rider would dream for.

All in all, it was a very uneventful day. In fact, it was downright boring, compared to yesterday when the whole outcome of the race changed. Today was perfect for me, though. I woke up tired, after working for two straight days trying to keep the jersey. Yesterday especially took it out of me. So today was a rest day for me…well, as much as you can rest in a 195km Tour stage. A break went early in the stage, and Casino had to ride on the front the whole day. It was nice to change roles with them: What a difference just sitting in, compared to riding on the front.

The break was caught with about 30km to go, and that was when the race really began. The whole day our job was keeping Lance out of the wind and near the front out of trouble. Early in the race this job is easy; at the end of the race, it becomes nearly impossible. The sprinters are going crazy, the speed has tripled, and it never feels like you are far enough in the front to stay out of trouble. Making our job a

little easier is the fact that Lance is good at holding and fighting for position. He's not like some guys whose hand you have to hold the whole time or they're spat out the back. Lance knows how to battle to stay at the front.

Finally, we changed hotels. The start of this Tour de France has taken us nowhere. It's been like the Tour de Nantes. We have spent one week in the same hotel and haven't left the region after four days of racing. Pascal was loving it; it's his

TOM STEELS

hometown here. He's already excited for next year, because we have two or three stages in the same area, and we will also see the return of the team time trial.

Because of yesterday's crash and the high speeds to the finish, the organizers decided nobody would be eliminated for finishing outside of the time cut. There were a few groups that would have been eliminated, if the time-cut rule had been enforced. Pascal was in one of those groups. As it was, there were riders who finished 50 minutes behind and they still were allowed to start the next day. Two riders did not start this morning, though, because of injuries sustained yesterday. One was Jonathan, who got stitches in his chin and hit his head; and the other was Rabobank's Marc Wauters.

We are still leading the team G.C. and every day we do the team presentation at sign-on. So far, each of us has collected three Crédit Lyonnais lions. After today's team presentation, Christian had to stay on the stage for another award. Our young lad is now leading the *classement* for young riders. Verbrugghe (Lotto), who was leading, didn't make the split yesterday and lost 15 minutes. Christian now has a nine-second lead over Salmon (Casino).

Each day, La Française des Jeux is desperately trying to set up Jimmy Casper for a win. This young French rider scooped Zabel in the Tour of Germany. The team only has eight or 10 days for Jimmy to pull off a win before he stops. At 21 years of age, he is the youngest rider in the Tour.

I would think that if you didn't like cycling, July in France would be a nightmare. Every day the race is shown for about three hours live. Then, each night at 9 p.m. on Eurosport, we can catch a one-hour review of the race. They also show another recap of the race the next morning. The commentators for English Eurosport are David Duffield and Russell Williams. David just babbles all day long about nothing. You know how when you're watching ABC or ESPN, they go into all the cultural stuff instead of bike racing. That's exactly how Duffield is: He knows jack about racing, but babbles about hats, wine, roads, and other stupid stuff. Russell knows a little more. He used to race on the track, but has never done a Tour. Obviously, their commentary for three hours live leaves a lot to be desired. But, hey, even bad bike racing on TV is better than no bike racing on TV.

one of the Mapei team cars almost ran over Durand, giving his legs a glancing blow. The Lotto-Mobistar rider finished the stage, but was in no shape to attempt an attack on stage 3.

Another rider hoping to come through with a win at Laval was Italian icon Mario Cipollini, who was not having the best of luck with his sprints. On stage 1, in the tight finish at Challans, he got shut out on the final turn, and crossed the line in 29th. Then, in the 74-strong front group that arrived in St. Nazaire, his only lead-out man to survive the Gois causeway crossing, Salvatore Commesso, had to chase down an attack before the one-kilometer-to-go mark, and, riding solo, Cipollini was outsped by the better-protected Steels and Kirsipuu.

Now came the fast finish into Laval.

The day saw only one significant break, by local Brittany rider Frédéric Guesdon of La Française des Jeux and Italian Massimo Giunti of Cantina Tollo-Alexia, who attacked 36km out of Nantes, and were caught 38km from Laval. Race leader Kirsipuu's Casino team rode tempo for most of the 194.5km stage, and Telekom took over with 15km to go.

This time, Cipollini had his Saeco-Cannondale "red train" with him on the long downhill to Laval's Mayenne River. The strung-out peloton was moving at 70 kph heading into a sharp right turn at the bottom of the descent, where Cantina Tollo's Moreno Di Biase skidded into the hay bales.

As the Italian went down, his bike hit the wheel of Saeco lead-out man Gian Matteo Fagnini, and Cipollini, directly behind, had to slow right down. As a result, SuperMario lost his main helper and a dozen places...and by the time he worked his way back to the front, the sprint was already underway without him. He placed ninth.

In the end, the sprint was led out by La Française des Jeux, hoping for a first win by 21-year-old Jimmy Casper. A former world junior sprint champion, Casper has tremendous acceleration—which he displayed in netting four stage wins at the Tour of Germany. But after his teammates Damien Nazon and Lars Michaelsen led the charge, Casper was left to make the sprint from 200 meters out. With a slight head wind, it was much too far for the lightly built Casper. Zabel immediately took over the front, and looked as though he was going to take the win; but Steels launched his own sprint with 100 meters left, and rocketed to his second win in two days.

Hincapie, Durand and Cipollini would have to wait another day, and hope for a better turn of the dice.

STAGE 4
Laval–Blois • July 7

Speed kings

THERE WAS A TIME WHEN THE BIGGEST THRILL FOR CROWDS WATCHING A FLAT STAGE of the Tour de France were the free gifts being thrown out from vehicles in the publicity caravan. If they were lucky, the roadside fans might see a small breakaway group working hard several minutes ahead of the slow-moving pack, or perhaps be present when a local rider stopped to greet his family, after he had been given permission to temporarily ride ahead. That suited most spectators, as they then had plenty of time to enjoy a picnic, share a bottle of wine, and have some friendly conversation before heading home.

Times have changed.

Instead of seeing a big pack rolling along at perhaps a steady 35 kph for most of the day, the thousands of spectators who lined the long, straight roads between Laval and Blois on this fourth stage saw a long line of racers snaking along at 45 kph on the uphills, 55 kph on the flats, and close to 80 kph on the downhills. The locals barely had time to take their bread and cheese out of the picnic hamper before the racers arrived, well ahead of schedule. The result was the fastest stage in Tour de France history: 50.355 kph. And it could have been even faster....

Attack followed attack in the opening half-hour, with each one of them being pulled back before another was launched. The first 34km were covered in 38 minutes (almost 54 kph), before there was a short respite through the twisting streets of Sablé-sur-Sarthe. Then, on the other side of town, the attacks started again, with the next 19km taking 21 minutes (just over 54 kph).

There was a light breeze from behind, but not the powerful tail wind that helped produce the previous Tour stage record of 49.417 kph in 1993, on a 158km stage from Evreux to Amiens, when a series of breaks ended with a late solo winning move by Belgian Johan Bruyneel, now the Postal team's directeur sportif.

"We were yelling at Johan, 'Your record's going down for sure, buddy,'" recounted the USPS's Christian Vande Velde.

Not only did it seem that Bruyneel's mark would be shattered, but it also looked certain that the all-time stage record of 51.137 kph—set by Marcel Wüst in last year's Vuelta a España on a short 145.5km stage from Biescas to Zaragoza—would go. Especially when a breakaway was launched just before the first intermediate sprint at La Flèche, 59km into the stage.

The initiator was the ever-aggressive Belgian champion, Ludo Dierckxsens of Lampre-Daikin, who was joined by nine others—including, significantly, five who were within 90 seconds of race leader Kirsipuu: Spain's Alvaro Gonzalez Galdeano of Vitalicio (who was the best-placed on G.C., at 0:49); Italy's Daniel Nardello of Mapei (who was eighth at the '98 Tour de France) and Mario Scirea of Saeco-Cannondale; Frenchman Christophe Mengin of La Française des Jeux; and Belgian Fabien De Waele of Lotto-Mobistar. Also in the attack were Dutchman Leon Van Bon of Rabobank, Frenchman Anthony Morin of LFDJ, Italian Gianpaolo Mondini of Cantina Tollo and Russian hope Alexei Sivakov of BigMat.

With such dangerous riders in the break, Kirsipuu's Casino team soon began to chase, hoping to catch it before it developed into something more serious—which would have meant a much longer, tougher pursuit. So, after 10km of intense effort, the 10 leaders had gained only 20 seconds. Other teams joined in the chase, including the sprinters' teams of Crédit Agricole (Stuart O'Grady), Lampre (Jan Svorada) and Telekom (Zabel).

The gap went up to 24 seconds after 15km of effort...down to 18 seconds after 20km...up to 26 seconds after 24km...down to 18 seconds after 31km. It took the peloton just 33 minutes to complete those 31km, an average of more than 56 kph! "That's where it really hurt," said Vande Velde. "It was single file for like 20 minutes at 60 kph. *That* hurt...."

Again, the sprinters' teams joined in the chase. But not the Postal riders. Armstrong told his teammates that as soon as they reached a hill, the break would be caught. He was correct...almost. On the next short climb, eight of the lead riders did sit up and wait for the peloton, but Morin and Mondini stayed ahead.

Neither racer was a danger, and while the men in the peloton gratefully grabbed their food bags at the feed zone, the two leaders grabbed a five-minute lead within 12km. Morin and Mondini covered "only" 46km in the third hour, and opened up a maximum lead of 6:40.

It seemed a big margin, but when first Telekom, then Crédit Agricole and Saeco, opened the throttle again, the gap shrunk almost as quickly as it opened…and they were caught 6km from the finish.

The final hour was as fast as the first, and the hectic rush into Blois, alongside the wide waters of the Loire, was terrifyingly fast. "It was like the team pursuit, the last 4k," said Postal's Christian Vande Velde, a member of the U.S. track team. "I was thinking it can only be less than four minutes now…. It was unbelievable."

Also unbelievable was the way in which Saeco's red train set up Cipollini for the finish—a straight shot, a kilometer long, from the top of an ancient arched, stone bridge over the Loire. Commesso, Giuseppe Calcaterra and Scirea all played the lead-up roles, until the faithful Gian Matteo Fagnini was left leading out their leader with 350 meters to go. Cipollini began his sprint more than 200 meters from the line, and had so much power that a fast-finishing Zabel was still half a length behind when the Italian threw up his arms in triumph.

"The Lion King is still there," Cipollini

I know I'm a little late, but here's an inside tip for those of you who wager on the Tour or are involved in some type of fantasy Tour game. I can't predict if Cipo' is going to finish the Tour this year, but I do know that he is expecting his second child at the end of August, and *not* during the Tour, as many people have previously noted. Cipo' probably told everyone this so he could bail out of the Tour scot-free when he wants to.

Cipo' has now joined the ranks with the big guns by moving to Monaco. One difference is that he didn't move solely to avoid income tax. His move was based more on his inability to train and function in Italy, where his training and social life were continually being interrupted by *tifosi,* Italian fans. At every stoplight, drivers would stop Cipo' for an autograph or to talk about his Giro wins. In the mountains, drivers would pull him off the road to congratulate him and talk. If you know Italians, then you know how much they love to talk all day. I'm sure Cipo' knew it was time to move when he started having more chamois time than riding time.

Cipo' also joined the ranks of the big guns by winning today's fastest stage in Tour history. The final total was 195km done in 3:50 minutes, an average of 50.34. We all had 51 on our Vetta computers, but either way, the record still falls. From the gun, guys were racing full-out, trying to get in a break. Riders shot out of the pack as fast as you hear snap, crackle and pop, while eating a bowl of Rice Krispies. It was non-stop. The first hour we averaged 52 kph, and it looked like no signs of slowing down when a 10-man break went up the road. We chased for the next hour, and finally, through the feed zone, we caught the break and cruised for a little. But the final sprint was so fast that with one kilometer to go, whichever wheel you were on, you stayed there. The top five places never passed anyone; they finished one behind the other.

Maybe you noticed that some of the Spanish

riders, mostly Banesto, had red bandanas on today. This was to celebrate the running of the bulls in Pamplona. The party starts today, and tomorrow morning they let the bulls out into the city of Pamplona.

I found out that yesterday Tom Steels won a horse—a race horse whose mother won more than seven million French francs. I also found out that Lelli (Cofidis) won a horse before, and Pantani won two horses before.... I once saw a bull given as a prize in a race in Spain. And in the Tour of Poland, I once won a pig. I know it's not much of a comparison, but they both are animals. Today, we were joking about Tom's horse. We were saying that if it doesn't race well, we could have Dr. Mabuse train it, attorney Lavelot (the guy who represented all the French guys) be the horse's agent, and Dicky V. (Virenque) be its jockey. The horse would *have* to win.

A few days ago, *L'Equipe*, a big French sports paper, ran an article about how Lance demanded that the team have two camping cars at the Tour. It said that one of the camping cars was for Lance's own personal use. That story was complete bullshit, but now one of the camping cars is referred to as "Lance's camper." The Rabobank bus driver read the article, cut it out, and gave it to Johan. Rabobank, which is continuing for four more years, is trying to sell its bus so it can buy a new one. The team was teasing Johan about why we have two campers when we could have one big bus. Johan told the squad that the reason they are selling the bus is so that they can get two camping cars like us.

After the races and after dinner, each guy has a different way to relax . I mean, we only have six French channels on TV. We could sit around and just stare at the ceiling, but I think we would really go crazy. So for starters, we have our computers. Normally, Lance is the biggest abuser of on-line time,

but Johan banned him from bringing his computer to the Tour. So he and Kevin are without computers and on-line capabilities. Lance must be going through some severe withdrawal symptoms, cold turkey with no computer.

George has the best set-up: He has his computer and he has some killer portable speakers. George also has a portable CD player with an amplifier that takes eight D-size batteries. I think they are D, whatever the big batteries are called. We turn on this system and the whole hotel can hear it—it's great. George and I usually get on-line one time at night.

Christian is also doing an article every day; his are for the *Chicago Tribune*. He has one problem: He can't get on-line when in France, a major problem while doing the Tour. The reporter calls him each day and they talk out the article....

Jonathan had a bunch of writings lined up for the Tour, too, but couldn't see how he was going to do it. He had at least four or five different sites he was going to give reports to....

The computers may entertain us now, but on Motorola, it was baseball. The team kept gloves and balls in the mechanic's truck, and the soigneur would bust them out almost every night after dinner. Jim Ochowicz, our director on Motorola, had a wicked fast ball. I would get scared trying to catch his heat. One day during the Tour, in the back of a hotel, John Hendershot set up batting practice. He would hit fly balls to all our soigneurs running around in the outfield. It's always fun to watch the Euro guys try to catch and throw. It's a very unnatural act for them.

Our team is sponsored by Yahoo!, and if you go to Yahoo! sports, you will find Tour information at the top of the page. It's a big difference compared to other sites, where I always have to scroll down to find cycling or click on "other sports" to get cycling news. It's nice having the Tour front and center, the way it should be. Maybe some other sites will take notice.

said, to silence those critics who had said that his three defeats on the opening stages proved that he had lost his magic touch. Indeed, the only thing he looked like losing was his privileged place on the Saeco team, when it took a reported different direction in 2000.

But for now, Cipollini had not only taken another stage, he had also put his name in the record books as the fastest stage winner in Tour history—and given the fans something to talk about on their way home. Even though there was no time for a picnic.

STAGE 5
Bonneval–Amiens • July 8

New mood

A DIFFERENT TONE, A DIFFERENT MOOD HAD BEEN APPARENT SO FAR IN THIS TOUR. It was almost a week into the race and the only hint of scandal had been a rumor on prologue day that—depending on whom you spoke to—one, two or three riders had registered above the UCI's designated 50-percent hematocrit level in the pre-breakfast blood tests. The rumor proved false, having probably been triggered by the fact that some riders have certificates proving that their natural, historic hematocrit percentage is over the limit.

Before this fifth stage, another rumor was making the rounds. French sports newspaper *L'Équipe* had just "revealed" that an unnamed source had told a reporter that one of the four urine samples taken after the prologue had come out "positive." For the first time, a new testing procedure was used to detect corticoids (artificial cortisone), and, according to the source, the test was successful on one rider's sample.

Those tested after the prologue were three randoms, Dane Bo Hamburger of Cantina Tollo, Colombian José Castelblanco of Kelme and Spaniard Manuel Beltran of Banesto...and stage winner Armstrong. European journalists being European journalists, they immediately assumed that the "positive" must be Armstrong, and that the organizers had done a cover-up job—even though corticoids are routinely used (with medical certification) for treating tendon injuries, inflammation and asthma.

So these were the rumors circulating as the 4000-strong Tour family gathered in Bonneval, a jewel of a medieval town set in the middle of the Kansas-like wheat fields of the Beauce region.

The meeting point each day for the race entourage is the so-called *village départ*. On this day, the village was in and around the centuries-old St. Florentin Abbey. Through its dark-stone 13th century gatehouse, one walked into a mixture of moods created by ushers in colorful

Tough day at the office

Moses Maloney, I am one tired puppy tonight. Today was the second longest day of the Tour, and after yesterday's record-breaking ride, I figured we might just cruise a little. It started off that way, but only for a measly 3 kilometers. I think it took Jacky Durand that long to talk someone into attacking with him. At kilometer three, Jacky and one of his Lotto teammates launched one of Jacky's patented attacks. Jacky is known for attacking at the gun and going long for the suicide break. In the neutral zone, I even told Kevin to go find Jacky and sit on him—that way, for sure he would make the break.

Jacky's attack took 10 guys with him, and no one in the peloton cared. We went from riding 27 kph to riding 28 kph, as the break went away from us. There was no interest on anyone's part to race or chase down the break. So we just let it go, while everyone tried figuring out which teams had a guy there and which ones didn't. Everyone was gambling, waiting to see who would have to work first, as the break went from two, four and then six minutes up the road. The losers at this poker game were the teams going for the G.C. in the race. It was too far to the finish for the sprinter teams, and whoever had a guy in the break didn't have to work.

The agreement was that each team with G.C. hopes would put three guys on the front to start chasing: Mapei for Tonkov, ONCE for Olano, Cofidis for Julich, and our team for Armstrong. The team that didn't participate was Polti, which had no guy in the break and for some stupid reason wouldn't ride. Man, I hate Virenque....

We hit the front at about kilometer 25 and

MARIO CIPOLLINI

rode in a head wind for 180km. It was not a fun day at the office, and I'm sure it was pretty boring to watch on TV. Finally, for the last 20km, the sprinter teams took over to polish off the job. Cipo' was in true form again, winning the sprint a bike length in front of Steels.

The battle for the green jersey is heating up. It's a battle between Steels and Kirsipuu; there is only a three-point difference. Each mid-sprint carries points of six, four and two. On top of that, Steels is still 17 seconds out of the lead, and Cipo' is a measly 32 seconds from the yellow. Tomorrow is a short stage of 175km, so the mid-race sprints will be important to anyone going for the yellow or green jersey. The pressure is mounting for Zabel to win, and also for Jimmy Casper to win, because he won't be riding many more stages. Last year Zabel did not win any stages, but he did manage to win the green jersey.

For Cofidis, one of the best things that could have happened was the crash on the causeway a couple of days ago, which cost both Rinero and Meier six minutes. Actually, it was the best thing for Bobby, too, for now there is just one leader on the team. Before, there was a question about who would work for whom once the Tour hit the mountains. With Rinero and Meier far down on G.C., there should be no question as to who the leader is for the mountains and the Tour.

Tomorrow, we have a late start and that means a late wake-up. I'm sure I'll wake up like lead in the bed, but at least I'll have as many hours as I need to get up and going. GOOD NIGHT!

medieval dress, a weirdly menacing troupe of verdigris-painted mummers with camouflaged stilts and tentacle-like fingers, and a string quartet playing a *diversimento* by Vivaldi.

The historic theme continued through the day, with the race passing three of Europe's most magnificent Gothic cathedrals, at Chartres (29km), Beauvais (169km) and Amiens (where the stage finished). Coincidentally, these three points marked the stage's three transitions.

An attack was made right from the start by Lotto's Durand and Thierry Marichal. They were joined by eight others, and as they raced into Chartres, already had a lead of 6:15. The two best-placed men in the break were: at 1:04, Crédit Agricole's Jens Voigt, winner if the Critérium International stage race in March; and, at 1:05, one of race leader Kirsipuu's team colleagues, Frédéric Bessy. Bessy's presence meant that Casino had no reason to chase, which put pressure on the main Tour contenders, since Voigt was a potential outsider if the breakaway were allowed to run riot.

With this in mind, for the next 140km, riding in echelons to combat the unfavorable wind, four teams worked laboriously to cut back the deficit: Postal Service for Armstrong, Mapei for Tonkov, Cofidis for Julich, and ONCE for Olano. The gap was down to 1:30 by the time they sped by the magnificent west front of Beauvais Cathedral, and the 10-man break split up shortly afterward.

Over the remaining 65km of this long, difficult stage, three riders from the break went on ahead: Marichal, Rabobank's Van Bon and Lampre's KoM leader Mariano Piccoli. Yet even though they received reinforcements in the shape of giant Swede Magnus Bäckstedt of Crédit Agricole and BigMat Frenchman Carlos Da Cruz, the leaders never gained more than a minute over a Casino-led pack.

The gap was just 22 seconds when Bäckstedt left the break with 12km remaining, but he was caught within sight of Amiens Cathedral's 367-foot-high spire, just 6km from the finish.

By this point, the sprinters' teams were in full flight, with the familiar protagonists again having their respective leadouts. The sprint was a difficult one to judge by the riders, as the finishing straight was a lengthy 1.7km, narrowing to a width of about 20 feet in the final kilometer.

"The straight sprints are always dangerous," said Hincapie, whose words proved true when the young French hope, Casper, suddenly sat up at the height of the sprint, almost causing the American to fall.

Meanwhile, Cipollini was getting the royal treatment from his red train, which was holding strong in the center of the road. The other contenders were fighting it out on Cipollini's right, with Zabel this time starting his sprint too early, allowing first McEwen and then

Steels to zip past between the German and the barriers. But neither they nor a late-charging Kirsipuu could match Cipo' and his eventual, totally focused move.

The Lion King's second impressive victory took the headlines at Amiens…but there was still talk about the "positive" test from the prologue. A statement issued that evening by the UCI then seemed to close the speculation. It reiterated that all anti-doping tests at the prologue were negative, and pointed out that certain substances—but not naming corticoids—can be used for therapeutic reasons, with certain restrictions. In other words, the medical treatment received by Beltran after a recent crash, or the asthma product used legitimately by Hamburger, might well have sparked the debate.

So the speculation ended for the moment, but the Tour still had a long way to go. Most people were hoping that the new mood would prevail.

STAGE 6

Amiens–Maubeuge • July 9

The focus

ATTEMPTING TO WIN A MODERN TOUR DE FRANCE DEMANDS AN EXTRAORDINARY effort from the contender—and also from his team. "We have just one focus," said a weary Tyler Hamilton, after finishing this sixth stage near the back of the peloton. Throughout the stage, like the rest of his Postal Service teammates, Hamilton had focused on looking after his team leader, Armstrong. Whatever it took.

Each day in this opening week posed different challenges for the team workers. Stage 1 saw the Postal men riding tempo for most of the day to defend Armstrong's yellow jersey. Stage 2, for Hamilton, was a fight for survival, after he crashed heavily before the infamous Gois causeway and battled through his pain to finish with the second group, six minutes behind the leaders. Stage 3 may have been relatively easy, but then came that record-setting stage 4, which forced everyone to race at their limit just to finish in the pack.

For the Postal team, though, stage 5 was probably the hardest in terms of work load, towing the peloton for more than three hours to close a six-minute gap on a dangerous 10-man break. And that was done on a course of constant ups and downs, through the twisting streets of dozens of small villages and towns, while often fighting head winds on exposed roads between wheat fields.

So when this sixth stage began with a 13-man break forming within the first five minutes, the Postal men again faced the prospect of an unpleasantly long chase. This time, the potential threats in the attack were two Italians: veteran Alberto Elli of Telekom and former Motorola rider Andrea Peron of ONCE.

Postal's Andreu, Vande Velde, Meinert-Nielsen and Deramé were soon riding at a fast tempo with their colleagues on Mapei, but the gap still grew to 40 seconds after 10km. So the rest of the Postal team, including Armstrong, moved up, formed a full paceline…and took another 10km to close down the break.

The stage was now up in the rolling hill country of the Somme, where much of World War I was fought out in mud-filled trenches, and where neatly tended graveyards and memorials for fallen British, Canadian, Australian and American troops are now the only reminders of that black period.

The hills put a different perspective on the stage, and a split saw 23 men move clear, shortly after the initial break was caught. "(The break) was an accident more or less," said the principal rider in the attack, Armstrong. "There was a lot of wind…just following the wheels. But it worked out to be not so bad, as we had to do a lot of work before that…and the other (teams) now had to work."

Besides, the new break included such strongmen as yesterday's threat, Voigt, Telekom's Udo Bölts, Stéphane Heulot of La Française des Jeux and Patrick Jonker of Rabobank, along with Armstrong's teammate, Hamilton.

While the attack gave the other Postal

FRANKIE'S DIARY @ July 7 @ Maubeuge

Positioning and personnel

A little note about yesterday: You probably were thinking that if we had had a guy in the break, then we would not have had to work. Don't get me wrong: We missed the break, but that would not have solved our problem. Lance is our guy, and if one of us had been in the break, we still would have had to work in the pack. A few of us—Tyler, Pascal and Peter—are 15 minutes down already; and a few of us—George, Christian and me—can't climb with the big guns…so it would have been no advantage for us to be there.

Today I felt like I never got off the bike. I chased all day yesterday, and today started out the same way. After maybe 5 kilometers, the attacks started, and right away a group of 10 went up the road. Again we had no one, and we immediately started a chase with the full team. This time the chase was 100-percent full-out, trying to catch those guys as quickly as possible. It was pure hell for all of us and a maximum effort. I was suffering big-time because my legs still weren't recovered from the day before. I think we chased for about 20km. Near the end, even Lance was helping us pull—I think he felt sorry for us, seeing how badly we were sucking wind…. I know we should have had a guy in the break.

After catching the break, the attacks started flying. It was like doing a classic. We had huge crosswinds and full echelons, with everyone fighting for position—which made it very hard for everyone. In the end, the result was the same: a field sprint.

Some of the most dangerous sprints are head-wind sprints, and today's was another example. The final 20km were into a strong head wind. This enabled everyone to keep swarming to the front, because the speed was not high enough to string out the pack. In the sprint, Cipo' took off first, with Svorada on his wheel. Steels started coming up and totally slammed into Svorada, almost taking him down. In the same pedal stroke, Steels continued to move over and almost take Svorada's wheel out, while pushing him into the barriers. Then, with Steels sprinting next to Cipo' for the win, he ran into Cipo' and caused him to swerve a bit. Steels was a one-man wrecking crew today. If it wasn't for Svorada's bike-handling ability, there would have been guys all over the ground…. George got up there for the sprint, but Minali took a hand-sling from one of his teammates and the guy who got shot backward went right into George. In the end, Steels won, but was disqualified. So the win went to Cipo'—three in a row!

Tomorrow's objective is simple: Keep Lance as fresh and rested as possible. Not that that's any different from what we've been doing this whole week. Lance hasn't put his head in the wind for one second, which is the way we want it. And we want him to finish tomorrow as if he didn't even ride that day. That might be hard, considering the stage is 230km. The time trial is the next day, which will be the first critical and deciding day in setting up the G.C. guys. We need three guys to go for it in the time trial, so we can keep the team G.C. But as I told Christian, "I don't do TTs." This is where we will really miss Jonathan. After the TT, we hit the mountains, and once we're in the mountains, you either keep up or get dropped—it's that simple.

The staff is a critical part to our success—not only at the Tour, but all year long. Here at the Tour, because we have nine riders, we have three mechanics and four soigneurs. Two of the soigneurs are in charge of the hotels. This means transporting and placing the luggage in each rider's room, so when we arrive all they do is give us a key and everything is there. They're also in charge of putting water in all the riders' rooms and setting up the feed room. After each race, all of us are usually starving, so we have

an area—sometimes in the hallway or in a room—where we have cereal, cookies, drinks and fruit waiting. The two hotel soigneurs also set up the massage tables for all the soigneurs, and track down the maids for extra towels and sheets for the massages.

The other two soigneurs are in charge of the feed zones at the races. They have to make all the race food for the start of the race, as well as the food that will go in the *musettes* at the feed zone. Usually, the night before, they prepare all the bottles with water, and with Cytomax for during the race and Metabol for after the race. We go through a lot of bottles each day. One of the soigneurs is also in charge of setting up the breakfast table, with all the plates, bowls, forks, coffee, cereal and bread. This is so we don't have to get up 10 times trying to locate a fork or knife. Normally, they would also help out with the dinner; but for the Tour, we have a chef here to help us: Willy Balmat from Switzerland, who previously worked with Motorola for the Tour.

What a difference having a chef makes. Sure, the food is better, but the biggest difference is that we get the food quickly. Instead of waiting around for an hour eating bread, as soon as we sit down, the pasta arrives. This is one of the biggest advantages of having a helper in the kitchen. We get to eat the right food quickly.

The mechanics also have their tasks split up. One mechanic drives the truck to the hotel and works on the bikes, gluing tires, getting TT bikes ready, and so on. The other two mechanics work the race: One sits in the first car, and the other in the second car. Working in the first car is more stressful, especially in the flat races. The second car never sees the front, so that mechanic and driver usually take turns driving, so each can get a nap in the back of the car. The most time-consuming job for the mechanics—the one they all hate, but the most important—is the gluing of tires. They wash the bikes day-in and day-out, but I get the feeling they hate tubulars. I'm sure a mechanic's dream would be a team on clinchers. Forget about it!

men a chance to follow wheels for a change, this was not the case for Hamilton. "It was hard driving the break," said the New Englander, who was still covered in bandages and bruises from his stage 2 crash, with a particularly painful tendon injury in his right calf.

The 23-man group was 42 seconds ahead by the time it swept through the village of Cappy, just after Bray-sur-Somme. Julich's Cofidis team was leading the chase, and the speed was such that a few riders were dropped from the pack, including climbers Benoît Salmon of Casino and Hernan Buenahora of Vitalicio. The gap closed to 14 seconds, but started to open up again on the Cat. 4 hill out of Cappy, causing Olano's ONCE team to join in the chase. That extra help finally brought back the Armstrong break, after it had held strong for about 15km.

Despite the undulating terrain, and strong cross- and head winds, 43.6km were covered in the first hour. The attacks continued, but now the sprinters' teams controlled affairs—until the time-bonus sprint at Marquaix, after 61km, where Kirsipuu added to his lead by outspeeding Zabel and Hincapie. Soon after, starting a 20km-long tail-wind section, a successful break was made by Spaniard Francisco Cerezo of Vitalicio, who was joined by three French riders: national champion François Simon of Crédit Agricole, former Paris-Roubaix winner Frédéric Guesdon of La Française des Jeux, and Casino's Gilles Maignan—who was there to sit on the break and force other teams to chase.

The move was well-timed, and, blown by the wind, the four built up a 3:30 lead by St. Quentin, where the course turned left onto the Paris-Roubaix route for about 20km. Back with the crosswinds, the pack was reluctant to chase; and by the feed zone, 70km from the finish in the northern French city of Maubeuge, the gap had soared to eight minutes. This meant that Simon, only 50 seconds back of Kirsipuu on overall time, was the temporary yellow jersey, although, as a non-climber, he was no real threat to the main contenders.

And so a familiar pattern unfolded: a small break trying to ride as hard as it could, followed by a strung-out pack led by the sprinters' teams and moving about 3 kph faster. This time, it took the chasers 90 minutes of effort to run down the breakaways. Their demise came 8km out of Maubeuge, from where the Telekom and Saeco teams shared the pacemaking, along a four-lane highway into town. The speed gradually increased, while the road narrowed, until it was only about 20 feet wide between metal barriers. At more than 60 kph, with a fast downhill a kilometer from the end, the passage seemed even narrower, leaving very little room to maneuver.

The final 300 meters provided as exhilarating and spectacular a sprint as you are likely to see. This time, Jan Svorada was getting the main lead out from two of his Lampre teammates, while Cipollini again followed Fagnini's wheel. At about the 200-meter mark, Fagnini sat up and moved right, causing those behind him to adjust their lines. Steels veered left, partly cutting off Zabel, and then the Belgian again moved away from his line, bumping shoulders with Svorada—who came incredibly close to the barriers on the right, perhaps even touching them with his elbow. Steels achieved his goal of getting past Cipollini on the left, to cross the line marginally ahead of the Italian, with Zabel in third.

Svorada had skillfully avoided disaster, but the judges decided that Steels was culpable anyway, and the Belgian was relegated to last place in the pack, and docked 30 seconds and 25 points from his overall tally. Cipollini was now ahead in the sprinters' opening-week challenge: Cipollini, three wins; Steels, two wins; and Kirsipuu, one.

STAGE 7
Avesnes-sur-Helpe–Thionville • July 10

7 of 7, 4 of 4

BACK IN 1997, A SERIES OF MASS PILEUPS HAPPENED ON NARROW ROADS at the end of the early stages of the Tour. At the time, the organizers blamed the crashes on riders using Spinacci clip-on bars, going too fast, and not being in control of their bikes. But given that all of the pileups were on stages ending at towns of 5000 population or less, the poor choice of roads was almost certainly the biggest factor.

The Tour didn't have the same problems in the first week this year. All went well, except for a couple of small pileups that happen any year. However, a too-conservative choice of roads also made this opening week too predictable. The only stage that produced any time gaps was the second, when a combination of factors caused the peloton to split on the now-infamous Passage du Gois. But even that stage saw 74 riders sprinting for the win, while the rest of the week saw almost the whole field still together at the end of every stage.

This seventh stage was no exception, with Cipollini taking a fourth straight stage, a feat last achieved by French sprinter Charles Pélissier in 1930 (the record is five straight by Luxembourger François Faber in 1909). And yes, the stage, once again, did end on fast, flat roads that made a field sprint almost inevitable. In fact, never before has a Tour started with seven straight field sprints. They may be spectacular, but where were the hilly run-ins that have frequently produced exciting finales—with significant time gaps—in years past?

They weren't in this seventh stage, which traveled from an old coal-mining area at Avesnes-sur-Helpe to the steel-making city of Thionville. The 227km route followed a single, wide *route nationale* for most of the day, before turning onto a narrower *departmen-*

Food for thought

Given the amount of talking at the table this morning, I can safely say that we are tired. There wasn't a lot of talking between us, just a lot of eating…. The first thing that goes into anyone's mouth is always the coffee. Some days it's good, and some days it's downright unhealthy. It was great earlier in the season when Dylan Casey was around. He always brought some fresh Peets coffee that we would mooch off of him. Pascal is our one non-coffee drinker; he's a hot-chocolate man…. After the coffee, we usually go into the cereal, before having some pasta and eggs. Then we usually go back to the cereal, to top everything off. We go through a minimum of 25 boxes of cereal each week. I have every edition of every toy prize found in a cereal box. I'll never have to buy my kid another toy.

Today was the longest…no, second longest… no, third longest day of the Tour. What's the difference when the stages are 227, 230 and 233 kilometers? To me, they're *all* long, so it doesn't really matter which day is the "longest." Today's stage was 227km, and nobody wasted any time getting the legs going. As usual, the attacks went from the start, and it took two hours till things finally settled. The only thing to settle a peloton is for a small group to get away; today, it was a BigMat rider. After he built up a lead of seven minutes, Jacky Durand decided to try and bridge the gap. Casino just kept riding a slow tempo, because the BigMat rider was 17 minutes down.

For today's race, there were more people watching and lining the roads than for any of the earlier stages. The course went next to Belgium and Luxembourg, so I'm sure all the cycling fans from there made their way down to watch the race. But an increase in spectators generally means an increase in crashes. The crowds just don't realize how fast we are moving and how we take up the whole road. It's unbelievable how many baby carriages, bike wheels, camera stands and coolers we are dodging all the time, simply because they are left in the road.

Today, Garzelli (Mercatone Uno) hit a spectator, got spun back into the pack, ping-ponged off a couple of guys, and then shot out into a field. I'm sure he will be messed up tomorrow….

As Jacky got close to the first rider in the break, the BigMat rider sat up to wait for him. They could work better together than separately, especially since there were 100km to go. But Jacky never seems to learn, so they were caught again at the end. He either never learns or he just doesn't care. Actually, I think he attacked so he could gain points in the most-aggressive-rider competition. If this race had an award for the most stupid rider, Jacky would win hands down.

With 10km to go, we caught the break, and the Telekom and Saeco guys started their trains for the field sprint. (Before I get to the sprint, I have to note that Zabel took a bad spill in the middle of the race. He cut his chin badly and got a load of road rash.) In the final sprint, the Saeco guys took over, with Cipo' taking off for the line. When Zabel went to start his sprint, he pulled both his feet out and landed straight on the top tube. It was amazing he didn't crash. Watching it later on TV, it looked like his wheel locked up and that stopped the pedals, causing both of his feet to come out right away. Cipo' won—*again*— fourth time in a row.

Since the break was nine minutes up the road and we were just cruising, Christian and I decided to have some fun as we entered the feed zone. We were trying to throw our water bottles into the open hatchbacks of cars that were lined along the road. I missed both times, but Christian landed one right in the back of a red Honda. George, being the nice guy that he is, decided he was going to toss one of his bottles to a guy waiting on the side of the road. He gently tossed it at him—and it hit him square in the chest. It almost knocked the guy out. George didn't realize that when you're going 40 kph, a water bottle can became a bullet when you throw it at someone. Even worse was that the bottle was half-full!

After yesterday's race, we saw Tom Steels after dinner. When George saw him, he wasn't sure what to say—none of us were. So George asked, "Bad news, huh?" Tom said, "Yeah, it's impossible to argue with those guys." I would think it *would* be hard to argue, especially if you're in the wrong.

Cipo' has won four times, but I don't think he will ride even one mountain pass. His next big goal will be to even out his tan lines at the beach. For the end of the season, he has the idea of going to the track world's in Berlin at the end of October, to ride the pursuit. That will be interesting to watch. Speaking of pursuits, Boardman is still mumbling on about retiring. He was spewing to me about how his recovery is no good and how he can't come up to his old winning ways. It got depressing listening to him; it's obvious he wants out.

Tomorrow is the time trial. The first guy goes off at 10:30 a.m., and the last takes off at about 4 p.m. It's an all-day affair. Anybody going for a good ride in the overall will be pulling out the stops tomorrow. No more sitting on the wheels and resting and waiting. Look for the top 20 to completely change after tomorrow is done…. For me, it's the start of my two-day rest block. I will cruise the TT, and we fly out the next morning. Normally, I'd say wish us luck; but in this case, wish Lance luck.

tale road 40km from the finish. It seemed like there would now be some challenging climbs; but instead of taking the race over one of the many ridges that surround Thionville, the organizers took it into town on valley roads for the most part. In particular, the course could have turned left at Knutange, 14km from the finish, and climbed a steep 4km hill that would have almost certainly stopped Cipo's red train from rolling, and offered some other rider a chance for the stage win.

One can think back to 1995, when on a similar stage—the day before the first long time trial—Miguel Induráin attacked with Johan Bruyneel on a hilly run-in to Liège for a spectacular winning break. Two years before that, in the same part of France as this stage, an exciting breakaway over another hilly run-in saw Armstrong score a memorable stage victory at Verdun.

It's often said that the riders make the race, not the terrain. But on this first week of the 1999 Tour, there was no shortage of enterprising attackers; there was only a shortage of courses that could give them any real hope of success. The organizers will have to do a better job in the future, unless they want every opening week to be a string of stages won by a select group of super-sprinters….

On this second Saturday of the Tour, the most enterprising attacker was Lylian Lebreton, a 27-year-old Frenchman who is known as a pretty decent climber—41st in last year's Tour. He came close to winning the Grenoble stage of this year's Dauphiné Libéré, just losing out to Festina's Laurent Madouas after a marathon two-man breakaway.

Lebreton chose a similar tactic here. After a series of attacks in the opening 20km—through the rolling, wooded countryside where the annual Grand Prix de Fourmies takes place—BigMat's Lebreton went clear with compatriot Heulot of La Française des Jeux. Australian champion Henk Vogels of Crédit Agricole got within seven seconds of joining them, but soon drifted back to the peloton, which was 45 seconds behind by the first intermediate sprint at Hirson after 29km.

For the next 20 minutes, the gap hovered around the one-minute mark, until Casino decided that it was safe to let two men move ahead on such a long stage with strong crosswinds, even though Heulot (28th, at 1:21) was a potential G.C. danger to race leader Kirsipuu.

So, after averaging 44 kph for the first two hours, Lebreton and Heulot were seven minutes ahead. Heulot then decided that another three-or-so hours on the attack would not be the ideal preparation for the next day's time trial, and, in any case, the less-dangerous Lebreton would have a better chance of succeeding on his own. At the same time, the ever-willing Durand decided that he'd be able to replace Heulot at the front. He did, but it took him two hours of effort before the leader sat up and waited for Durand.

Once together, the new pair had a lead of 6:31, with just less than 60km to go. However, while the two leaders rode as hard as they could for the remaining hour and a quarter, the sprinters' teams again acted as if they owned the stage—which they did; but there was no need for the arrogance they displayed. At one point, when Thierry Bourgignon and another BigMat colleague of Lebreton moved into the paceline in a legitimate tactic to slow down the tempo, Saeco's Commesso dismissively waved Bourgignon out of the way. The humbled French veteran started to protest, but knew it wouldn't get him anywhere.

And so the repetitive end-of-stage scenario was repeated, and the peloton overtook Lebreton (after 198km in front) and Durand, just inside the 5km-to-go mark.

For once, though, it wasn't a straight-in finish. There were two left turns in the final kilometer, so there was one long line entering the final straight, 200 meters from the line. As usual, Fagnini was leading out Cipollini, who was being closely followed by Zabel. At last, the German seemed to be in the right position at the right time for a sprint that was his ideal distance. So with 120 meters left, Zabel—who seemed to have shaken off the effects of a heavy fall he had suffered about an hour earlier—began his final sprint a split-second before Cipollini, and seemed sure to get his first Tour stage win since Pau in 1997.

But about two rev's into his violent effort, Zabel's left foot unclipped from the pedal, followed almost immediately by the right, as his body was thrown forward onto the top tube and stem. Somehow, Zabel kept upright, even though all he could do was coast to the finish…and watch helplessly as Cipollini romped to his fourth consecutive win, three or four lengths clear of a persistent O'Grady, with Kirsipuu again in third.

The Lion King's win might have been well merited, but it seemed that even the 32-year-old Tuscan was becoming bored by his success, when he said in the post-stage press conference, "As for the sprint, I'd rather have beaten Steels or Zabel than O'Grady."

And if the organizers had included a hill or two at the end, perhaps someone completely different would have had a chance of winning. Maybe next year….

STAGE 8
Metz TT • July 11

The Armstrong margin

FIVE-TIME TOUR DE FRANCE WINNER BERNARD HINAULT ONCE SAID that his success in time trials was due, in part, to his reconnoitering the course: "I ride the course to memorize it, and when it comes to racing it, each feature replays like a video in my head." The importance of his words were played out vividly—and cruelly—on this stage 8 time trial in Metz.

So confident in his form and ability was world time trial champion Olano that he didn't think it was necessary to look over the 65.5km circuit, which started and finished in Metz, and included three distinct forays into the surrounding hills and valleys. Instead, the Basque star relied on the information brought to him by his ONCE-Deutsche Bank directeur sportif Manolo Saiz, who inspected the course following the previous day's stage to Thionville.

As for another favorite, Julich, when asked a few days earlier whether he had made a visit to see the course, the American said, "No. I'll have a look at it the night before."

Olano's and Julich's attitudes—which would come to haunt them—were in sharp contrast to that of prologue winner Armstrong. Back in April, the Postal Service rider had made a special trip to Metz with his team director Bruyneel and mechanic Julien DeVries—Greg LeMond's former wrench. Armstrong rode two laps of the course, in the rain. He rode it a third time on the actual morning of the race, an hour before the first rider began.

Armstrong felt that these inspections were vital to his success.

As he later said, "All three times that I rode it, I rode it alone, and I really tried to train on it as if I was racing…in taking the corners at somewhat race speed, taking the descents at race speed…totally focusing on it. Like I said, I was totally alone, so there was no one else to talk to and nothing else to do except look at the course."

The result was that Armstrong knew which gears to use on each of the many climbs, which lines to take into every corner and bend, and where he needed to slow down for dangerous turns. Another advantage he had on his opponents was starting near the end of the field, so he would know how his splits compared with the previous top times. And, more specifically, director Bruyneel armed himself with kilometer-by-kilometer times of Postal's other top time trialist, Hamilton, who would finish his race about an hour before Armstrong was due to start.

When Hamilton set out at 1:30 p.m. on a humid and hot, mostly overcast day, the best time was the 1:12:08 set an hour-and-a-half earlier by Britain's Chris Boardman—who really needed to try for a win here after his disappointing prologue. His average speed of 47 kph appeared to be pretty good for such a testing course….

After about 6km on flat city streets, the course went over its first short hill, before swinging left for the 1.4km-long, 3.8-percent Côte de Lorry-les-Metz, climbing through an old residential neighborhood where crowds were massed on doorsteps and garden walls. By the top, after 9.5km of racing, the plucky Hamilton, his injuries still patched from his stage 2 crash, hurtled through the time check in 12:17—18 seconds faster than Boardman.

Starting two minutes behind Hamilton was another race favorite, Zülle, who reached the checkpoint in 12:20. Clearly, Hamilton was going well, and his splits would be totally valid for Armstrong to measure his progress against.

After this first checkpoint, the road, now in thick woodland, continued to climb on a slightly rougher surface, leading to a short, steep drop and an immediate uphill, before dropping again into narrow streets at Amanvillers, after 15km. Here, there was a tight, double-left turn, leading onto a smooth two-lane road that went gradually downhill for the next 8km, snaking through a forest of pine and birch trees. The course then turned right in the streets of Rozerieulles, almost back in Metz itself, to the start of the main climb: the 3.5km, 4.6-percent Côte de Gravelotte, a three-lane highway that in places was turned into a single lane by the encroaching crowds.

The second checkpoint was at the 1059-foot summit (an elevation change of just over 500 feet), 26.5km into the race. Hamilton was still holding strong here with a split of 34:35 (42 seconds up on Boardman); but the chasing Zülle, now fully into his impressively smooth style, was 17 seconds faster than Hamilton.

After the Gravelotte climb, the road dipped down steeply—where the strongest riders were spun out on their 55x11 top gears at almost 100 kph—before going up another short, steep climb where the biggest crowds of the day were watching. It was here that Virenque was temporarily blocked by publicity vehicles that were trailing the rider he was about to catch.

For Zülle, however, this was where he started to put time on Hamilton. After making another sharp left turn in Gravelotte, there was a short climb before the fastest downhill of the course, which became progressively steeper, before reaching the right bank of the Moselle river, at Ancy. Here, the course turned right, with the wind, for 3km, and then crossed the river on a narrow bridge to the third checkpoint at 42.5km—14km from the finish.

By this check, Zülle was a minute faster than Hamilton—whose light build saw him struggle riding into the wind over the mainly flat finale—and the American was caught by the powerful Swiss 5km from the end. Zülle finished in 1:09:34, easily the fastest, with Hamilton's 1:12:07 putting him in second for the moment.

These times were still the best when the last batch of riders set out from Metz, including Julich (at 3:22 p.m.), Moreau (3:44 p.m.), Olano (3:50 p.m.) and Armstrong (3:52 p.m.).

This was the testing moment for Julich, whose preparations for the Tour hadn't been the best. He was hoping that a week of fast racing had given him the form and rhythm he needed for a great time trial. He soon knew, though, that this was not going to be the case. Julich was 28 seconds slower than Hamilton by the first checkpoint, and 1:18 behind his fellow American atop the Gravelotte climb.

Perhaps in trying to make up for lost time, and not having ridden the course at race speed, Julich went too fast on a deceptively curving left turn on the steep descent toward the Moselle river. He hit the curb, lost control of his bike, and landed heavily on his chest and left arm at about 90 kph. Because it was not possible to get an ambulance to him or land a helicopter where he crashed, Julich was still lying on the grass, stunned by his fall, as all the remaining riders went by.

When Moreau passed the fallen American, he was level on time with Hamilton, but finished as fast as Zülle for an excellent 1:10:41. Behind the French hope came the battle that the tens of thousands of fans had been waiting for: Olano versus Armstrong.

The Postal Service leader felt ready for the challenge—and he was hungry for success: "I really wanted to get the jersey back," he later said. "I'd never aspired to getting the yellow jersey or winning the Tour de France, but having had (the jersey) the first day, it changed everything for me. And...I *wanted* the jersey."

That motivation was visible in Armstrong's eyes as he sat on his bike in the start house, staring down the Avenue Ney, to where a rainbow-jersey-clad Olano had just disappeared from sight. For Armstrong, this, more than any other moment, was where the Tour began. "I started as hard as I could," he said. So hard, in fact, that he flew the first 10km, staying in his 55-tooth big ring up the first climb, to roar through the first split in 12:02. It was easily the fastest, 15 seconds up on Hamilton, and already 18 seconds faster than his rabbit, Olano.

On reflection, Armstrong thought he may have started a little *too* fast. "I remember seeing the signs that said 40km to go," he said, "and I was already tired, I don't know, I'm in trouble.... "

Fortunately, that 40km sign came on the long gradual downhill, where he was able to get a second breath, while using his knowledge of the course to still ride at the limit. His one scare came early into this descent, when a youth in a yellow T-shirt ran across the road between the advance motorcycle gendarme and Armstrong. But it proved to be just a momentary distraction.

His focus now was the Gravelotte hill—which was given a Cat. 3 rating, with each rider's climbing time being taken for the KoM competition. When talking about this a few weeks before, Armstrong had said it was an out-the-saddle climb. Well, he climbed the early part *in* the saddle, still in the big ring, his hands pulling on the arm rests of his aero' bars. When it steepened, his hand moved to the drops, but his chain remained on the 55x19, and he stood on

The time trial

Lance is in yellow, and he won it back confidently. Early this morning, Lance went and took a preview of the course, so he would know what to expect. Actually, this was his second time seeing the course.

This morning, Pascal got the raw end of the deal for the time trial. His departure time was 10 in the morning, so he didn't get to sleep in. But in Pascal's eyes, he got the best part of the deal: He got to watch the Formula One race in Silverstone *and* to see Lance win another stage in the Tour.

The 56km TT course contained two climbs: a Cat. 4 that was 1.5km long and a Cat. 3 that was almost 4 kilometers. The three riders with the go-ahead in the TT were Tyler, Kevin and, of course, Lance. The rest of us were supposed to try and take it easy, without getting eliminated by the time cut.

The course was very windy today. The first part was windy, while the middle part had the hills, and the last part, which was flat, ended in a strong head wind. It was a course for a strong, fit rider, who could hammer the gear into the winds. Needless to say, George was caught by his chasers: Olano and Lance. After *my* time trial, I went to the camper and George asked what time I did. I told him around one-hour-16. He said okay, I'll set my watch for one-hour-15. Sure enough, George crossed the line at one-hour-15.

In the TT, Lance started out fast and strong. He had the fastest time at the first two check points. And after the fourth check point, he had a 1:14 lead over the current leader, Zülle. He was killing *everyone*. Olano crashed in a small corner and lost maybe 30 seconds, but it ruined his rhythm. Almost right away, Lance was on top of Olano and leaving him behind. Crashing and being caught must have been a blow to Olano's motivation: He ended up more 2:22 back.

Lance lost time to Zülle in the final head-wind stretch, but still managed to beat him by almost a minute.... Our other hit man in the TT was Tyler, who, for the longest time, was second behind Zülle. Tyler did a great ride, ending up fifth in the stage. It's too bad he crashed on the causeway, since otherwise he would have been up there in the G.C. Then again, the same could be said for Zülle....

The biggest upset in the overall was the crash of Bobby Julich. On a sweeping downhill turn, he lost control—or skidded out—and crashed badly. Nobody but Bobby knows just how he crashed. I've heard conflicting stories that report everything from broken ribs to a broken elbow—to nothing broken at all. I do know that his Tour is finished, before it even got started for him.

Tomorrow, on our rest day, we fly to the Alps. We have to leave early in the morning to take a bus to the airport. We then fly to Geneva and take an hour-long bus ride to the hotel. Then we have to try and go ride in the mountains for at least three hours. It's a long, stressful rest day. Why three hours? Because the day *after* the rest day is a big mountain day, and we have to make sure our bodies don't shut down from race mode. We probably will do a couple of efforts to keep the legs awake and ready for Sestriere.

This first week has seen some bad crashes, lots of close calls, and some very nervous riders. Everyone has the same orders from their directors: Be represented in the break. This makes for a lot of fighting to get to the front and stay there. Because of this craziness, almost everyone wears a helmet. Maybe one or two wear hairnets, like Lars Michaelsen (La Française des Jeux), but I'd say that 99 percent wear hardshells. O'Grady, Boardman, Vogels, Moncassin, Boogerd and Lance, have custom-painted helmets. Lance's has a painting of Texas, with a lone star in the middle. George had a Captain America helmet all last year, after he won in Philly.

One helmet that is different from most is the Rudy Project helmet. These are the ones you see on TV that are pink and have a visor on the back. The visor is interchangeable from the front to the back.

Most of the guys have the visor in the back, but if they wanted to, they could have a visor in the front *and* back. Miguel Induráin had a Rudy Project helmet that had an attachment that allowed it to hook to the handlebars. This was for when he was in the mountains, so he could take off his helmet and attach it the bars securely, without worrying about it.

Each day in the back of the results, the penalties of the day are listed. Penalties are handed out to the riders and their teams for many different reasons. The most common reasons are for motorpacing, irregular feeding, disrespect to a commissaire, pissing in front of people, and forgetting to sign in. These fines are usually about 50 Swiss francs (about $35); and every day the UCI makes money off of someone—that's guaranteed. Irregular feeding means giving food or clothing to a rider when the team car is not behind the commissaire's car. In the back of the peloton, there is a red Fiat that has one of the head commissaires in it. This car is always supposed to be the first car behind the pack; if you pass it without permission, you get a fine.

The UCI also hands out fines to the publicity caravan, press cars and press motorcycles. The main reason the press cars get fined is for not having moved their parked cars before the start. Sometimes you'll see certain press motorcycles kicked out of the Tour for one day or maybe two. The reason can be for endangering a cyclist, excessive speeding, or not listening to the commissaires. There are many times when a motorcycle will not get off the front of a break or a chasing peloton, and so allow motorpacing to take place. If this happens, they are kicked out for a day.... The time I remember the UCI *really* getting rich was when Cipo' would always wear different team clothing. He would get hit for about 500 Swiss francs (about $350) each time, and the team would also get a 250 SF ($175) fine.

the pedals, displaying incredible power,

Armstrong was indeed the fastest rider up the 3.5km climb, and at the summit, his overall split was 33:34. This put him 44 seconds ahead of next-best Zülle…and an enormous 1:23 up on Olano—who was now only 37 seconds ahead of Armstrong on the road.

"I knew I was catching Olano, as we had radio communication, Johan (Bruyneel) and I," said Armstrong. Still, he was surprised to come upon the Spaniard as quickly as he did—the reason being that Olano paid for his not checking the course beforehand by overshooting the left turn in Gravelotte, plowing into the plastic-covered hay bales, and being stopped as he went over the bars in slow motion.

Olano soon remounted his bike, but he was still not back into his rhythm when Armstrong came up behind him on the descent, where Julich was still lying on the roadside, attended by the race doctor and his team helpers.

Armstrong saw that his U.S. rival was out of the race, but he immediately had to focus on the task at hand: overtaking Olano. "I came up to him on a downhill, so it was gonna be tough to go past him," he said, before explaining: "In the beginning, when I passed him, I was pushing too big a gear, trying to get away, and I was killing myself…. It was difficult psychologically, because I knew that he was behind me and…all I could hear was his team car yelling at him. And that's hard on the mind. So I then went back to turning a lower gear at a higher cadence, and went back to doing my own race."

With Olano behind him, Armstrong could again focus on the challenge thrown down by Zülle—whom the Texan still regarded as his biggest rival in the Tour. Through the 42.5km checkpoint, Armstrong's time of 50:30 (an average of 50.5 kph!) was 47 seconds ahead of Zülle. And after the next 9km section, into the wind, the gap was 1:14.

Despite this advantage, it was clear that his early charge was slowly catching up with Armstrong, because he was unable to get away from his six-minute man, Steels, whom the American had caught with 10km remaining. And in the last flat 5km, through the streets of Metz, Zülle pulled back 16 seconds. So Armstrong won the time trial by 58 seconds from the Swiss star, while Olano's crash cost him third place, which went to Moreau.

Even more than the prologue, and despite all his preparations and expectations, this victory astonished Armstrong. It had been a total effort. "I definitely have never been this fatigued after a race," he admitted. "Yes, I'm happy, but I'm so tired it hasn't sunk in…I'm blown away more than I've ever been."

PROLOGUE TT: Le Puy du Fou. July 3.

1. Lance Armstrong (USA), U.S. Postal Service, 6.8km in 8:02 (50.788 kph); 2. Alex Zülle (Swi), Banesto, 8:09; 3. Abraham Olano (Sp), ONCE-Deutsche Bank, 8:13; 4. Christophe Moreau (F), Festina, 8:17; 5. Chris Boardman (GB), Crédit Agricole, 8:18; 6. Rik Verbrugghe (B), Lotto-Mobistar, 8:20; 7. Alex Vinokourov (Kaz), Casino, 8:23; 8. Santos Gonzalez (Sp), ONCE-Deutsche Bank; 9. Laurent Brochard (F), Festina, both s.t.; 10. Gilles Maignan (F), Casino, 8:25.

Others: 14. Christian Vande Velde (USA), USPS, 8:27; 15. George Hincapie (USA), USPS, 8:28; 16. Stuart O'Grady (Aus), Crédit Agricole, s.t.; 18. Tyler Hamilton (USA), USPS, 8:29; 19. Jonathan Vaughters (USA), USPS, s.t.; 20. Pavel Tonkov (Rus), Mapei-Quick Step, 8:30; 22. Bobby Julich (USA), Cofidis, s.t.; 46. Frankie Andreu (USA), USPS, 8:39; 65. Axel Merckx (B), Mapei-Quick Step, 8:43; 73. Erik Zabel (G), Telekom, 8:46; 85. Kevin Livingston (USA), USPS, 8:49; 90. Ivan Gotti (I), Polti, s.t.; 107. Fernando Escartin (Sp), Kelme-Costa Blanca, 8:53; 109. Richard Virenque (F), Polti, s.t.

Teams: 1. U.S. Postal Service (USA), 24:57; 2. ONCE-Deutsche Bank (Sp), at 0:04; 3. Crédit Agricole (F), at 0:19; 4. Festina (F), at 0:20; 5. Banesto (Sp), at 0:21.

STAGE 1: Montaigu—Challans. July 4.

1. Jaan Kirsipuu (Est), Casino, 208km in 4:56:18 (42.119 kph); 2. Tom Steels (B), Mapei-Quick Step; 3. Erik Zabel (G), Telekom; 4. O'Grady; 5. Silvio Martinello (I), Polti; 6. Jimmy Casper (F), La Française des Jeux; 7. Nicola Minali (I), Cantina Tollo-Alexia; 8. Hincapie; 9. François Simon (F), Crédit Agricole; 10. Moreau, all s.t.

Others: 13. Jay Sweet (Aus), BigMat-Auber 93; 19. Robbie McEwen (Aus), Rabobank; 34. Olano; 41. Julich; 42. Armstrong; 45. Paolo Savoldelli (I), Saeco-Cannondale; 48. Vande Velde; 49. Merckx; 65. Laurent Dufaux (Swi), Saeco-Cannondale; 70. Zülle; 80. Escartin; 81. Vinokourov; 82. Gotti, all s.t.

Overall: 1. Armstrong, 214.8km in 5:04:20; 2. Zülle, at 0:09; 3. Olano, at 0:11; 4. Moreau , at 0:15; 5. Boardman, at 0:16; 6. Kirsipuu, s.t.; 7. Verbrugghe, at 0:18; 8. O'Grady, at 0:20; 9. Vinokourov, at 0:21; 10. Gonzales, s.t.

STAGE 2: Challans—St. Nazaire. July 5.

1. Steels, 176km in 3:45:32 (46.822 kph); 2. Kirsipuu; 3. Mario Cipollini (I), Saeco-Cannondale; 4. Zabel; 5. Casper; 6. Hincapie; 7. Jan Svorada (Cz), Lampre-Daikin; 8. Martinello; 9. O'Grady; 10. Simon, all s.t.

Others: 21. Olano; 22. Angel Casero (Sp), Vitalicio Seguros; 23. Merckx; 24. Vinokourov; 28. Armstrong; 32. Dufaux; 34. Savoldelli; 35. Escartin; 41. Stefano Garzelli (I), Mercatone Uno-Bianchi; 42. Julich; 48. Richard Virenque (F), Polti; 53. Pavel Tonkov (Rus), Mapei-Quick Stedp; 54. Livingston; 57. Giuseppe Guerini (I), Telekom; 67. Vande Velde, all s.t.; 72. Andreu, at 0:48; 76. Jean-Cyril Robin (F), La Française des Jeux, at 6:03; 82. Zülle; 87. Gotti 88. Boogerd, all s.t.

DNF: Vaughters and Marc Wauters (B)m Rabobank.

Overall: 1. Kirsipuu, 390.8km in 8:49:38; 2. Armstrong, at 0:14; 3. O'Grady, at 0:22; 4. Olano, at 0:25; 5. Moreau , at 0:29; 6. Steels, at 0:31; 7. Hincapie, at 0:32; 8. Vinokourov, at 0:35; 9. Gonzales, s.t.; 10. Andrea Peron (I), ONCE-Deutsche Bank, at 0:37.

STAGE 3: Nantes—Laval. July 6.

1. Tom Steels (B), Mapei-Quick Step, 194.5km in 4:29:27 (42.310 kph); 2. Erik Zabel (G), Telekom; 3. Stuart O'Grady (Aus), Crédit Agricole; 4. Nicola Minali (I), Cantina Tollo-Alexia; 5. George Hincapie (USA), U.S. Postal Service; 6. Jimmy Casper (F), La Française des Jeux; 7. Robbie McEwen (Aus), Rabobank; 8. Silvio Martinello (I), Polti; 9. Ello Aggiano (I), Vitalicio Seguros; 10. Mario Cipollini (I), Saeco-Cannondale, all s.t.

Others: 14. Jaan Kirsipuu (Est), Casino; 20. Axel Merckx (B), Mapei-Quick Step; 24. Lance Armstrong (USA), U.S. Postal Service; 27. Abraham Olano (Sp), ONCE-Deutsche Bank; 28. Bobby Julich (USA), Cofidis; 30. Laurent Dufaux (Swi), Saeco-Cannondale; 39. Stefano Garzelli (I), Mercatone Uno-Bianchi; 47. Alex Vinokourov (Kaz), Casino; 57. Christian Vande Velde (USA), U.S. Postal Service; 59. Alex Zülle (Swi), Banesto; 63. Fernando Escartin (Sp), Kelme-Costa Blanca; 64. Richard Virenque (F), Polti; 69. Pavel Tonkov (Rus), Mapei-Quick Step; 73. Ivan Gotti (I), Polti; 82. Tyler Hamilton (USA), U.S. Postal Service; 112. Kevin Livingston (USA), U.S. Postal Service; 113. Paolo Savoldelli (I), Saeco-Cannondale; 117. Frankie Andreu (USA), U.S. Postal Service, all s.t.

DNF: Javier Pascual Llorente (Sp), Kelme-Costa Blanca.

Overall: 1. Kirsipuu, 585.3km in 13:18:59; 2. Steels, at 017; 3. O'Grady, at 0:20; 4. Armstrong, s.t.; 5. Olano, at 0:31; 6. Hincapie, at 0:34; 7. Christophe Moreau (F), Festina, at 0:35; 8.

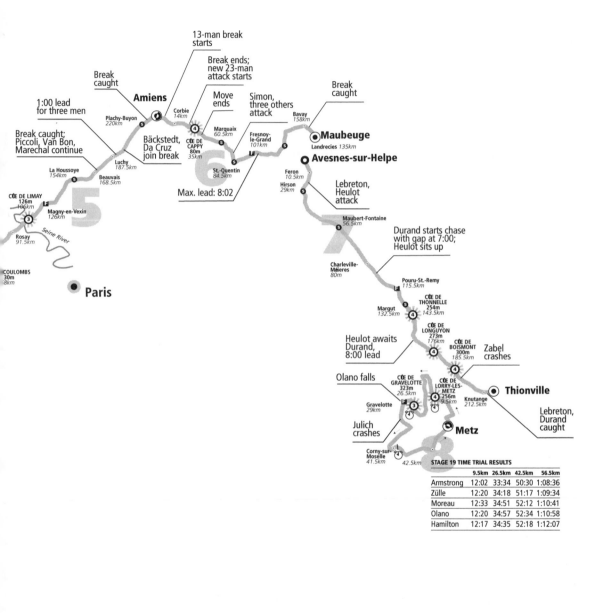

13-man break starts

Break ends; new 23-man attack starts

Move ends

Simon, three others attack

Break caught

Break caught

1:00 lead for three men

Amiens

Corbie
14km

Bäckstedt, Da Cruz join break

Plachy-Buyon
220km

Bavay
158km

Maubeuge

Break caught; Piccoli, Van Bon, Marechal continue

Luchy
187.5km

Beauvais
168.5km

CÔE DE CAPPY
80m
35km

Marquaix
60.5km

Fresnoy-le-Grand
101km

Landrecies 135km

Avesnes-sur-Helpe

La Houssoye
154km

St.-Quentin
84.5km

Feron
10.5km

CÔE DE LIMAY
126m
106km

Magny-en-Vexin
126km

Max. lead: 8:02

Hirson
29km

Lebreton, Heulot attack

Rosay
91.5km

Seine River

Maubert-Fontaine
56.5km

Durand starts chase with gap at 7:00; Heulot sits up

COULOMBS
30m
8km

Paris

Charleville-Mézieres
80m

Pouru-St.-Remy
115.5km

CÔE DE THONNELLE
254m
143.5km

Margut
132.5km

Heulot awaits Durand, 8:00 lead

CÔE DE LONGUYON
273m
176km

CÔE DE BOISMONT
300m
185.5km

Zabel crashes

Olano falls

CÔE DE GRAVELOTTE
323m
26.5km

CÔE DE LORRY-LES-METZ
256m
9.5km

Knutange
212.5km

Thionville

Gravelotte
29km

Julich crashes

Lebreton, Durand caught

Corny-sur-Moselle
41.5km

42.5km

Metz

STAGE 19 TIME TRIAL RESULTS				
	9.5km	26.5km	42.5km	56.5km
Armstrong	12:02	33:34	50:30	1:08:36
Zülle	12:20	34:18	51:17	1:09:34
Moreau	12:33	34:51	52:12	1:10:41
Olano	12:20	34:57	52:34	1:10:58
Hamilton	12:17	34:35	52:18	1:12:07

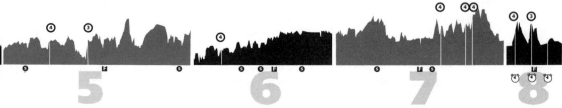

WEEK 1

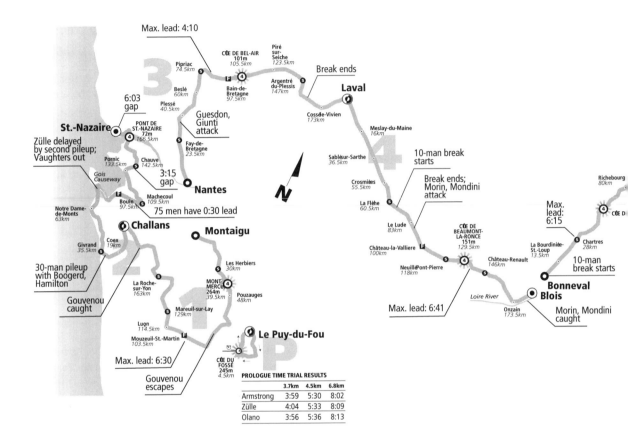

Max. lead: 4:10

CÔE DE BEL-AIR
101m
105.5km

Piré-sur-Seiche
123.5km

Pipriac
74.5km

Beslé
60km

Plessé
40.5km

Bain-de-Bretagne
97.5km

Argentré-du-Plessis
147km

Break ends

Laval

Cossé-le-Vivien
173km

6:03 gap

PONT DE ST-NAZAIRE
72m
166.5km

St.-Nazaire

Zülle delayed by second pileup; Vaughters out

Pornic
133.5km

Gois Causeway

Chauve
142.5km

3:15 gap

Guesdon, Giunti attack

Fay-de-Bretagne
23.5km

Nantes

Machecoul
109.5km

Bouin
97.5km

75 men have 0:30 lead

Notre Dame-de-Monts
63km

Challans

Montaigu

Coex
19km

Givrand
35.5km

30-man pileup with Boogerd, Hamilton

Gouvenou caught

Les Herbiers
30km

La Roche-sur-Yon
163km

MONT-MERCU
264m
39.5km

Pouzauges
48km

Mareuil-sur-Lay
129km

Luçon
114.5km

Mouzeuil-St.-Martin
103.5km

Max. lead: 6:30

Gouvenou escapes

Le Puy-du-Fou

CÔE DU FOSSE
245m
4.5km

Meslay-du-Maine
16km

Sablé-sur-Sarthe
36.5km

10-man break starts

Crosmières
55.5km

Break ends; Morin, Mondini attack

La Flèhe
60.5km

Le Lude
83km

CÔE DE BEAUMONT-LA-RONCE
151m
129.5km

Château-la-Valliere
100km

Neuillé-Pont-Pierre
118km

Max. lead: 6:41

Château-Renault
146km

Loire River

Onzain
173.5km

Richebourg
80km

CÔE D

Max. lead: 6:15

La Bourdinière-St.-Loup
13.5km

Chartres
28km

10-man break starts

**Bonneval
Blois**

Morin, Mondini caught

PROLOGUE TIME TRIAL RESULTS

	3.7km	4.5km	6.8km
Armstrong	3:59	5:30	8:02
Zülle	4:04	5:33	8:09
Olano	3:56	5:36	8:13

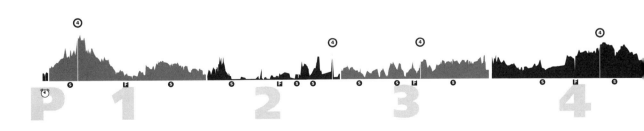

P   1   2   3   4

Zabel, at 0:40; 9. Vinokourov, at 0:41; 10. Santos Gonzales (Sp), ONCE-Deutsche Bank, s.t.

STAGE 4: Laval—Blois. July 7.

1. Cipollini, 194.5km in 3:51:45 (50.355 kph); 2. Zabel; 3. O'Grady; 4. Steels; 5. Kirsipuu; 6. Minali; 7. Christophe Capelle (F), BigMat-Auber 93; 8. Damien Nazon(F), La Française des Jeux; **9. Hincapie**; 10. Jay Sweet (Aus), BigMat-Auber 93, all s.t.

Others: 26. Vinokourov; **33. Julich**; 36. Olano; **48. Andreu**; 52. Dufaux; 56. Boogerd; 60. Merckx; 62. Escartin; **70. Armstrong; 77. Hamilton**; 79. Zülle; 80. Garzelli; 85. Virenque; 90. Tonkov; 91. Gotti; 94. Guerini, all s.t.

Overall: 1. Kirsipuu, 779.8km in 17:10:40; 2. O'Grady, at 016; 3. Steels, at 0:21; **4. Armstrong, at 0:24**; 5. Zabel, at 0:32; 6. Olano, at 0:35; 7. Hincapie, at 0:38; 8. Moreau, at 0:39; 9. Cipollini, at 0:44; 10. Vinokourov, at 0:45.

STAGE 5: Bonneval—Amiens. July 8.

1. Cipollini, 233.5km in 5:36:26 (41.638 kph); 2. Steels; 3. Kirsipuu; 4. Robbie McEwen (Aus), Rabobank; 5. Zabel; 6. O'Grady; 7. Minali; 8. Capelle; 9. Nazon; 10. Jan Svorada (Cz), Lampre-Daikin, all s.t.

Others: 15. Hincapie; 32. Olano; 37. Merckx; 38. Vinokourov; **42. Vande Velde; 44. Julich**; 55. Garzelli; 57. Boogerd; **70. Armstrong; 71. Hamilton**; 74. Virenque; 75. Dufaux; 83. Guerini; **86. Livingston**; 87. Escartin; 93. Gotti; 98. Zülle; 103. Tonkov; **148. Andreu**, all s.t.

Overall: 1. Kirsipuu, 1013.3km in 22:47:00; 2. Steels, at 0:17; 3. O'Grady, at 0:24; **4. Armstrong, at 0:32**; 6. Zabel, at 0:40; 7. Olano, at 0:43; 8. Hincapie, at 0:57; 9. Moreau, at 0:47; 10. Vinokourov, at 0:53.

STAGE 6: Amiens—Maubeuge. July 9.

1. Cipollini, 171.5km in 4:11:09 (40.971 kph); 2. Zabel; 3. Kirsipuu; 4. Svorada; 5. Nazon; **6. Hincapie**; 7. Martinello; 8. O'Grady; 9. Minali; 10. Lars Michaelsen (Dk), La Française des Jeux, all s.t.

Others: 36. Olano; 46. Boogerd; **55. Vande Velde; 58. Julich**; 61. Merckx; 64. Savoldelli; 77. Zülle; 82. Vinokourov; 85. Escartin; 87. Tonkov; 92. Virenque; 96. Dufaux; 110. Gotti; **114. Hamilton; 116. Armstrong; 125. Livingston**; 131. Garzelli; 137. Guerini; **152. Andreu**, all s.t.

Overall: 1. Kirsipuu, 1184.8km in 26:57:55; 2. Cipollini, at 0:26; 3. O'Grady, at 0:38; 4. Zabel, s.t.; **5. Armstrong, at 0:46**; 6. Olano, at 0:57; 7. Hincapie, at 0:58; 9. Steels, at 1:01; 9. Moreau, s.t.

STAGE 7: Avesnes-sur-Helpe—Thionville. July 10.

1. Cipollini, 227km in 5:26:59 (41.653 kph); 2. O'Grady; 3. Kirsipuu; 4. Henk Vogels (Aus), Crédit Agricole; 5. Svorada; 6. Nazon; 7. Capelle; 8. Casper; **9. Hincapie**; 10. Simon, all s.t.

Others: 23. Vinokourov; 27. Zabel; 29. Steels; 34. Olano; 41. Boogerd; 44. Merckx; **47. Vande Velde**; 52. Dufaux; 54. Escartin; **60. Julich; 62. Andreu**; 74. Virenque; **75. Livingston**; 76. Gotti; 80. Tonkov; 82. Zülle; 89. Guerini; 91. Savoldelli; 110. Garzelli, all s.t.

Overall: 1. Kirsipuu, 1411.8km in 32:24:46; 2. Cipollini, at 0:14; 3. O'Grady, at 0:34; 4. Zabel, at 0:44; **5. Armstrong, at 0:54**; 6. Olano, at 1:05; **7. Hincapie, at 1:06**; 8. Steels, at 1:09; 9. Moreau, s.t.; 10. Simon, at 1:12.

Stage 8: Metz TT. July 11.

1. Armstrong, 56.5km in 1:08:36 (49.416 kph); 2. Zülle, 1:09:34; 3. Moreau, 1:10:41; 4. Olano, 1:10:58; **5. Hamilton, 1:12:07**; 6. Chris Boardman (GB), Crédit Agricole, 1:12:08; 7. Alvaro Gonzalez Galdeano (Sp), Vitalicio Seguros, 1:12:17; 8. Jens Voigt (G), Crédit Agricole, 1:12:18; 9. O'Grady, 1:12:21; 9. Laurent Brochard (F), Festina, s.t.; 10. Dufaux, 1:12:32; 11. Andrea Peron (I), ONCE-Deutsche Bank, 1:18:35; 12. Daniele Nardello (I), Mapei-Quick Step, 1:12:48; 13. Santos Gonzales (Sp), ONCE-Deutsche Bank, 1:12:52; 14. Casero, 1:13:11; 15. Luis Perez Rodriguez (Sp), ONCE-Deutsche Bank, 1:13:15; 16. Magnus Bäckstedt (S), Crédit Agricole, 1:13:18; 17. Tonkov, s.t.; 18. Pavel Padrnos (Cz), Lampre-Daikin, 1:13:32; 19. Gilles Maignan (F), 1:13:34; 30. Massimiliano Lelli (I), Saeco-Cannondale, 1:13:49.

Others: 22. Livingston, 1:13:55; 24. Savoldelli, 1:14:05; 30. Kirsipuu, 1:14:27; 37. Garzelli, 1:14:45; 38. Merckx, 1:14:47; **42. Hincapie, 1:15:03**; 46. Virenque, 1:15:06; 48. Vinokourov, 1:15:08; 50. Escartin, 1:15:12; 54. Guerini, 1:15:40; 71. Cipollini, 1:16:17; **73. Andreu, 1:16:18; 75. Vande Velde, 1:16:26**; 101. Gotti, 1:17:32; 103. Boogerd, s.t.

DNF: Julich.

Overall: **1. Armstrong, 1468.3km in 33:34:16**; 2. Moreau, at 2:20; 3. Olano, at 2:33; 4. O'Grady, at 3:25; 5. Gonzales Galdeano, at 4:10; 6. Voigt, s.t.; 7. Dufaux, at 4:19; 8. Peron, at 4:22; 9. Gonzalez, at 4:37; 10. Nardello, at 4:46.

WEEK

2

In the valley
of the shadow....

AFTER SEVEN DAYS of sprint finishes, bookended by time trials
won by Lance Armstrong, the
Tour reached the Alps in a climate
of disbelief. Armstrong and his
supporters had to pinch themselves to believe that he really did have the Tour de France
yellow jersey. The rest—including the skeptics whose outlook had been soured by
cycling's ongoing doping problems—did not believe that a cancer survivor could return
so quickly to the top of his sport. This faction was saying: Surely, he will crack in the
mountains; time trials are one thing, the Galibier and L'Alpe d'Huez are another....

There was time to reflect on this dilemma on the rest day in Le Grand Bornand, a
small alpine ski resort tucked into a green valley at the foot of the Col de la Colombière.
After arriving there from Metz late morning, having a light lunch and riding with his
teammates for two-and-a-half hours in the mountains, Armstrong strolled from his hotel
across the crowded street to a marquee that housed that day's press room. It was 5 p.m.,
the evening before the Tour entered the mountains.

After his team announced that agreements had been signed with the U.S. Postal Service
and Trek to extend their sponsorships through the end of 2001, and that Armstrong, too,
had re-signed for two years, the main in the yellow jersey fielded questions for a half-hour.
He was first asked how he could come back from cancer so strongly.

"I was a halfway dead man," he said. "I was put back together by the best doctors
in the world, and I feel better now than I ever felt before. So perhaps there was some ill-

ness there for a while that I was competing with, and training with, and having to live with; but when I finally rid myself of the cancer, perhaps it helped me...."

He was asked about his opposition. Armstrong replied, "Zülle is perhaps the most dangerous rider, because he has big class, and even though he's seven minutes behind, he could.... In '95, he was nine minutes behind (Induráin) after the first time trial, and he finished second (overall in Paris)."

And what about coping with the pressure of being the race leader, and the center of attention? How was he handling that? "I have had a lot of tense and confusing times in my life," he said, "and having the yellow jersey is a wonderful thing, but it's certainly not the most stressful thing that's ever happened to me. So perhaps, again, the illness and the situations of the past are helping me now...."

Then, of course, he had to address the questions about drugs in cycling. This is what Armstrong said on this rest day: "I think we all have a responsibility to change the image of the sport...I do...the other 170 riders do...the UCI does...the journalists do... because I think we all love the sport. and we're all here for that reason.... Either it's out job or its our passion, or its both. Now, we can choose to do one of two things. We can try and break down the sport that's been around forever...and break down a Tour de France that's been around forever...or we can try and repair it. Unfortunately, there's still some people that want to see it go away, want to tear it down. I'm not one of those people. I want to be part of the renovation. My story is what it is...and I try my best on the bike...and hopefully it *is* good for the sport. I hope *so*. But at the same time, I think the courage and the hard work of the other riders is also good for the sport.... It's not a crooked sport. It's a healthy sport, it's a good sport. It's a wonderful, traditional sport...."

That was how a positive, confident Armstrong began the second crucial week of the Tour—a week starting with perhaps the two most grueling mountain stages of the 86th Tour de France.

STAGE 9
Le Grand Bornand–Sestriere • July 13

Lance in the ascendancy

MOST EUROPEANS WATCHING ARMSTRONG APPARENTLY TOYING with his opposition on the climb up to Sestriere at the end of this first mountain stage could not believe what their eyes were telling them. In order to describe the insolent manner in which the Texan first rode away from main rival Zülle, then closed down an attack by ace climbers Escartin and Gotti, and finally rode away from them all to score a superb stage victory, they had to search their memory banks. They could remember similar rides by great Tour winners like Induráin, Hinault, Greg LeMond and Eddy Merckx. But how was such a performance possible, they asked, from a rider who had always floundered in the Tour's high mountains?

Those European observers were entitled to their views. After all, the last time they had seen him at the Tour de France, in 1996, Armstrong abandoned the race the day before it even reached the Alps. His best effort, they remembered, was his finishing the '95 Tour in 36th place, more than an hour behind winner Induráin.

But what they didn't recall, or didn't want to, was how Armstrong always possessed explosive strength on the uphills. One can think back to his first full season as a professional cyclist in 1993, when Armstrong took solo victories in the world's and nationals, each time making his winning move on a steep climb. It was also his climbing strength that earned him a World Cup win in San Sebastian and a Tour stage victory at Limoges in 1995, and won him the Flèche Wallonne in '96.

And those continentals probably never knew about Armstrong's phenomenal climbing demonstrations in mountain stages at the Tour DuPont, most notably on North Carolina's rugged Beech Mountain. Those successes, like the ones in Europe, came prior to Armstrong's fight with cancer, at a time when he weighed a hefty 180 pounds—a size that, for his 5-foot 11-inch height, prevented him from repeating his hill-climbing prowess in the longer, higher mountain passes.

Then came the cancer that threatened his life, but from which Armstrong emerged, in his own words, as "a better rider than I was before...certainly a better person." With a body now weighing closer to 160 than 180 pounds, he has automatically gained 10 percent in his power-to-weight ratio—and that's not taking into account his improved training methods, and a new focus on climbing, which both have helped to increase his power output.

Despite all these factors, the U.S. Postal Service leader still had to translate the theory into practice. He still had to defend the Tour yellow jersey in the mountains for the first time in his life, and do it in what some considered to be the race's most challenging stage.

It's *pièce de résistance* was the Col du Galibier, the legendary 8677-foot peak on whose slopes the Tour was played out in 1998—when Marco Pantani attacked to drop Ullrich and Julich on the stage to Les Deux-Alpes. That finish was only 43km (including one climb) from the Galibier summit; this year, 68km (and two climbs) separated the Galibier from Sestriere, giving rise to very different tactics.

One similarity was heavy rain in the closing part of the stage, but thankfully the worst of the conditions didn't arrive until well after the Galibier, which was climbed on mainly dry roads, after a menacing thunderstorm only skirted the mighty mountain pass. Because of the more distant finish, this year's stage was tactically very different. Instead of deciding the whole race, the Galibier became a climb that filtered out the weaker riders.

One who was found lacking was Olano, who was dropped by Armstrong's group 8km from the top, when Livingston was leading a successful chase for the yellow jersey, to catch a potentially dangerous attack by Polti's Virenque and the two Kelme climbers, Escartin and Castelblanco. By the summit, not in the clouds this time, Olano was about a minute behind the 10-strong Armstrong group, a situation that would dictate the tactics for the rest of the stage....

First over the Galibier was Spaniard José-Luis Arrieta of Banesto, who had been sent ahead by his team leader Zülle in a five-man break that gained 6:15 by the foot of the Col de Télégraphe—which in effect is also the foot of the Galibier, because only 5km separate the top of the Télégraphe from the start of the Galibier. Starting this combined 30km of climbing, Arrieta soon left behind the rest of the break, and managed to keep a lead of 1:40 over the Galibier summit.

On this first major obstacle of the Tour,

FRANKIE'S DIARY © July 12 © Le Grand Bornand

Rest day talk

We took a bus, flew, took another bus and then rode. We didn't arrive to the hotel till about 1 p.m., and then we went riding for two-and-a half hours over the first part of tomorrow's course. Talk about a lot of people: Our hotel is in the middle of Le Grand Bornand. The place is packed, and it's pure gridlock outside.

On the way to the hotel I called Bobby, to see how he was doing. He flew to Nice early this morning from Metz. In Nice, he is going to the hospital again to get a full check-up on his injuries. The main thing that he's worried about is his elbow. It may be broken; but even if it isn't, something is torn inside. He says he has no movement at all with it. His other serious problem is massive bruising or a hematoma in his chest area. He said it's painful to breathe, much less move around. He realizes, though, that at the speed he was going, he is lucky only to have the problems he has. I wish him a speedy recovery. [Julich had hairline fractures of two ribs and the elbow's radius bone.]

Now that the first week is over, the sprinters will be in survival mode. They have made their mark in this first week, showing everyone who was in charge. One sprinter who was not here who could have possibly put a stop to Cipo's four consecutive wins was Jeroen Blijlevens (TVM). Blijevens has always been a threat in the Tour, especially in the longer stages. In this year's Giro, he dominated the early stages, winning three times. His decision to quit the Giro in the last week was based solely on keeping his sprinting legs for the Tour. If he knew that his team would be prevented from riding the Tour, I'm sure he would have tried for another stage win in Milan. Meanwhile, Cipo' can count his blessings that Jeroen didn't get a chance to show his colors at the Tour.

Yesterday's time trial was something special. Lance dominated the stage in the same way Induráin used to crush the opposition. Lance averaged 49.3 kph on a hilly, windy circuit. He went up the Cat. 3 climb in a 55x19, while I used a 45x19. Lance was waiting for no one to take that yellow jersey— except for him. He told us that after he passed Olano, he knew that Olano was sitting behind him. The first part of the race he had all the press motorcycles around him, but after he passed Olano, they were nowhere. That's because the motorcycles were not allowed to pass Olano until the gap grew big enough so that Olano would not get a draft.

George said that when Lance's lead motorcycle passed him, the driver, all excited, said to George, "Lance is coming, Lance is coming!" Even the cops are fans. When Johan caught up to Saiz—the ONCE director who was following Olano—they drove next to each other for about 5 kilometers. It was like the student and the teacher squaring off, since for three years, Johan rode for Saiz on team ONCE.

The French spectators seem to have a new game. It's a dangerous game for themselves and for the riders. There seems to be a competition going on regarding who can run in between the lead car and the charging peloton. People are darting across the road at the last possible moment, right before the group speeds by. In Lance's ride, in particular, one kid tried to run in between the lead motorcycle and him. Lance had to swerve a little to avoid the kid.

You might also have noticed the many banners for Piccolli—the Lampre rider leading the KoM competition. It seems like there are more banners for the Italian than there are for their favorite French rider, Virenque. The reason it's like this is because there is a daily award given out by the Lampre team. Each day while driving the race course, the marketing people select their favorite banner supporting Piccolli. Lampre then gets the supporter's address and sends them a climber's polka-dot jersey. It sounds simple, but considering how many fans are watching the Tour, the odds of getting noticed can't be that good.

Zabel is okay after his injuries the other day. It's incredible that he took the start today in the TT. I saw him at dinner and was asking him what had happened. He received 10 stitches to his chin and has a very sore groin, after landing on his top bar and stem. He said that he had a couple of stones lodged in his pedal after his first crash, and his cleats did not completely lock into the pedals. When he started the sprint, his foot came straight out. He said he had to set up some new shoes, because the leather got ripped off from the soles somehow. He is one tough German.

Mark Gorski, our manager, has been our second director driving the second team car throughout the race. He hasn't seen much action lately, because the peloton has always been finishing together. Now, that will all change. With the mountains arriving tomorrow, the peloton will be split into many groups, giving the second directors a critical job of keeping the riders fueled and warm. I have two rain bags, one in the first car and one in the second. Both contain pretty much the same things, such as rain jacket, gloves, hat and vest. I haven't needed anything from the first car yet, but I guarantee you I'll be digging into that second bag. Mark is responsible for all the riders not in the first group. He has to drive in between the groups, taking care of riders with water, food and clothes, if it's needed. The first car always stays with the first group or the leader on the team…. I can remember a few mountain stages when I was stranded in a group that my second director forgot about. Freezing on a downhill or bonking during a mountain stage is no way to get through a Tour. I guess you could say that during the mountain stages, the second car is my lifeline.

Armstrong's Postal team rode impressively: Andreu pulled for the first 10km of the Télégraphe, before sitting up and letting Hincapie take over. Then, on the Galibier, according to Armstrong, "Kevin (Livingston) pulled for 19.5 of the 20 kilometers."

Once at the top, Arrieta stopped to don a rain jacket, then waited for the chasers, who shed Castelblanco on the fast descent, while Livingston also dropped back when the rain jacket he had been handed up got tangled in a wheel. The resultant nine-man lead group was comprised of Banesto's Zülle, Arrieta and Beltran; Polti's Virenque and Gotti; Kelme's Escartin and Carlos Contreras; Saeco's Dufaux; and race leader Armstrong.

"It wasn't a good situation for me, with a couple of Banestos, a couple of Kelmes, a couple of Poltis (in the group)," Armstrong later said. "But they were very anxious in getting away from Olano, so they worked, and I was able to ride easy."

On the long descent, Olano was a minute back in a chase group of 27 riders, led down the valley road by four of his ONCE riders, who were trying desperately to keep their team leader in the top three overall. It proved to be a classic chase, with most of the work ahead being done by Zülle's lieutenants Beltran and Arrieta—who sat up when he reached the short hill up into Briançon, with the gap up to 1:20.

Now came the Cat. 2 Montgenèvre climb, opening with a false flat, and culminating with 7km of steep switchbacks. Overhead, menacing clouds were about to unleash a rainstorm that would increase in intensity for the next couple of hours—and would most affect the *gruppetto*, a half-hour back, and last man on the road, Aussie Jay Sweet, who had been alone since the early slopes of the Télégraphe.

While Sweet was just starting the Galibier descent, the eight-strong lead group was fighting a gusting head wind on the early slopes of the Montgenèvre; and it looked like Olano's men might succeed when the gap was cut to 54 seconds. Then the grade steepened, and Beltran went to work for Zülle, along with Escartin and Gotti, to re-establish a 1:25 lead.

All this played in Armstrong's favor, who was able simply to follow the others, without digging deep: "On the Galibier, I was comfortable but I didn't feel super…but I always ride good in these cold, wet conditions, and on a day like this you automatically eliminate 50 percent of the opposition." Armstrong then said he looked at his rivals' faces, and "it looked like they were suffering a little bit."

Suffering or not, Gotti and Escartin sped clear of the other six leaders on the steep, curving descent of the Montgenèvre. They were not taking too many risks, as the now heavy rain was making conditions extremely treacherous.

This was confirmed when there was a crash in the big chase group. Among those who came down were Tonkov and the two Postal climbers, Hamilton and Livingston.

"It was a left turn…a little off camber…I was following Olano," Livingston reported. "We got in the turn, and I thought, 'This looks slick.' And the next thing my front wheel slid out. My bike went to the right, and I went out sliding head first…. I couldn't believe how fast I was going. I saw the guard rail coming, with the pillars—and I actually changed my direction (to go) in between 'em, under the rail.

"I didn't hit my head, I was lucky. I was thinking, 'You idiot, you don't have your helmet on.' I'd taken it off just before."

Hamilton later described his own fall: "One guy goes down…you touch your brakes…I just slid for ever, and then crashed into the barricades. Kevin went down, too, so I thought, 'Do I wait (for him)?' But we were only a minute behind Lance…so I just got on my bike as fast as possible and went. I thought it was important to still ride, just in case there was a problem (for) Lance."

Armstrong, however, said he was having "good feelings on the last climb." So 2 kilometers into the 11km ascent to the finish in the Italian ski resort of Sestriere, with the two leaders 32 seconds ahead of Armstrong's group, the American decided, "I didn't want Gotti and Escartin to go too far."

Impressively, Armstrong smoothly crossed the gap, while Zülle had also taken up the chase. On reaching the lead pair, the race leader quickly countered a smart attack by Gotti—the Giro winner who was hoping to score a stage victory here on home soil. Armstrong then went to the front to control the pace, and when he saw Zülle latching on to the break just inside 7km to go, the Postal leader accelerated.

"I wasn't trying to attack," Armstrong said. "Johan (Bruyneel) told me on the radio that I had a gap, so I rode a little faster tempo. Then he told me the gap was bigger, so I tried to go…."

So, on a flatter part of the step-like climb, Armstrong shifted onto his 53-tooth big ring, and went hard, out of the saddle, to create a 12-second gap. Twelve seconds became 30 seconds at the 5km-to-go point, and became 43 seconds a kilometer later. Riding through the icy rain, his yellow jersey blackened by tire spray, Armstrong kept up the pressure, looking invincible. But Zülle was slowly closing on him, cutting the gap to 37 seconds with 3km left.

Armstrong later said that, in hindsight, his move "was too early because the last 3 kilometers I was suffering…. It was just exhaustion. I was running out of fuel. It gets hard after 220 kilometers, with a finish at 2000 meters."

Zülle chased all the way to the line, finishing with his mouth wide open, 31 seconds after Armstrong. It was another minute before Escartin and Gotti appeared, and 2:27 until Beltran showed up with Virenque and Contreras. Olano lost more than three minutes,

Dufaux three-and-a-half, and Tonkov— who chased hard after his crash—a solid five minutes.

Hamilton, with cuts on his arm and leg, finished the stage in 25th, at 6:31, while Livingston came in three minutes later, in 26th. Describing his reaction to his frightening crash, Livingston said, "I was sort of out of it for a second, and then I got it back together." What he found was a smashed front wheel, with no team car in sight. Livingston gratefully accepted a wheel from the Polti team car.

The same descent claimed other victims, including Cipollini, who fell heavily into the guard rail. So the stunned winner of four stages didn't finish the stage, as he had said he would to honor his Italian fans waiting at the finish. One sprinter who did finish was Sweet, who battled through the rainstorm alone, to cross the line almost an hour behind Armstrong. The young Aussie arrived in Sestriere well outside the time limit, but his bravery impressed the judges who allowed him to stay in the race.

At the other end of the day's spectrum, Armstrong's demonstration impressed the world. Many were shocked, too; but the way the Texan saw it, his beautiful victory was just reward for many months of hard work preparing for this moment. Yet he was in no way boastful of his feat. After saying that his team was "superb," he told a packed press room, "I'm still nervous and still don't think the race is over. The others

FRANKIE'S DIARY © July 13 © Sestriere

Wet day in the Alps

What a day: I've been colder, hotter and more tired, but I don't think I've ever been more wet. For some reason, the mountains in the Tour seem to go along with bad weather. Today was a classic. At the start we did our team presentation again, and we all received another lion. When I came off the stand, Willy, our chef, asked me for my lion. I wasn't very happy with him. You see, I already gave him a lion, but he thought so much of it that he left it on a curb and lost it. So, this is his second lion. But enough of that: The lions are over, because we lost our team G.C. today. When we came off the team presentation, we saw the Saeco guys rolling up to sign on. They were all dressed like Julius Caesar, wearing togas and with vines around their heads—but Cipo' wore a gold crown. They also had on gold jerseys and shorts commemorating Julius Caesar's birthday. Today was his 2099th birthday.

The day contained four major climbs. The plan was that if a break went, Pascal, Christian and Peter would do tempo on the flats before the first big climb, to keep the gap in check. I was to lead up the first 12km climb, the Col de Télégraphe. Then George was supposed to lead up, as much as he could, on the 18km Col du Galibier. When George died, Tyler would take over, and that left Kevin and Lance to handle the last two climbs.

For once, the race started out slow. After 40km, a break went with four guys, none of them dangerous. We could lose nine minutes and *still* have the jersey. Pascal, Christian and Peter took over and pulled until the bottom of the climb. I took over on the Télégraphe and was pinned by kilometer one. I don't know who thought I was a climber. Anyway, I quit pulling about two kilometers from the top; I just couldn't keep going. The pack was still together and George had to finish off the last part of the climb that I couldn't do. George then led to the bottom of the Galibier, but that was when Kelme started attacking, so George got spit out after four or five kilometers. Tyler and Kevin took over until the second-to-last climb, when Lance got away in a small break. Lance was with Virenque, Gotti, Zülle, Escartin and some Banesto guy.

In the back, already a minute down, was Olano—with Tyler and Kevin sitting on his wheel. On the final climb, Lance showed no mercy: He attacked and rode away from everyone. Zülle was the only one to respond and was able to keep within 30 seconds at the finish. Lance won—again, very convincingly. Olano, the second-place guy on G.C., is now six minutes back.

Lance, Kevin and Tyler were lucky weather-wise. They escaped the worst of the storms that the rest of the team met 30 minutes behind them. It was weird: As we climbed the mountains, the rain would start; then as we got higher, the hail would fall; then by the top it was cold, but dry. The same thing would happen down the other side: hail, rain and then dry.

ABRAHAM OLANO

The last climb up to Sestriere was 10 times worse than the previous mountains. I have never been in a bike race where it rained so hard. There were rivers flowing down the road with so much water that when it hit our wheels, it would make a wave. We were soaked, but then the hail started pelting us. It was strong and painful. I was almost laughing, 'cause I couldn't believe how bad a day it had turned out to be.

With all this rain, for some reason I couldn't get my brakes to work. I had to go real slow down the last hill, because no matter how hard or long I pulled on my brakes, I couldn't stop—I could only slow

down a little. By the bottom of the hill, I was just hoping there were no more corners, since my luck had probably run out because of all the times I drifted to the edge of the road.

I'm not sure if it was because of their brakes, but both Kevin and Tyler crashed. Actually, Kevin crashed Tyler, if you want to get technical. Kevin just slid his front wheel out and whoever was behind him also stacked it. They are both okay…. Cipo' also took down a bunch of guys. He was flying down the hill, which was wet and slick, and crashed into the guardrail. So Julius Caesar didn't make it to the finish.

Some guys have all the luck: They pick the right day to show up for the Tour. Today, our team sponsor Thom Weisel showed up and drove in the first car with Johan. He got to see every piece of action, all the way up to Lance crossing the line with his hands in the air. I also saw Greg LeMond today; he's here with his Tour group. I talked with him while he was hanging out in the *village départ*. He was all dressed in cycling gear, so I assumed he was either going or coming from a ride with his tour group.

Tomorrow is another big mountain day.
What's the problem? Trying to get six of us over the 25km climb that comes at kilometer 60. It's a 220km stage with three big climbs, and the last one is Alpe d'Huez. Everyone wants to win there, so I'm sure the climbers will be attacking like it's the last day. I'm nervous, just like I was this morning.

will be back and they will be better than they were today. They're all scrappers and they will make life hard for us. I respect all of them 100 percent."

Armstrong has been a champion since he first began his cycling career. On this rainy summit in the Alps, he simply reached another step in his ascendancy.

STAGE 10

Sestriere–L'Alpe d'Huez • July 14

Up to the challenge

THE 21 TURNS TO L'ALPE D'HUEZ HAVE SEEN TOUR DE FRANCE BATTLES as spectacular as the road itself, which climbs 3664 feet in 13.8km up the near-vertical side of the Romanche valley. Two years ago, the protagonists were Ullrich and Pantani, with the young German toiling successfully to defend his yellow jersey, as he chased, but didn't catch, the runaway Italian. Back in 1992, the stage winner was American Andy Hampsten, who left behind the rest of a break that formed on the preceding Croix de Fer climb. And in 1986, of course, the traditionally huge crowds on L'Alpe d'Huez witnessed the memorable hands-holding finish of LeMond and Hinault that clinched the American's first triumph in the Tour.

Now, 13 years later, it was time for another American to prove that he had the strength to stay in the yellow jersey. Or, more to the point, did Armstrong and his American *teammates* have the strength to control once more a 200km-plus mountain stage through the Italian and French Alps? At Sestriere, Armstrong came through unscathed, to score a monumental victory. But having lost his climbing partner Jonathan Vaughters back in the Vendée, and with lieutenants Livingston and Hamilton both suffering heavy falls the day before, would the team be up to the task it had carried out so efficiently over the Galibier?

Motivated by having the yellow jersey in the team, the Postal men knew that this 220.5km stage would be long and hard—with the Alpe waiting to challenge them at the end. The first of the team on duty was youngest member Christian Vande Velde, who was now facing the hard reality of the Tour after his euphoric start—each morning in the first week, he was on the podium for leading the best young rider competition, and the team race. Here in the Alps, on a warm, windy day, life was much harder for Vande Velde: "Working on the front doesn't make it any easier," he commented. "I had to ride all the way to the first climb...like 45k into a head wind, on a downhill.... That sucked."

During the second hour, climbing the steep and long Mont Cénis Pass, Vande Velde passed the baton to his French teammate Pascal Deramé. Although this was the highest mountain of the day, and much of it at a 10-percent grade, Mont Cénis was too far from the finish to elicit any attacks. Yet even though the climbing pace was a pedestrian 20 kph, a few riders were dropped, including a sick Axel Merckx of Mapei, who abandoned the Tour.

Over the bleak summit, there was a brief sprint for the KoM points taken by Russian Dmitri Konyshev of Mercatone Uno-Bianchi. Then, at the foot of the wide, curving descent, a hopeful attack was made by two Frenchmen, BigMat's Thierry Bourgignon and La Française des Jeux's Heulot—after all, this *was* Bastille Day, the French national holiday.

Their long-distance move made life easier for Armstrong's men, as others would be less likely to attack—as long as the Postal team set a high enough tempo down the 60km of gradual downhill before the Croix de Fer. This was Frankie Andreu's job, which he did well enough to hold Heulot and Bourgignon—riding against a strong head wind—to a maximum lead of 11:20.

Ahead loomed the 29km-long Croix de Fer, which climbs in three parts, separated by two short downhills. It's a spectacular road, sometimes carved into the side of a deep gorge or tunneled through rocky escarpments, before emerging into a high, grassy alpine valley. Here, the riders can look up and see the final 8km of the climb, angling across the mountainside in a staircase of eight switchbacks.

By this point, after initial pulls by Andreu and Hincapie, Postal's Livingston had towed the dwindling pack to within eight minutes of Heulot and Bourgignon—who were being chased individually by Cofidis's Roland Meier and Mercatone Uno's Stefano Garzelli.

"Kevin (Livingston) wasn't feeling too hot, so he decided to switch with me," said Hamilton, who would be the last Postal rider to stay with Armstrong. "Kevin did a lot of work on the Croix de Fer, and I did just a little bit at the top."

"I was a bit off today," Livingston agreed. But his last pulls before dropping off the pace brought the race leader's group to within 6:12 of the break, with Meier still chasing in between. All the race leaders were still in the Armstrong group, which Hamilton led for most of the 30km descent, and along the valley floor to the foot of L'Alpe d'Huez. Starting the final ascent, the group was about to catch the obstinate Meier, while Heulot's and Bourgignon's lead had been cut to 4:35.

Many of the Alpe's early pitches are as steep as 14 percent, which proved too much for first Bourgignon, then Meier. They were both overtaken by a quickly disintegrating group that was being led at an impressive clip by the youthful Hamilton, his jersey unzipped to his waist, the sun glinting on the sweat dripping from his tanned brow.

Three minutes ahead with 10km still to climb, Heulot was holding strong, inspired by the thousands of French fans, willing him to win on this now blazing 14th of July The 28-year-old Breton, who was 13th overall in the 1998 Tour, was showing incredible resilience after almost four hours at the front. But Heulot was fighting a strong head wind for most of the climb, and his lead was down to two minutes when Hamilton eased back halfway up.

Attacks were now coming from Escartin, Tonkov and Zülle, to which Armstrong was having to respond on his own. "I was more tired than the day before," Armstrong later stated. "But I never felt in danger. My only problem was that the 19 (sprocket) wasn't working, so I was having to use the 17 when there were attacks, and the 21 or 23 the rest of the time. I would have liked the 19…."

The yellow jersey was able to respond to the climbers' accelerations, but they were too much for Olano, who lost contact at the same time as Hamilton. Meanwhile, Heulot was clearly struggling, and seven men began to close in on him: Banesto's Beltran and Zülle, Kelme's Escartin and Contreras, Mapei's Tonkov, Polti's Virenque and Postal's Armstrong. And by the time the French hero was caught, just inside 4km to go, the group had been joined by Telekom's Guerini.

Up the Alpe

Talk about tired, I am completely wasted.
Maybe partly because of yesterday, and maybe because whatever was left over is now gone. Thank God, I'm sure everyone felt the same way, since we went easy over the first 25km climb at kilometer 60. Today was a 220km race, finishing up Alpe d'Huez, the most prestigious mountain stage. Besides everyone being tired from yesterday, a very, very strong head wind kept us in our place. It was very windy through the valley leading to the Croix de Fer, the second climb of the day. This climb was 30km long. We had Pascal and Christian ride tempo through the valley, to keep close to a break that went clear on the descent. It was a two-man break and we could give up 19 minutes, so there was no panic. Peter had the day off, as much as he could, to nurse a sore knee….

After the valley, we hit the Croix de Fer, and the plan was for George and I to do the first part, then Tyler and Kevin take over until the top. After that, it was just the finish climb, which Lance could handle himself. At the bottom of Croix de Fer, George and I started setting tempo. We were supposed to set a medium tempo just to keep things calm. On approaching the climb, Johan saw the Polti director was all nervous, and all the Polti riders were setting up near the front for the climb. He figured they were going to attack right away. Johan radioed George and I, and told us to go hard to screw up their plans. We hit the bottom and in about 200 meters, as usual, I was pinned. We pulled for about 5 or 6 kilometers alternating, and then I blew. George pulled for another couple kilometers and then left it for the real climbers.

It is so hard trying to climb with the climbers; it's like three times the effort for us. After I blew, a couple of guys caught me from behind, and then we caught George to finish going up the climb. We still had a good 15km to go. After going to my max and then trying to recover while still going uphill, I blew by the top. My muscles just did not want to work. Luckily, George went to the front of our little group and kind of got in the way to make them slow down. All I needed was a kilometer or two slower. I suffered, but I made it over.

Tyler ended up pulling up the last part of the climb and setting Lance up for the Alpe. They were in a group of about 15 when they hit the bottom, and then it was every man for himself. Near the top there were seven guys left and Guerini (Telekom) attacked and got away alone. Flying toward the finish with about 800 meters to go, he had it in the bag. Then all of a sudden an idiot with a camera popped out into the middle of the road—no exaggeration, the very middle—

TYLER HAMILTON

and tried taking a picture. Guerini had nowhere to go. There are so many people watching the riders that we sometimes have only a four-foot gap to go through. He hit the photographer and crashed—incredible. He got up and got on his bike, while the idiot was patting him on the back saying something like good job, way to go. The guy didn't even give him a push, he was still trying to talk with Guerini. I couldn't believe my eyes. Afterward, Guerini said it was no big deal. Yeah, it was no big deal because he still *won*; imagine if that would have cost him the win. Then it would have been a big deal, and the guy would probably be in jail.

Lance finished with a group of six with all the climbing favorites, except Olano. He's no climbing favorite, but he still is in second on the overall. Lance didn't really sprint. I think he probably could

have won, but at this point it's better to make some friends in the peloton than enemies. Olano lost more time and is now seven something down on Lance.

Yesterday I told you about all the Saeco guys wearing gold jerseys and shorts. Well, the UCI made a fortune off of them. Each one of them got fined and the team got fined. Including all the fines for yesterday, in just one day, the UCI made 8760 Swiss francs (about $6500). That's a lot.

I made a mistake last night thinking that we lost team G.C. We still had it this morning. The best team yesterday was Banesto, so I thought it would take over the team G.C. The problem was Banesto lost so much time on the causeway day that we still have a seven-minute lead on them. Maybe we lost it today. Either way, I got another lion this morning.

Even though I couldn't see straight at the bottom of Alpe d'Huez, I still was excited about doing it. The number of people and the party atmosphere there are incredible. There are rows and rows of people along the road the whole way up the 15km climb. The climb is full of switchbacks, each one numbered as you climb up starting with 21. At certain parts of the course, the road is only as wide as your handlebars. People are screaming their heads off at the first guys, and all the way to the last guys.

I have five minutes to send this, more tomorrow. We don't have phones in the room and the front desk is letting me use their fax machine.

As the grade steepened again, Heulot was dropped, and he was soon passed by two other chasers: Dufaux and Belgian Kurt Van de Wouwer of Lotto. Then, just inside 3km to go, Guerini made a darting attack that Tonkov and Zülle both tried to follow, without success. Maybe Armstrong, sitting comfortably, could have gone with the 28-year-old Italian, but there was no need to chase someone who was 11:42 behind him on overall time....

The other leaders also thought better of going into their red zone, and so Guerini was let go, while Dufaux and Van de Wouwer were able to catch back. Then, with 1.5km left, Tonkov took off after Guerini, but without much hope of catching the Italian.

That prospect suddenly changed when, about 800 meters from the finish, Guerini saw a spectator standing in the center of the road, waiting to take a photo of him. Both men realized at the same instant that they would have to take evasive action...and both, unfortunately, went in the same direction. To avoid being rammed, the fan held out his hands—and in doing so pushed Guerini off his bike!

Embarrassed, after watching the racer scramble to pick up himself and his bike, the spectator simply patted Guerini on the back as he struggled to clip his feet into the pedals. "For a moment, I really thought I had lost the race," Guerini later said. Fortunately, he had a big enough gap, and as he scampered off like a scared rabbit, the chasing Tonkov was still a couple of hundred meters behind.

And so the hawk-nosed, black-haired Guerini, who was expecting to be a workhorse for Telekom leader Jan Ullrich at the Tour, scored a prestigious stage victory and moved into the overall top 10.

As for Armstrong, he crossed the line with chief rivals Escartin, Zülle, Virenque and Dufaux, while adding 1:39 to his margin over second-placed Olano. The Tour was only half over, but the American and his team had accomplished what few thought them capable of: They had emerged from the Alps with the yellow jersey, almost eight minutes ahead of the opposition.

STAGE 11

Bourg d'Oisans–St. Etienne • July 15

Stage-win mania

REMARKABLY, WITH HALF THE 86TH TOUR DE FRANCE COMPLETED, only five riders could boast of having won a stage (Armstrong, Kirsipuu, Steels, Cipollini and Guerini) and only two of them (Armstrong and Kirsipuu) had worn the yellow jersey.

There was not much chance of the overall lead changing on this 11th stage—or any of the following three days. But stage wins were there for the taking…especially as only 12 riders were within 15 minutes of overall leader Armstrong.

For most riders in the peloton, winning a stage of the Tour is the key to a new respect…a new contract…a higher salary…or simply their survival in professional cycling. It has similar prestige to victory in a one-day classic, because of the Tour's larger, worldwide audience, even though it is generally easier to win a less-important Tour stage than a major classic.

So, within 5km of this 11th stage starting in the valley below L'Alpe d'Huez, the attacks began. Teams that had yet to win anything—especially Cofidis, Lotto, Mercatone Uno, Crédit Agricole and Vitalicio—were sending riders up the road. The early kilometers were gradually downhill, but against a strong, blustery wind, and yet the speed rarely dropped below 50 kph.

Every team, it seemed, was anxious to get in a break…and, at the same time, none of them wanted a break to form without them. That pattern continued on the wide roads through Grenoble, until Telekom (for Zabel) and Crédit Agricole (for points leader O'Grady) restored some control prior to the first intermediate sprint, outside the headquarters of the Dauphiné Libéré newspaper in Voury-Voroize, 58km into the stage.

The sprint result—1. Steels, 2. Zabel, 3. O'Grady—was reminiscent of the first week, but the deployment of each team had changed drastically. Neither Cipollini nor Kirsipuu remained in the Tour, so their respective Saeco and Casino teams were more focused on getting riders into breaks, than closing them down to favor their sprinters. As for Steels's Mapei teammates, their fist duty was to help Tonkov, seventh overall, stay out of trouble until the Pyrénées rather than work toward a field sprint each day.

With these different forces at work, the attacks continued until the race reached the 5km-long, Cat. 2 Col de Parménie. The pace on the climb—winding under oak and beech trees to the top of a ridge—was such that the peloton split in two. Some 40 riders were in the back group, while at the front a break was made by Lotto's Rik Verbrugghe. The 24-year-old Belgian was 30 seconds clear over the 1873-foot summit, with the second pack a further 50 seconds behind.

Verbrugghe attacked in the hope that others would join him, and this happened when five joined forces to close the half-minute gap: Mercatone Uno's Konyshev and Riccardo Forconi, Festina's Wladimir Belli and Laurent Lefèvre, and Lampre's Dierckxsens. None of the six leaders was a danger on G.C., but they were chased anyway by a peloton led by most of the Casino team.

Into the feed zone at 92km, with the stage less than two hours old and the wind now blowing from the right, Casino closed the gap to 12 seconds. It looked like the break was doomed, but Casino now launched its Kazakhstani star Vinokourov across the gap...and then eased back the pace. It was a classic move, coming when most of the riders were grabbing their feed bags; secondly, most were concerned that their teammates in the group behind (now 2:40 back) could be in danger of elimination if the peloton's insane pace continued. The result was a sudden slowing in the speed, allowing the delayed riders to return, as Armstrong's Postal team resumed its familiar role of riding tempo at the head of the pack.

The seven leaders were already two minutes clear; and the gap grew to 12 minutes by the time they crossed the Rhône River at Andance, with 60km left in the stage. Ahead lay the green mass of Mont Pilat, to whose conifer-forested ridge the course soon began to climb on narrow, winding roads. When about 10km from the top, where the road, not that steep, was twisting between open pastures, Vinokourov suddenly sprinted ahead. It was a confident move, but the two Mercatone Uno riders immediately chased with Dierckxsens. And as they closed on the Casino rider, Dierckxsens, winner of the Belgian road championship a week before the start of the Tour, made

FRANKIE'S DIARY © July 15 © St. Etienne

Luxuries of the Tour

The hotel we stayed in last night was a Club Med hotel at the top of Alpe d'Huez. Normally, they're closed for the summer; but because of the race, they opened up for three days. Tomorrow, they close the hotel again. Peter's dad, who is visiting the Tour, inquired how much it would be to stay for the night. It was almost $200. If you saw the rooms and the hotel, you would realize you'd have to be crazy to pay that for this place. The room was so small, George and I couldn't open either of our suitcases. The shower was a small stall in a closet, and I couldn't even close the door where the toilet was—that room was so small that when I sat on the toilet, my knees would hit the door in front of me. Hell, I couldn't even use the phone. I had to bug the rent-a-receptionist to let me use the phone line from the fax machine to send yesterday's article. I wrote the article right after the race, while waiting for a massage....

Tyler was the man yesterday! He pulled, pulled, and pulled on the mountain. He rode a great race for Lance, leading halfway up Alpe d'Huez—till the Banestos started attacking. Our climbers are doing a great job protecting Lance in the mountains. Kevin was feeling a little under the weather after crashing hard the day before. Normally, Tyler would work first, then Kevin; but they switched yesterday because Kevin was not 100 percent. This is something that is important with any team: communication.

Yesterday, going up Croix de Fer, we had a mishap on the team. About 4 kilometers from the top, when the road gets narrow, our first team car died. It stopped dead in its tracks, blocking all the team cars behind it. Johan, shit, couldn't believe this was happening to him. He tried turning the key four or five times—and nothing. Not even the little lights on the dashboard were lighting up. After a few more tries the engine finally turned over. Who knows why, but then again, the cars *are* Fiats.

After two days of riding in the mountains, the guys were attacking today like it was the first day. They're crazy. We started at the bottom of Alpe d'Huez and the first 40km were a false flat downhill. Maybe everyone thought they had good legs. It took two hours of attacks before finally a break went. That was what we were waiting for. We had to wait for the right combination of guys to go up the road. We figure no Banesto, ONCE or Telekom. No Banesto and ONCE because when we ride slow, if the break gets too much time, they will have to protect their second and third place on G.C. And no Telekom in case they decide to go for the stage win in a sprint. They would have to chase, because they would not have a rider up the road.

What ended up in the break were two Festinas, two Mercatones, a Lampre, a Casino and a Lotto. It was good for us. Our job now was to ride tempo, slowly! I needed a rest day and this was probably the closest thing I could have asked for. The break went up the road to 20 minutes. Obviously, everyone else in the pack did not mind a little rest also. The Lampre guy won the race. That's a pretty big flick: two teams with two guys and the solo rider wins. I'm sure their directors won't be happy.

Tonight we are staying in a clone of the Olympic Training Center in Colorado Springs. I'm sleeping in the bottom part of a bunk bed. I can't even sit up to type this, I have to lie down or I'll hit my head. I guess the bonus is that we can at least open one suitcase and go to the bathroom in private. Oh, the luxuries of the Tour.

Another car story: Willy, our chef, usually drives part of the course on his way to the team's hotel. He likes to wave at all the people and honk the horn at all the Americans standing on the side of the road. When our soigneurs were going from the start to the feed zone, they passed Willy. When they saw Willy, our soigneurs pointed at his front car tire, motioning that there might be a problem. Willy, a nervous guy to begin with, got all panicky and drove straight to a garage to find out what the problem was. Willy told the mechanic to check everything: tires, oil, water, coolant, whatever. The guy told him nothing was wrong. So Willy took off, headed back on the course and started waving again. Then our soigneurs saw Willy again, while going from the feed zone to the finish hotel. Again they motioned to his front wheel. Willy started freaking, trying to yell at them through the car window and waving his hands all over the place to find out what was wrong. Finally, the soigneurs broke down and started laughing. They were messing with Willy because they know his nervous nature, and sure enough, he got hooked. At breakfast, all Willy could talk about was what bastards those soigneurs are. He still doesn't forgive them.

In yesterday's race, two riders switched to special bikes made for climbing. Virenque switched to a bike with smaller wheels and so did Olano. Olano's bike with the smaller wheels weighs seven kilograms. The reason for switching? I'm not sure. Lance says it's to save weight and it makes the bike stiffer. Maybe there are some other technical reasons. If Jonathan were here, he would probably have some data showing the torque versus power versus speed, all in a colored graph. He loves numbers.

a hefty counterattack, surprising the others. More than 25km remained, but Dierckxsens didn't hesitate in his move, knowing that the final 18km was a fast downhill into the streets of St. Etienne.

"My solo break in the national championship was similar," the shaven-headed Dierckxsens later said. "For a long time I was only 15 or 20 seconds ahead, and then the gap opened."

The Lampre man went so fast on the ultimate descent that he was 1:20 ahead at the kilometer-to-go archway, while the four still chasing slowed before their sprint for second—which went to Konyshev from Vinokourov, Belli and Verbrugghe.

At 34, Dierckxsens is one of the older members of the peloton, but he's in only his fifth season as a professional. So this Tour stage win—added to his Belgian title—should have brought him not only greater recognition, but also the prospect of several more years of high-paying employment...but those hopes came tumbling down a couple of days later. When Dierckxsens reported to the anti-doping control after the stage, and was asked by the UCI medical inspectors whether he had used any products that might show up on his analysis, he told them of a doctor's prescription for a product called Synachtin he had used for treating a knee injury several weeks earlier. The product contained corticoids, the artificial form of cortisone, that was now being tested for. Dierckxsens urine test was negative, but because he "admitted" using a product that has a potential doping use, he was considered "positive" and was sent home by his Lampre team.

In the Belgian champion's case, he may have won the stage, but lost most of its prestige.

STAGE 12

St. Galmier–St. Flour • July 16

In control

EVERY DAY AT THE TOUR DE FRANCE, AS A STAGE GETS UNDERWAY, one of the organizers comes on Radio Tour to announce the number and length of the stage, the number of starters, and any other pertinent information. There were two extra items, somewhat connected, read out by race director-general Jean-Marie Leblanc, as 158 riders rolled out of St. Galmier for this semi-mountain stage to St. Flour. The first: "There is one non-starter, No. 152, Christophe Bassons of La Française des Jeux." The other: "Between 7 and 8:20 this morning, 40 riders from eight teams were given blood tests, including the U.S. Postal team, and no rider was declared 'inapt.'"

Place your order

You can bet the riders will be trying for a win today. After yesterday, they realized that the peloton is willing to let a group go away and stay away for the win. This provides lots of incentive for opportunists. And it makes it a real pain in the ass for us, because every director has told his riders, "Now we can win a stage; make sure you make the break."

The real incentive to make the break is the prize waiting for the winner. Earlier in the Tour, a horse was awarded, and today the grand prize is a cow. Think about it: You could feed your whole town. Actually eating your cow would be risky, though, after what happened in Belgium with the dioxins and the whole mad-cow disease from England. Here's the Belgian story, in short: Some guy put contaminated oil into feed for animals. As a result, all meat from Belgium—including chicken—and eggs, butter and milk, and pretty much everything else except beer, contained cancer-causing dioxins. True to Belgium, they tried to cover the whole thing up. So I would pass on the cow.

We started the day with a small detour on our way to breakfast. The first stop for five of us was with the UCI vampires. How they pick which riders to test and which get to let sleep is beyond me. I can assure you that Lance was one of the five tested.

Yesterday's, today's and tomorrow's stages all enter an area called the Massif Central. These stages are extremely tough because all you do is go up or down all day long. The courses are full of 5- or 6-kilometer climbs, most not categorized, from start to finish. There is never a place to relax, rest and get your legs back.

Well, today was exactly one of those days. The stage started off with a 16km climb. The riders went ballistic! Guys who can't climb were attacking like climbers, and the guys who *could* climb just

attacked harder. The entire way up the climb there were always groups of four or five attacking in front of us. Sometimes groups of 20 would go up the road. We would set tempo to try and control or slow things down, and they would still attack. It was a nightmare. Our morning meeting's decision was to let any break go up the road—but we didn't expect 50 guys to try and get away! Finally, after a lot of chasing and tempo riding, a group of 10 or 12 got away. Even after they had seven minutes, guys would still attack from our group. They were all out to destroy us.

We had Christian, Pascal and George do most of the tempo work today. I blew my engine taking care of the first two big climbs. It took me a while to recover after that. Peter is nursing a sore knee, so we are trying to keep him fresh. At the finish, the first group arrived something like 12 minutes ahead of us. But we were able to lose 19 minutes today and still keep the jersey. The closest rider on G.C. was Heulot (La Française des Jeux). An ONCE rider won, which I think is good. Now that they have a stage win, maybe they will help us control things in the race. We both have the same objectives.

I'll tell you this, fetching water bottles is no fun. It always seems that when the pack is racing is when everyone runs dry. When I go back to the car, Johan will hand up enough bottles to give each guy one. I stuff them wherever I can—the pockets, in the collar and up the back of the jersey. I can't put them in the front of the jersey, because then the bottles hang and you can't pedal. The worse is when the car hands you up a bunch of water: You bust your butt going to the front, and then the guys ask if you have Revenge. Then, if you bring just Revenge, someone will want only water, because he already has the energy drink on his bike. It's like they think it's a ride-up menu: Just place your order.

Bassons, 25, is the former Festina team rider who made a reputation as Mr. Clean, an athlete who was recognized for not taking performance-enhancing drugs. His stand had been praised by the public, but he stepped into troubled waters with some ambiguous statements he made on doping in a Tour diary he penned for the French national newspaper, *Aujourd'hui*. Race leader Armstrong had been drawn into the debate, and the resultant pressure on Bassons had apparently caused him to quit the race. In his column, Bassons had questioned whether anyone could win a stage of the Tour without artificial help, intimating that Armstrong was not a clean rider. It was ironical that the morning Bassons left the race, Armstrong was among the riders who passed the UCI test—his second hematocrit check of the Tour—while all six of the urine tests the Texan had undergone also proved negative.

In addressing the rumors, Armstrong said, "We have nothing to hide. If anything, we shouldn't be talking of all the planning we did for this Tour. We should be hiding that, because if people copy our system, then we wouldn't have an advantage. For instance, did anyone else ride the stage to St. Flour?"

Indeed, during their reconnaissance trip to the Alps in May, Armstrong, Hamilton and Livingston extended it to include the St. Galmier-St. Flour stage through the hills of the Massif Central. By riding the whole 220.5km, the Postal men knew every climb and descent on a stage that was potentially dangerous for a team defending the yellow jersey.

In theory, if a dangerous rider got in a break on one of the first two climbs between kilometers 20 and 50, the defending team would likely have a long, difficult chase that could leave it open to a timely counterattack. That's why the Postal riders went to the front on the first slopes of the first climb: the 16km, Cat. 2 Croix de l'Homme Mort, out of Montbrison. Even so, they still had to deal with a non-stop barrage of attacks, which saw Armstrong himself infiltrate one 10-man move. One of the attacks involved Polti's Gotti and Kelme's Contreras, another Lotto's Van de Wouwer, while Mercatone Uno's Garzelli and Kelme's Castelblanco featured in yet another.

In the end, the Postal riders *did* contain the most dangerous attacks on the two climbs...before allowing two (less dangerous) groups to ride clear on the flat roads leading to the day's third climb. The best-placed rider of the 12 who went up the road was Bastille Day hero Heulot—who began the stage in 21st place, 20 minutes behind Armstrong. With 79km covered, the 12 joined forces with two riders—Italian veterans Lelli of Cofidis and Alberto Elli of Telekom—who had already been out front for more than an hour-and-a-half.

With the 14-man break established, the Postal riders dropped into their now familiar paceline, pulling the pack over hill and dale at a tempo fast enough to discourage any more attacks, while keeping the gap to less than 12 minutes going into the final hour.

The American team's seeming stranglehold on the race was too much for Giro winner Gotti, who perhaps realized that he was not going to get anything positive out of this Tour and quit in the feed zone. As for the men fighting out the stage win, eight moved clear when a gap developed on a fast, twisting section of road about 30km from the finish. From these eight, on the day's final Cat. 4 climb, Basque rider David Etxebarria of ONCE broke clear, and was eventually chased by Elli, Simon and De Wolf—who could never get closer than 26 seconds on the long, rapid descent toward St. Flour.

Etxebarria, 25, a former winner of the Tour de l'Avenir, looked as though he was finally going to get the reward for his many years of service for Laurent Jalabert at ONCE—if he didn't falter on the 2km-long climb up to the finish, located in the old part of St. Flour, atop a 300-foot-high basalt outcrop. The young Spaniard raced up the smooth 5-percent hill expecting to get caught any second; but even though French champion Simon impressively left Elli and De Wolf, he could make no impression on Etxebarria.

Heulot rolled home in ninth place, 1:34 down, and his 11-minute gain lifted him into sixth place overall, one place and 53 seconds ahead of fellow Frenchman Virenque.

But the big winner, again, was Armstrong. As if to emphasize the Postal team's control, Hamilton set a fierce pace up most of the climb into St. Flour, with the rider in the yellow jersey then easily going with the last-minute accelerations of Zülle and Zabel—whose 15th-place points were enough for him to overtake O'Grady for the green jersey.

STAGE 13

St. Flour–Albi • July 17

The longest day

IT'S A GREAT DAY FOR A PICNIC AT THE TOUR DE FRANCE. Work's over for the week, the weather is perfect (low humidity, temperatures in the 90s), and the Tour is traversing one of the most scenic regions of the country. Why not drive up the stunning Lot Gorge to Entraygues on this exhilarating Saturday morning, find a cool spot under the shady oak trees on the Cat. 2 Côte de la Moissetie, and set up the picnic table by mid-morning? The schedule printed in the local paper says the race is due on the climb at 1:42 p.m.

The last time the Tour came this way was in 1983, when Dutchman Henk Lubberding led a breakaway group up the Montsalvy hill, the other side of the valley from here, and he went on to win the stage in Aurillac. That stage started in Albi, where this year's stage 13 will finish. There was also an Albi-Aurillac stage in 1968, when the Italian they called Mad Heart, Franco Bitossi, was first up Montsalvy and in Aurillac. Then there was 1959, when the Tour was contested by national teams, and the Spanish climber Federico Bahamontes led a crucial breakaway up Montsalvy, and the French national team's Henry Anglade took the stage. That was a great Tour, won by Bahamontes.

This Moissetie climb is not as tough as Montsalvy—which is about 600 feet higher and a bit steeper. But the road up the Moissetie is just as narrow; it's 6km long and almost 6

Hot-foot hell

I woke up sleepy, sore, tired…. This was *not* the way to start off the morning. Then, I looked at today's profile and my morning only got worse. Today we are dealing with four Cat. 4s, two Cat. 3s, and one Cat. 2. The profile looks like the jagged edge of a saw. We are already figuring out how many days are left in this race. We figure you can't count the last day, you don't count the time trial, you don't count the rest day, and you can write off the stage to Bordeaux (it's dead flat). That only leaves a handful of days left…granted, a few of those days will contain a lot of suffering.

I don't know if the story of the day should be about how hot it was or about how hard the start was—again! The riders knew a break would stay away today, but their problem was how to get in the break. At kilometer zero, the attacks started. What pissed me off is that Colombo (Cantina Tollo) made the first attack. It wasn't even an attack: He jumped ahead of the group and looked back to make sure some other riders were reacting, and then he pulled off. He just wanted to get the shit started. Well, he did a good job. The start of the course was over some one-kilometer rollers, and following all the attacks, it practically killed me. I did not have good legs at the start, and after following a couple of attacks I found myself in the middle of the pack, hanging on. Luckily, our dead boy from yesterday, Kevin, had great legs and he took control of the pack on the small climbs.

Finally, a group of 15 went up the road and we hit the front to try and control things right away. It worked: The break built up a lead of two minutes quickly, and that sort of calmed things in the pack. Once the pack realized we didn't care if this group went up the road, we could lose 35 minutes, Polti decided to chase. I'm not sure why, but I think Virenque was worried about his climber's jersey; the second-place guy was in the break. Then Polti stopped after maybe 5 kilometers, and Festina started. I think they didn't have a guy in the break, so they wanted to bring it back. But they blew up big time almost immediately.

That finally left the job to us, a 240km paceline between four of us. It was George, Pascal, Christian

SALVATORE COMMESSO

and me riding tempo all day long. George figured that if we each took one-kilometer pulls, we would each have to pull only 60 times. By kilometer 180, the break was around 19 minutes and Kelme got nervous and started chasing. Lanfranchi (Mapei) was moving close to taking over Escartin's spot on G.C. This was perfect for us: no more working and finally a chance to sit on. Kelme rode the whole rest of the way in. The break ended 22 minutes up on the peloton. Commesso (Saeco), the Italian champion, won the race in front of another Italian, Serpellini (Lampre).

The distance was a factor today, but the heat is what played havoc on everybody. It was 40 degrees C (over 100 degrees F), and in spots, the temperature on the road was 48 degrees. It was so hot that the road was melting wherever it was exposed to the sun. We were riding through tar most of the last part of the day. At the finish I had tar and gravel all over the edges of my tires. No wonder I felt like I was sticking to the road. With the extreme heat, I also get hot foot and some saddle sores. When it's very hot, my feet swell in the cycling shoes, causing them to hurt. It mostly happens on the bottom of the big toe; it feels like you're pressing on lots of pins and needles. I feel like a cat with my chamois problems. You know how a cat pushes and presses on a pillow for about five minutes before it lies down—that's how I am with my saddle. It takes a while to get comfortable, but once I'm locked in, I'm ready to go.

We have just gotten through two critical days in the Tour. Team-wise, it was very important for us not to make mistakes and end up wasting a lot of energy during the race. The team is feeling better, and we can now see a speck of light at the end of the tunnel…. On the negative side, we did lose Peter Meinert today. He has had a bad knee for four days and has been suffering big time trying to stay in the race, hoping it would get better. Nothing usually gets better during the Tour. Today, he stopped; his knee is visibly swollen and he will be going home tomorrow. He may not be here for the last week, but he did a lot for us in the first week….

We received the Tour mail today and, as expected, Lance got a lot. Pascal received a bunch of letters; George got a few; and even Christian got more than one letter. I received one letter—don't laugh; it's better than none at all. My super fan letter turned out to be extra special: It was from my wife. But if you rule out family as qualification for "getting letters," I would be back down to zero. In my book, though, family letters are the best letters.

percent; and the tar will probably be melting when the race comes through in the hottest part of the day. They say it'll be about 36 degrees in the shade (that's almost 97 degrees Fahrenheit).

In the old days, stages like this one used to have a bigger impact on the race, because the strongest guys almost always tried to get away on one of these semi-mountain days—especially when it was hot, like today. But from the radio, we hear that a similar break as happened yesterday at St. Flour has already developed. They say that 16 riders were already clear when they got to Chaudes-Aigues, after about 20km. Then, on that big climb out of the Truyère valley, the Russian Konyshev was dropped, leaving 15 in front; on that same hill, the Postal's Danish team man Peter Meinert-Nielsen was dropped, suffering from a swollen knee, and had to abandon the Tour. None of the leaders is dangerous to the race leaders, the best in the break being the young Italian on the Mapei team, Paolo Lanfranchi, who's about 35 minutes behind on overall time.

Anyway, with a big group away like that, there'll be two chances to see some racing; and the peloton will probably be riding pretty slowly here. It'll be easy to pick out that American who's in the yellow jersey...and everyone will want to see Virenque. It's good that he's in the race; and even better that he's wearing the polka-dot jersey. Probably good for him that he's not involved with that Festina outfit...they say he joined an Italian team this year.

It shouldn't be long before they arrive. Maybe they'll need some water, it's so hot now. They even watered the roads just now, where the tar is melting.

There seem to be a lot of Italians in this front group.... And what was the time gap that loudspeaker van said just now? Eleven minutes? *Mon dieu*, here they come already!

There's supposed to be a couple of French guys in this break. Yes, there's Lebreton, in that red-and-yellow BigMat jersey; he's the one who was caught after that long break with Jacky Durand on the stage before the time trial. Maybe he'll have better luck today. And there's Mengin—he's a teammate of that rider who doesn't like doping. Bassons. Pity he had to drop out of the race; he comes from around these parts.

It looks like four Italians are at the front. Yes, one is the Mapei guy, Lanfanchi...another, in that pink-and-blue jersey, is Piccoli. He's the rider who had the polka-dot jersey before Virenque. And, there's Piccoli's Lampre teammate Marco Serpellini. And just behind them, the one wearing the Italian champion's jersey.

What's his name? Oh yeah, Commesso. He looks too young to be in the Tour…and a bit too fat. Still, he looks pretty good on the bike.

This break sure is moving fast…they're already faster than the 41-kph schedule. That's some speed for such a hilly opening…and there's a lot more hills ahead. They still have to climb across the ridges between the Aveyron, Viaur and Tarn valleys. In fact, this is the Tour's longest stage. Not quite as long as some they used to ride in the old days, but 236 kilometers is far enough on a hot day like this…. From here, they have another 140km…about three-and-a-half hours. That gives us time to get back home to see the finish on TV….

What TV eventually shows us is an attack from the lead group by Banesto's Vicente Garcia Acosta, on the hill climbing away from the Viaur, 40km from the end. On the ensuing downhill, he is joined at first by Commesso and then by Serpellini. Racing hard up the next hill, the two Italians drop Garcia Acosta, and the pair is soon racing down into Albi—where its ancient brick, fortress-like cathedral stands proudly above the city's clay-tiled roofs and nearby fields.

On the run-in to town, Serpellini twice tries to jump away from the baby-faced Commesso, but each time the Italian champion matches his jump—and then easily wins the final sprint. With Commesso's happy face still filling the screen, there's time to make some tea before the peloton arrives in 22 minutes. It's been a long, hot day….

STAGE 14
Castres–St. Gaudens • July 18

Another stage, another chance

WHEN, WITH A WEARY SMILE, THE NOW VETERAN RUSSIAN DMITRI KONYSHEV was expressing his joy at winning in St. Gaudens—a fourth consecutive looka-like stage—another veteran racer, in the background, was expressing his frustration by thumping his handlebars. This was Massimiliano Lelli, the Cofidis team rider who had worked hard in the opening week for his team's star Julich; and since leaving the Alps had featured in countless attacks, most notably when he started the marathon stage 12 break with fellow Italian Alberto Elli. Lelli came in sixth that day.

On this 14th stage—which began in heat-wave conditions and ended in thunder showers—it was Konyshev who made the early attack, with another break-away specialist, Jacky Durand. These two moved to a 1:50 lead in the rolling, opening kilometers; but when the gap suddenly fell to 20 seconds on the sun-baked climb at Fendeille, 55km into the stage, it looked like their efforts had been in vain.

Then, just after the summit, racing on a narrow back road between two long lines of fans, four men took up the chase: Lelli, Belli, Mapei's Gianni Faresin and Telekom's Steffen Wesemann. They linked up with Durand and Konyshev at kilometer 60...and the Postal riders immediately fell into their familiar pace-setting mode, seeing that the closest man on G.C. was Belli, 26 minutes behind Armstrong.

The six raced together into the foothills of the Pyrénées; they swept through the phenomenal Mas d'Azil cave—a 1377-foot long, 164-foot wide natural tunnel beneath a limestone ridge—with a 12-minute lead; and they raced through a sharp rainstorm before the finish in St. Gaudens.

They were still together as they reached the outskirts of town, where, with 6km to go, former Italian Tour of Lombardy winner Faresin broke the deadlock with a sharp acceleration—immediately matched by Konyshev.

FRANKIE'S DIARY © July 18 © St. Gaudens

Another tempo day

Early this morning, I woke up sweating and knew we would have another hot day like yesterday. I wasn't even out of my hotel room and I think I had already lost a liter of water. At the start, the temperature was already 35 degrees C (95 F), and the road temp was 45 C. It was hot!

As for the race, it was the same ol' stuff. It must be God-awful boring to watch on the television. Guys attack at the start; we chase them down; more guys attack; and finally, a break goes away. We rode tempo all day between Christian, George and I. I gave Pascal the day off; he was completely wasted. He has not had a day off since day one. Today, on the first climbs, he was going backward, and then he got ridden off of some wheels from guys in the break. It was bad. I had to tell him three times to stay off the front and sit in. Kelme and Banesto took over the chase with 30km to go. They have to protect their second, third and fourth positions. The lead rider in the break was Belli at 26 minutes. I think Konyshev (Mercatone Uno) won, and we came in 15 minutes down.

The coolest thing about today's stage was that we rode through this tunnel-like cave [called Mas d'Azil]. It was like riding the "It's a Small World" ride at Disneyland. It was the lights and all the open space that made it seem like the amusement ride. Near the end of the race, a 10-minute torrential downpour interrupted the hot weather. I got my Carnacs clean without even having to wash them after the race.

There is one other thing that is pretty incredible to watch: the camera guys on the motorbikes trying to turn around and film while riding the bike backward. The most incredible team is ESPN. Their camera guy literally stands up with one foot on the pegs and the other on the back of the bike, while

LUDO DIERCKXSENS AND DMITRI KONYSHEV

looking through a camera lens. It looks like he is going to fall off at any moment. I think they have signals to let each other know what is happening. If the camera guy pulls on the driver's shoulder, that means for him to slow down. If he pulls right or left, then that is for the driver to move right or left. If there is a corner coming up—remember, we are going usually 50 kph—the driver taps the camera guy's leg to signal him he has to stop filming and turn around and sit down. They probably have a bunch more signals.. I should ask them the next time I see them.

Today, the team received lots of gifts. I don't know why today, but we sure will use everything we got. We now have Peets coffee for tomorrow's breakfast; Mary dropped off some of her famous chocolate turtles; the soigneurs got us peanut butter; and I even got a new outfit for my baby boy. All in all, it was a great day. At the finish, a fan gave George a Postal jersey and a mountains jersey to sign. We passed them around and Christian was like, "Heck I need a jersey,

I'm just gonna put this in my bag." It was funny…maybe you had to be there.

Tomorrow is our rest day, yeah! We will probably ride two to three hours on some climbs. Tomorrow is also a memorial remembering Fabio Casartelli on the climb where he passed away. Lance will be going by helicopter with Jean-Marie Leblanc. Today is the date that Fabio died. After Lance goes to the memorial, we will go training. Then, in the afternoon, Lance has another press conference. I guess he is kind of busy on his rest day.

Also today, Peter went home. He flew out of Toulouse and then back to Denmark. I believe he will return for the last day in Paris. After all, he did most of the work in the first weeks, when Lance opened up a big enough gap to hold on to the yellow rather comfortably. Plans are already being made for Paris. We all feel the same way, though: It's too early and still long enough away that making plans might be jumping the gun. It's like being in a bike race and saying how you never puncture in races, then bam, you puncture.

With the gap at 11 seconds, Lelli went after them, and slowly began reeling them in. But he started his pursuit too late, and he could only sit and watch as the final sprint played out in front of him.

Konyshev was a fine sprinter early in his career: He beat Sean Kelly to the silver medal in the 1989 world's behind Greg LeMond; then, in the following two years, he won three stages of the Tour—including the sprint on the Champs-Elysées made famous by Djamolidin Abdujaparov's spectacular crash into the barriers. Konyshev hadn't won much since then, but he clearly had too much speed for Faresin; while Lelli, despite being on great form, would have to try another day.

STAGE 9

Le Grand Bornand—Sestriere.

July 13.

1. Armstrong, 213.5km in 5:57:11 (35.863 kph); 2. Zülle, at 0:31; 3. Escartin, at 1:26; 4. Gotti, s.t.; 5. Manuel Beltran (Sp), Banesto, at 2:27; 6. Virenque, s.t.; 7. Carlos Contreras (Col), Kelme-Costa Blanca, at 2:29; 8. Kurt Van de Wouwer (B), Lotto-Mobistar, at 3:10; 9. Olano, s.t.; 10. Dufaux, at 3:30; 11. Nardello, at 3:33; 12. Guerini; 13. Casero, both s.t.; 14. Benoît Salmon (F), Casino, at 3:43; 15. Bo Hamburger (Dk), Cantina Tollo-Alexia, at 3:46; 16. Mario Aerts (B), Lotto-Mobistar, at 4:24; 17. José Castelblanco (Col), Kelme-Costa Blanca, at 4:34; 18. Garzelli, at 4:51; 19. Roland Meier (Swi), Cofidis, s.t.; 20. Moreau, at 5:04.

Others: 23. Tonkov, at 5:04; **25. Hamilton, at 6:31; 26. Livingston, at 9:15**; 54. Merckx, at 18:02; 60. Boogerd, s.t.; 68. Savoldelli, at 21:12; **87. Hincapie, at 34:36**; 90. Vinokourov; **107. Andreu, both s.t.; 146. Vande Velde, at 40:29**.

DNS: Minali; Casper.

DNF: Kirsipuu; Cipollini; Fagnini; Roberto Conti (I), Mercatone Uno-Bianchi; Michele Coppolillo (I), Mercatone Uno-Bianchi; Gines Salmeron (Sp), Vitalicio Seguros.

Overall: 1. Armstrong, 1681.8km in 39:31:07; 2. Olano, at 6:03; 3. Moreau, at 7:44; 4. Zülle, at 7:47; 5. Dufaux, at 8:07; 6. Nardello, at 8:39; 7. Casero, at 8:54; 8. Escartin, at 9:01; 9. Virenque, at 10:02; 10. Tonkov, at 10:34.

STAGE 10

Sestriere—L'Alpe d'Huez. July 14.

1. Guerini, 220.5km in 6:42:31 (32.868 kph); 2. Tonkov, at 0:21; 3. Escartin, at 0:25; 4. Zülle; **5. Armstrong;** 6. Virenque; 7. Dufaux,; 8. Van de Wouwer, all s.t.; 9. Beltran, at 0:32; 10. Contreras, at 0:49; 11. Heulot, at 1:43; 12. Olano, at 2:04; 13. Vinokourov, at 2:13 14. Salmon, s.t.; 15. Andrea Peron (I), ONCE-Deutsche Bank, at 2:42; 16. Casero; 17. Nardello, both s.t.; **18. Hamilton, at 2:45;** 19. Georg Totschnig (A), Telekom, at 3:47; 20. Steve De Wolf (B), Cofidis, at 4:00.

Others: 26. Moreau, at 5:32; 27. Gotti, s.t.; 31. Hamburger, at 6:18; 33. Garzelli, at 7:22; 45. Boogerd, at 12:27; **57. Livingston, at 22:18; 63. Hincapie, at 24:51; 71. Andreu, at 27:48; 155. Vande Velde, at 34:20**.

DNS: Spruch

DNF: Merckx; Svorada; Savoldelli; Padrnos; Van Bon; Raivis Belohvosciks (Lit), Lampre-Daikin.

Overall: 1. Armstrong, 1902.3km in 46:14:03; 2. Olano, at 7:42; 3. Zülle, at 7:47; 4. Dufaux, at 8:07; 5. Escartin, at 8:53; 6. Virenque, at 10:02; 7. Tonkov, at 10:18; 8 Nardello, at 10:58; 9. Guerini, at 10:57; 10. Casero, at 11:11.

STAGE 11

Le Bourg d'Oisans—St. Etienne. July 15.

1. Ludo Dierckxsens (B), Lampre-Daikin, 198.5km in 4:34:03 (43.459 kph); 2. Dmitri Konyshev (Rus), Mercatone Uno-Bianchi, at 1:26; 3. Vinokourov, s.t.; 4. Belli, at 1:28; 5. Verbrugghe, at 1:33; 6. Laurent Lefèvre (F), Festina, at 3:53; 7. Riccardo Forconi (I), Mercatone Uno-Bianchi, at 5:07; 8. Zabel, at 22:18.; 9. McEwen; 10. Gianpaolo Mondini (I), Cantina Tollo-Alexia, both s.t.

Others: 20. Virenque, at 22:21; 21. Olano, at 22:22; 23. Moreau; **25. Hincapie;** 26. Dufaux; **31. Armstrong;** 36. Escartin; 37. Casero; **40 Hamilton;** 46. Tonkov; 53. Zülle; 61. Guerini;. **71. Livingston, all s.t.; 103. Vande Velde, at 22:47; 125. Andreu, at 23:12**.

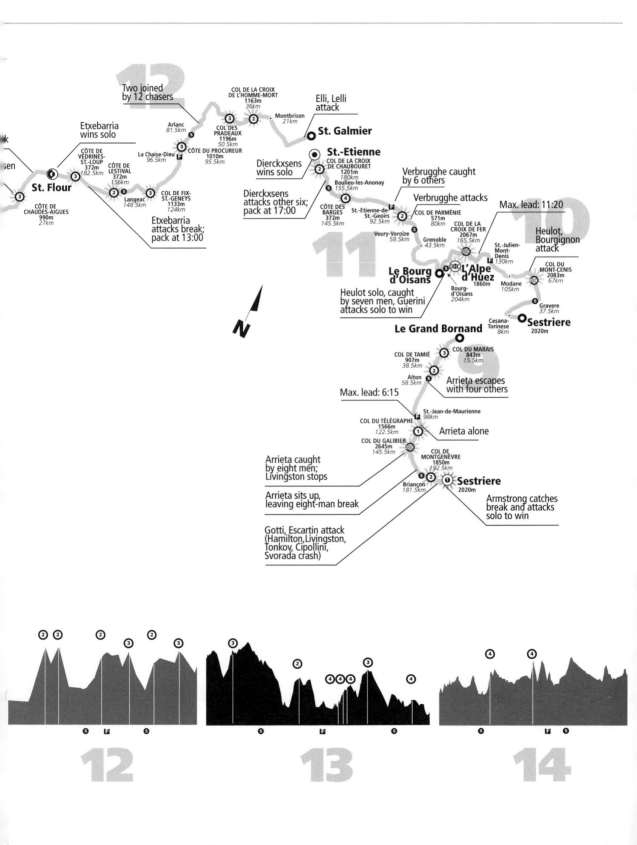

12

Two joined by 12 chasers

COL DE LA CROIX DE L'HOMME-MORT
1163m
36km

Montbrison
21km

Elli, Lelli attack

Arlanc
81.5km

COL DES PRADEAUX
1196m
50.5km

COL DU PROCUREUR
1010m
95.5km

St. Galmier

Etxebarria wins solo

CÔTE DE VÉDRINES-ST.-LOUP
372m
182.5km

CÔTE DE LESTIVAL
372m
156km

La Chaise-Dieu
96.5km

St.-Etienne

COL DE LA CROIX DE CHAUBOURET
1201m
180km
Boulieu-les-Anonay
155.5km

Dierckxsens wins solo

Verbrugghe caught by 6 others

St. Flour

Langeac
148.5km

COL DE FIX-ST-GENEYS
1133m
124km

Dierckxsens attacks other six; pack at 17:00

CÔTE DES BARGES
372m
145.5km

St.-Etienne-de-St.-Geoirs
92.5km

COL DE PARMÉNIE
571m
80km

Verbrugghe attacks

Max. lead: 11:20

10

CÔTE DE CHAUDES-AIGUES
990m
27km

Etxebarria attacks break; pack at 13:00

Veury-Voroize
58.5km

Grenoble
43.5km

COL DE LA CROIX DE FER
2067m
165.5km

St.-Julien-Mont-Denis
130km

Heulot, Bourgignon attack

COL DU MONT-CENIS
2083m
67km

11

Le Bourg d'Oisans

L'Alpe d'Huez
1860m

Modane
105km

Gravere
37.5km

Heulot solo, caught by seven men, Guerini attacks solo to win

Bourg-d'Oisans
204km

Cesana-Torinese
8km

Sestriere
2020m

Le Grand Bornand

COL DE TAMIÉ
907m
38.5km

COL DU MARAIS
843m
15.5km

Aiton
58.5km

Arrieta escapes with four others

Max. lead: 6:15

St.-Jean-de-Maurienne
98km

COL DU TÉLÉGRAPHE
1566m
122.5km

Arrieta alone

COL DU GALIBIER
2645m
145.5km

COL DE MONTGENÈVRE
1850m
192.5km

Arrieta caught by eight men; Livingston stops

Arrieta sits up, leaving eight-man break

Briançon
181.5km

Sestriere
2020m

Armstrong catches break and attacks solo to win

Gotti, Escartin attack (Hamilton, Livingston, Tonkov, Cipollini, Svorada crash)

N

12

13

14

WEEK 2

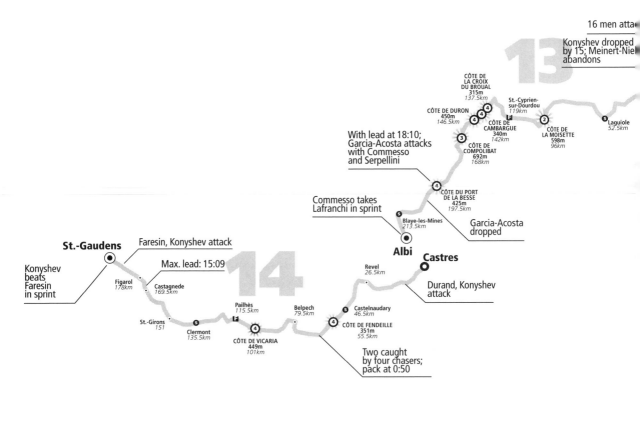

13

16 men atta●

Konyshev dropped
by 15; Meinert-Nie●
abandons

CÔTE DE
LA CROIX
DU BROUAL
315m
137.5km

CÔTE DE DURON
450m
146.5km

CÔTE DE
CAMBARGUE
340m
142km

St.-Cyprien-
sur-Dourdou
119km

CÔTE DE
LA MOISETTE
598m
96km

Laguiole
52.5km

With lead at 18:10;
Garcia-Acosta attacks
with Commesso
and Serpellini

CÔTE DE
COMPOLIBAT
692m
168km

Commesso takes
Lafranchi in sprint

CÔTE DU PORT
DE LA BESSE
425m
197.5km

Garcia-Acosta
dropped

Blaye-les-Mines
213.5km

Albi

Castres

St.-Gaudens

Faresin, Konyshev attack

Max. lead: 15:09

14

Revel
26.5km

Konyshev
beats
Faresin
in sprint

Figarol
178km

Castagnede
169.5km

Durand, Konyshev
attack

Pailhès
115.5km

Belpech
79.5km

Castelnaudary
46.5km

St.-Girons
151

Clermont
135.5km

CÔTE DE FENDEILLE
351m
55.5km

CÔTE DE VICARIA
449m
101km

Two caught
by four chasers;
pack at 0:50

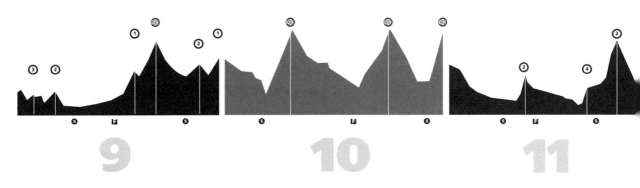

9

10

11

DNF: Moreno Di Biase (I), Cantina Tollo-Alexia.

Overall: 1. Armstrong, 2100.8km in 51:10:28; 2. Olano, at 7:42; 3. Zülle, at 7:47; 4. Dufaux, at 8:07; 5. Escartin, at 8:53.

STAGE 12
St. Galmier—St. Flour. July 16.

1. David Etxebarria (Sp), ONCE-Deutsche Bank, 201.5km in 4:53:50 (41.145 kph); 2. Simon, at 0:25; 3. Alberto Elli (I), Telekom, at 0:33; 4. De Wolf, at 0:40; 5. José Castelblanco (Col), Kelme-Costa Blanca, at 1:11; 6. Massimiliano Lelli (I), Saeco-Cannondale, at 1:18; 7. Frédéric Bessy (F), Casino, at 1:24; 8. Marc Lotz (Nl), Rabobank, at 1:32.; 9. Heulot, at 1:34; 10. Didier Rous (F), Festina, at 1:50.

Others: 15. Zabel, at 12:35; 16. Zülle; **19. Armstrong**; 20. Dufaux; 21. Escartin; 22. Tonkov, all s.t.; 25. Virenque, at 12:37; 27. Olano; 30. Moreau; 36. Casero; 42. Guerini; **55. Hamilton, all s.t.; 101. Andreu, at 14:54; 102. Livingston; 103. Hincapie, both s.t.; 106. Vande Velde, at 19:45**.

DNS: Christophe Bassons (F), La Française des Jeux.

DNF: Gotti; Johan Verstrepen (B), Lampre-Daikin; Magnus Bäckstedt (S), Crédit Agricole.

Overall: 1. Armstrong, 2302.3km in 56:16:53; 2. Olano, at 7:44; 3. Zülle, at 7:47; 4. Dufaux, at 8:07; 5. Escartin, at 8:53.

STAGE 13
St. Flour—Albi. July 17.

1. Salvatore Commesso (I), Saeco-Cannondale, 236.5km in 5:52:45 (40.226 kph); 2. Marco Serpellini (I), Lampre-Daikin, at 0:02; 3. Mariano Piccoli (I), Lampre-Daikin, at 2:07; 4. Paolo Lanfranchi (I), Mapei-Quick Step; 5. Roland Meier (Swi), Cofidis; 6. Christophe Mengin (F), La Française des Jeux; 7. Miguel Peña (Sp), Banesto; 8. Javier Pas-

cual Rodriguez (Sp), Kelme-Costa Blanca, all s.t.; 9. Lylian Lebreton (F), BigMat-Auber 93, at 2:12; 10. Francisco Cerezo (Sp), Vitalicio Seguros, s.t..

Others: 16. Zabel, at 22:24; 23. Olano; 28. Tonkov; 31. Moreau; **36. Armstrong**; 37. Casero; 39. Zülle; 48. Dufaux; **46. Hamilton**; 49. Escartin; 50. Virenque; 60. Guerini, all s.t.; **68. Andreu, at 22:32; 75. Livingston; 129. Vande Velde, at 22:55; 135. Hincapie, at 23:01**.

DNF: Peter Meinert-Nielsen (Dk), U.S. Postal Service.

Overall: 1. Armstrong, 2538.8km in 62:32:02; 2. Olano, at 7:44; 3. Zülle, at 7:47; 4. Dufaux, at 8:07; 5. Escartin, at 8:53.

STAGE 14
Castres—St. Gaudens. July 18.

1. Konyshev, 199km in 4:37:59 (43.952 kph); 2. Gianni Faresin (I), Mapei-Quick Step, s.t.; 3. Lelli, at 0:04; 4. Steffen Wesemann (G), Telekom, at 0:51; 5. Jacky Durand (F), Lotto-Mobistar; 6. Belli, both s.t.; 7. Zabel, at 13:27; 8. O'Grady; 9. Christophe Capelle (F), BigMat-Auber 93, at 2:12; 10. Mondini, all s.t..

Others: 16. Moreau; 27. Olano; 30. Casero; 35. Guerini; 42. Escartin; 49. Tonkov; 50. Zülle; 51. Virenque; 55. Dufaux; **60. Armstrong; 61. Hamilton; 78. Andreu; 91. Hincapie; 92. Livingston, all s.t.; 150. Vande Velde, at 15:17**.

DNF: Oscar Pellicioli (I), Polti; Marco Artunghi (I), .Mercatone Uno-Bianchi.

Overall: 1. Armstrong, 2737.8km in 67:23:28; 2. Olano, at 7:44; 3. Zülle, at 7:47; 4. Dufaux, at 8:07; 5. Escartin, at 8:53.

THE TOUR
THROUGH THE LENS
OF GRAHAM WATSON

In week one, Lance Armstrong (far right) powered toward the podium by taking the prologue time trial; Jaan Kirsipuu (right) reflected upon six days in yellow; and Bobby Julich (above) made a dramatic exit at Metz.

PRECEDING PAGE Battered by a wind from the right, broken by a pileup a kilometer before, the rear part of the field negotiates the 14-foot-wide Passage du Gois causeway on stage 2 of the Tour de France. Alex Zülle was in one of these groups, on his way to losing six minutes and any hope of overall victory.

Into the Alps, Mario Cipollini (far left) could look back at four consecutive sprint stage wins; Armstrong (above) confirmed his leadership at Sestriere; and Tyler Hamilton (left) pulled the yellow jersey and rivals up L'Alpe d'Huez.

Climbing men: Giuseppe Guerini (above) took the glory at the Alpe; David Etxebarria (top) claimed a cow at St. Flour; Fernando Escartin (far right) made Armstrong and Zülle suffer in the Pyrénées; and Richard Virenque homed in on a fifth polka-dot jersey.

Eyes front: Zülle (far right) headed for second at
Futuroscope; Ludo Dierckxsens (right) won at St. Etienne
and then headed home; Laurent Dufaux (above) raced
toward fourth overall; and Livingston (top), followed here
by Wladimir Belli, looked toward a promising future.

PRECEDING PAGE
High above the clouds on the mighty Tourmalet pass,
only the best could follow the hot wheels of Postal's
Kevin Livingston.

Paris lap of honor for (left to right) Postal's Pascal Deramé, Christian Vande Velde, Armstrong (tailed by sponsor Thom Weisel), George Hincapie and Hamilton; Erik Zabel celebrated his fourth consecutive green jersey, first with his son then with the yellow and polka-dot kings; while Armstrong was flanked by Zülle and Escartin on the podium.

NEXT PAGE
Journey's end for Lance
and Kristin Armstrong.

WEEK

3

Paris on the horizon

A S FAR AS THE RACING was concerned, Lance Armstrong came through the Tour's second week in a position of strength. He had confounded the critics by winning solo in Sestriere, where—as he predicted—Alex Zülle emerged as his main rival; and then worked hard with his team to defend the yellow jersey on four difficult days through the Massif Central to the foot of the Pyrénées. In doing so, Armstrong had endeared himself to most of the Tour's other teams by allowing them the chance to shoot for stage wins. But, still, on the second rest day, at St. Gaudens, the naysayers were still trying to belittle Armstrong's accomplishments with their insinuations that no one can win the Tour de France without the aid of performance-enhancing drugs.

So, on his rest day that began with a helicopter ride to pay homage to his late teammate Fabio Casartelli at a mess on the Portet d'Aspet mountain, and continued with a two-hour training ride in a persistent drizzle, Armstrong devoted the afternoon to the media. His main forum was a 5 p.m. press conference at an auditorium in Tarbes—where he appeared a little weary, not answering the questions with his usual completeness. No wonder. Just before the conference, Armstrong had been grilled in a one-on-one interview by *L'Équipe* sportswriter Pierre Ballester, whose full-page story appeared in the next morning's edition....

Most of the 59 questions posed in the interview concerned drugs and associated subjects—including the circumstances of the withdrawal from the Tour of Christophe ("Mr. Clean") Bassons. Armstrong answered most of the time with patience and candor, but clearly became annoyed when Ballester kept pushing the same question or, out of context, suddenly swung the conversation back to doping. In fact, many of Armstrong's answers were either interrupted or ended by the journalist.

Perhaps Armstrong's most effective answer was: "There is nothing against me, except some insinuations. If you discover a bag full of dope in my room, okay, you would have proof. But that's not the case. It never will be. These insinuations are an insult to me, to my family, and to the cancer community. Believe me, my proof is my performance."

To this, Ballester responded: "But in truth no one is going to believe you if you say that doping is not a real, obvious problem...."

Armstrong's response: "Sure there's a problem. But, once more, I can't speak about things I don't know."

Ballester: "Let's speak about facts then. Is...."

Armstrong: "That's not what you have done concerning me."

Ballester: "How's that?"

Armstrong: "Your articles and your accusations have been reprinted around the whole world. Even the local paper in Austin, they've put the things you've written about me on their front page."

And so it went on....

Near the end of the interview, Ballester asked how Armstrong would reply to those who saw him climb the cols toward Sestriere with mouth closed and no sign of fatigue on his face.

Astonished, the American replied, "Who, me?"

"Yes, you," the reporter answered.

"But good god, that was a hell of an effort! I was gasping for air through my nose, my mouth, my ears.... But you can't show that. You know, at moments like that, tactics are everything. If you make a face, your competitor may not see that directly, but his directeur sportif, who has a TV in his car, will soon see that you're suffering. You know when the cameras are focused on you. You have to be aware of that."

By the end of the interview, the reporter and the paper's readers were aware that Lance Armstrong was the real thing. He was a bona-fide leader of the Tour de France—and he intended to confirm that whenever he had the opportunity on the remaining six stages into Paris....

Another rest day

I need to inform everyone of our new sponsor: peanut butter. The same day our soigneurs found some peanut butter in the store, we started getting gifts of peanut butter. The last few visitors who came from the States brought some; and today at our hotel, we received a Fed-Ex package with about six huge cans. We have enough peanut butter for the rest of the Tour—and for the upcoming Vuelta. Everyone says thanks….

Today is our rest day and as usual, it's hectic. We left for our ride around 11 a.m.; it was late on purpose so we could keep the feeling of a race schedule. It's amazing how after riding every day for five and six hours, how fast two hours goes by. It seemed like I was done even before I got started. The ESPN guys started off with us for some filming, but "started" is the key word here. After a half-hour, they went up the road to pull off, so they could film us coming at them. As we passed the van, we noticed they pulled off right into a ditch. Afterward, we asked them how they got out. They said they tried getting the neighbors to help them, but all the neighbors were like antiques: They were too old to walk, much less drive.

Today was the ceremony at the Casartelli memorial. They held a small mass in memory of Fabio. I saw Jim Ochowicz afterward and he said it was nice. He said the memorial actually looks better now that it has aged a bit.

Lance held his press conference today. It was held in an auditorium and there were probably 100 journalists. Ironically, the first two doping questions came from two American journalists. Lance asserted his innocence and told all the journalists that his racing life, personal life, and health were open to questions. Not one of the journalists who had previously bad-mouthed him in the papers asked one question. Lance also talked about how hard it is having the jersey. All the extra obligations with the press, fans, and the Tour have made it more difficult for him to get his rest.

I've talked about our staff before and about how key they are to helping us. The mechanics and soigneurs are in charge of different guys on the team. Julian, the head mechanic, is in charge of Lance's and Kevin's bikes. Juan is in charge of my bike and George's; and Jeff is in charge of Tyler's, Christian's and Pascal's. This way, if there is a problem, we know whom to talk to about changing or fixing something. It used to be that we would tell whichever mechanic we saw, but things would never get done. The same division of the riders is with our soigneurs. Lance and Kevin are with Emma; George and I with Richard; Tyler and Pascal are with Ronnie; and Christian is with Peter. Peter is also an ex-rider from Belgium.

Besides the mechanics and soigneurs, we have many other helpers. We have Jean-Pierre Heynderickx—he used to ride for Collstrop—who drives one of the campers and also helps the mechanics. We have Stephan, Julian's son, whom you might have seen on television, providing the blocking for Lance going to and from the podium. Stephan loves plowing down people…. Of course, we have Mark Gorski and also Dan Osipow, who is in charge of handling all the press requests to get at Lance. We have Margo, who is from the U.S. Postal Service and helps Dan handle all the press stuff and all the invitees we have here. We have Louis, who is in charge of getting credentials for everyone and driving and picking up the invitees. And last but most important, whom I've mentioned before, is our Swiss chef Willy.

STAGE 15

St. Gaudens–Piau-Engaly • July 20

On the mountain

THREE IMAGES EMERGE WHEN THINKING BACK TO THIS FIRST, magnificently aggressive stage in the Pyrénées. The first was the ecstasy of Fernando Escartin as he reached the finish in the grandiose mountainscape of Piau-Engaly, a Tour stage winner for the first time in his long career. The second was the disillusionment of Jay Sweet, the Aussie sprinter who had been flirting with the time limit nearly every day, and finally found himself eliminated. And the third was the surprise of Lance Armstrong, a new yellow jersey on his back, as a French TV crew caught up with him on his way to an awaiting helicopter, to ask him about a new "doping" revelation.

To say that this day was emotional is like saying the Titanic sank. Early in the 173km stage, there were memories of Fabio Casartelli, when the race passed within a few hundred meters of the place where the Italian racer crashed and died descending the Portet d'Aspet mountain pass in 1996. Those thoughts were very fresh for Armstrong, who had attended a memorial service for his former Motorola teammate on the rest day, 24 hours earlier.

As if honoring those memories, the 149-strong peloton did not begin racing until it reached the top of the Cat. 2 Col des Ares, on the other side of the thickly wooded valley from the Portet d'Aspet. Then, with another five climbs ahead, all of them Cat. 1, it became clear that Escartin's Kelme team and Zülle's Banestos were going to do everything they could to challenge Armstrong and his Postals.

Two Banestos were in the very first 15-man attack on the Ares descent; and when another move happened on the first steep slopes of the 11km Col de Menté, among the seven aggressors were two from Kelme (José Gomez and Javier Otxoa) and one from Banesto (Jon Odriozola). Also there were ONCE's Andrea Peron, Vitalicio's Gonzalez Galdeano and the indefatigable Elli. Belgian Kurt Van de Wouwer of Lotto became the seventh member of the break when he replaced a waning Vinokourov over the summit, where the gap was up to one minute.

Sending teammates ahead in early breaks is a favorite tactic of the Spanish teams, and this move was a classic example.

On reaching the foot of the day's third climb, the 8km Portillon, after a tail wind blew them along the valley into Spain, the lead was up to 4:40. That was too much to give the break's highest-placed member, Italian Peron, who started the stage only 13:32 behind Armstrong; and it was clear that the American's teammates would have to increase their tempo.

"You do what you've got to do," Andreu said, in helping halve the gap on the smooth-surfaced Portillon. "I'm only doing a five-kilometer effort, and then I'm gone."

The effectiveness of the Spanish teams' tactics became clearer as the 20-strong chase group reached the 13km Peyresourde. With the gap at 2:50, a sudden acceleration came from Kelme's Contreras. When he was chased down, team leader Escartin counterattacked with teammate Pascual Rodriguez, along with Saeco's Dufaux, ONCE's Garcia and four others.

Further up the grassy mountainside, only Escartin, Dufaux and Garcia were left of the counterattack, while Otxoa briefly helped Escartin's raid as he dropped back from the front. The three men chasing caught the five ahead (after Odriozola had been dropped), to race over the summit 1:50 ahead of Armstrong's group.

The gap was 2:10 after a swooping descent off the Peyresourde, from where the riders could look across a wide valley to the crowds lining the switchbacks of the next climb, the Val Louron-Azet. At an average of 8.4 percent for its 8km, this was the steepest climb of the day. Escartin soon attacked, shaking off the persistent Dufaux and Peron, and crossed the summit 1:10 ahead of them.

Behind, under orders from the race leader, Hamilton and then Livingston made strong pulls, preparing the ground for an attack by Armstrong himself when the gap was almost three minutes. "I couldn't let Escartin get a lot of time," Armstrong later said. "I couldn't let him take four minutes, in case I had a problem later."

Only Zülle could match Armstrong's charge, and they went over the top 2:50 behind Escartin, who would continue his solo effort for the remaining 30km—the first 10km of it dangerously downhill, the last 20 painfully uphill—to the 5900-foot-high ski station of Piau-Engaly.

Six men recaught Armstrong and Zülle by the valley, but after one of them, Elli, had given a long, long pull, and with about 9km still to go, the American repeated his solo acceleration. He bridged to Dufaux 5km from the top, and then settled into a slower rhythm...which enabled Zülle and latecomer Virenque to catch him and Dufaux.

All the riders were struggling on these final kilometers—including Escartin, whose rocking, bow-legged style was becoming wilder as the finish approached. "I was afraid they would catch me in the last two kilometers, that's why I went all out," said the hawk-nosed Spaniard, who was heading for the finest victory of his 10-year pro career, which would also net him second place on G.C.

Escartin did lose a half-minute in the last grueling staircase of switchbacks, mainly due to a burst 2.5km from the end by Virenque that saw Dufaux gone for good, and to which only Armstrong and Zülle could reply.

Even Armstrong faded in the final pitch, to concede nine seconds to Zülle and Virenque; but that was due to a little hunger knock…and the energy he had burned in his two brave accelerations. "I guess I paid for it in the last two kilometers," said Armstrong, who seemed very content with what he had achieved.

The Texan's euphoria was somewhat deflated after the various protocol ceremonies and media interviews, as he headed on foot up the hillside to the helicopter waiting to fly him to his hotel. A pursuing French TV reporter asked Armstrong if he knew anything about the report by French newspaper *Le Monde*, which was saying a trace of corticoids had been found in one of the urine tests Armstrong had early in the Tour. "First I've heard of it," he replied. It wouldn't be the last….

While Armstrong and Escartin were leaving the mountain, as swirling clouds gathered on the granite peaks towering above the finish, a rider with No. 199 on his back was quietly, slowly struggling to the summit. This was Sweet, the Tour neophyte who had been reinstated to the race after finishing outside the time limit

More mountains

Well, it was the same ol' stuff again today. Guys attacked; we rode; they stayed away. You are probably thinking, "But wasn't it a mountain day?" You're right; I'm only kidding. Actually, today saw a shake-up in the overall standings….

Today, we had seven mountains to command and conquer. I'll start by letting you know that while the leaders were in "all wheel drive," Olano and Tonkov were in "park," and Vinokourov was in "reverse." Vinokourov is the one we are the maddest at. He's been attacking every day at every chance he gets, and we would always chase him down thinking he was dangerous. Now I know he was attacking just for something to do, and not for the overall.

This morning it was obvious that the peloton was very nervous. In the neutral section, guys were trying to stay in the front, and while we went slow, it was a battle to keep position. No one was talking or joking around like we would on some of the other days…. The first climb we went easy over. Pascal did a little tempo, but mostly sat on the front row making a wall across the road with the other riders. On the second climb, the attacks started. Guys would attack, get caught, and immediately get dropped. I don't know what they were thinking or doing. Christian was in charge of setting tempo on the second climb. Boy, did he have some climbing legs today. Sitting on his wheel I was uncomfortable, and when the attacks started coming around us, I only went 400 meters before I pulled off and let Kevin do the work. I got on the back of the group and made it over with the first 50 guys. Tyler was also in the back, getting his diesel engine warmed up.

On the third climb, Banesto went to the front trying to break up the group. I sat on the Banesto guy while he did tempo, and again the attacks started to fly. This time my legs had come around and I took over pulling to the top, controlling the attacks. A small group of seven had escaped earlier in the day, with no one dangerous; and with four more climbs coming, they would for sure be spit out the back later on.

I started the third-to-last climb in the front with Tyler, Kevin and Lance on my wheel. The group was now only 40 guys. I rode on the front till they started attacking again. After bringing back a couple of attacks, I decided to let the real climbers take over. Tyler and Kevin took turns riding tempo and controlling the rest of the climb. This climb, for some reason, was a sauna. It was much hotter than all the rest of the climbs, and guys were getting shelled quickly. This climb is also where Olano and Tonkov and many others decided to change gears and get spit out the back. At the same time, Escartin changed gears and went off the front.

On the second-to-last climb, Lance attacked 4

FERNANDO ESCARTIN

kilometers from the top with Zülle. Escartin had a two-and-a-half-minute gap and it was growing, because the guys with Lance were not racing, just waiting. At the bottom of the last climb, Lance was caught. Going up the last climb, Lance was comfortable, but he called up the car with 5 kilometers to go. He needed an Extran—he was bonking. He lost some time at the top in the last couple hundred meters. This was more from running out of energy than running out of legs…. It was a very difficult day to eat, because of the constant climbing and descending. I used a liquid diet to get through the day; no solid food at all.

Escartin won a little more than two minutes in front of Lance's chase group, and this moved him into second on the G.C.

Tomorrow is the last mountain day and for us, it's the last main obstacle before we pull this Tour thing off. I will admit I was nervous this morning because it was such a hard stage…and I'm sure it will be the same tomorrow.

The gruppetto was a big one today. Many riders are tired and the first chance they get to sit up, they do. Christian was making deals all day in the last group. Guys were so hot and desperate for water, they were begging Christian for water and they promised to buy him a beer in Paris. He has a about a case of beer waiting for him at the finish.

Prudencio, while riding in the group, spotted a two-liter bottle of Orangina sitting on a picnic table. When he spotted it, he yelled out, "Who want's some Orangina?" Of course, everyone wanted some; so Prudencio in one swoop swung over into the gravel and grabbed it off the picnic table. It was a party.

After the race, Lance got a helicopter ride off the mountaintop finish. The rest of us were waiting in the camper for our soigneurs to return so we could drive down the mountain. We were the last team to get off that mountain. It took forever. Luckily, we had a police escort, so we made up most of the time that we lost sitting up there doing nothing.

How many yellow jerseys do you get in a day? Answer: Each day you receive a short-sleeved jersey and a long-sleeved jersey in the morning. And after the race, you receive a clean, new, short-sleeved jersey for the podium presentation. Maybe sometimes you have seen the yellow jersey that is presented and fastened in the back. This jersey is awarded if it's going over your team jersey. It fastens in the back with Velcro, so you don't have to try and pull it over your head and look like a fool when it gets stuck.

in Sestriere a week earlier. This time, five minutes outside the 16-percent limit, the judges had no pity. He was out.

On reaching his team van, Sweet wearily sat on the tailgate, head down, a water bottle in hand, and coughed a bronchial cough. "Six hills is too much," he mumbled. "Everything is numb...."

"I gave it everything I had," he added. "I didn't give up.... I did 150k on my own...."

"The hardest was this one," he said, pointing at the Peyresourde on his rumpled stage profile card. "I was in big trouble there. I tried to cross to the *gruppetto*, and that's where I felt the legs go. Then, it was just survival...."

S T A G E   1 6
Lannemezan–Pau • July 21

Podium panache

EVERY MORNING, LESS THAN AN HOUR BEFORE THE START OF THAT DAY'S STAGE, all the U.S. Postal Service team riders would crowd into one of their two small camper vans for a meeting with directeur sportif Bruyneel. There, they'd discuss team strategy for the race ahead. "Our plan today is to get as many of us as possible over the Tourmalet in the front group," said team veteran Andreu, on emerging from the van in Lannemezan, the starting point of the final mountain stage. If that were accomplished, team leader Armstrong would have all the support he needed to defend the yellow jersey on the Tour's final climbs.

Armstrong also had to defend something else—his reputation—when he, too, emerged from the van, 10 minutes before start time, to face another battery of TV cameras and microphones. They all wanted to know the truth about the cortico-steroids that an article in *Le Monde* claimed were in the yellow jersey's urine sample after stage 1.

The explanation would have to wait, as on the agenda of this 16th stage were three mighty mountain passes: the 12km Aspin, 17km Tourmalet and the 21km combo of Soulor and Aubisque. These were among the first Pyrenean climbs to be included in the Tour de France, in 1910. Back then, the Tourmalet was just a rocky mule track; and all except one of the Tour riders walked their heavy, rudimentary bikes up the rugged mountain. The exception was Frenchman Gustave Garrigou, who received a 100-franc prize for riding all the way to the 6939-foot summit.

The Tourmalet's topography hasn't changed much in 90 years, except for a modern invasion of ski lifts and monstrous condo buildings on the climb's eastern slopes. The biggest changes have been in the road, which in recent years has been progressively widened and given a smooth, black pavement. The average grade on the eastern approach is still a challenging 7.5 percent, but that asphalt surface combined with light, narrow tires, nine-speed freewheels and featherweight titanium and carbon-fiber frames has greatly increased climbing speeds. The fastest rider this year climbed the Tourmalet at 21.64 kph (about 13.5 mph), probably four times the speed of those 1910 pioneers.

In past Tours, the Tourmalet has witnessed some great battles...and the launching of one still-talked-about exploit. On his Tour debut in 1969, Eddy Merckx led by a few seconds over the Tourmalet summit, but instead of being brought back on the descent, the Belgian pursued his effort, continued riding hard over the following Soulor and Aubisque climbs, and arrived at the finish in Mourenx, after a 130km solo, eight minutes ahead of the runner-up.

The course was similar this year, with the stage ending in Pau, 127km from the Tourmalet summit. But in today's techno-scientific environment, solo raids similar to Merckx's are rare. Indeed, on arriving at the foot of the Tourmalet this year, the complete field of 142 starters was still together. It didn't remain like that for long, though, as the attacks began as soon as the grade steepened on the early slopes between stone-fenced fields.

The Postals did their best to control things, but a pattern didn't emerge until the racers entered a thick bank of cloud, just beyond halfway. At this point, there was a break at the front, composed of Mapei's Tonkov, ONCE's Etxebarria and Peron, and Telekom's Elli; a group of leaders pulled by Postal some 40 seconds back; and a bigger group behind, featuring the disappointing Olano.

After emerging from the cloud into bright sunshine at around 6000 feet, the remarkable Elli (still in search of a stage win) forced the pace, to reach the summit five seconds ahead of Tonkov and Etxebarria, 10 seconds up on Peron, and only 23 seconds ahead of an 11-strong group that had been pulled impressively by Livingston for the final 5km. In this small pack were all the G.C. leaders except Olano, who was struggling again, some three minutes behind.

Descending back into the clouds on the other side, Elli was joined by Etxebarria and then Tonkov, while Peron drifted back to the Armstrong group—which doubled in size on reaching the valley floor, and doubled again when Olano's teammates brought up a pack that also included the rest of the Postal team—their goal accomplished—just before

FRANKIE'S DIARY ◎ July 21
◎ Pau

Exciting, but tough

It's over: Finally, the mountains are behind us.
What a nightmare, trying to be a climber when I'm
not. I will say this for the mountains, though: They
make for some exciting racing. Today we had
200km with three major mountains. The middle
climb, the Tourmalet, was the largest and hardest.
At our morning meeting, we decided that our main
goal was to get as many riders as possible over the
Tourmalet . After that, if we made it
over the last climb, then great; and if
we didn't, then that's life.

The first climb had all the
sprinters and guys who were dead
on the first row forming a wall from
one side of the road to the other.
This was great for us; we went slow
the whole way up. After descending
for maybe 10km, we reached the
base of the 20km Tourmalet. As
soon as we were about to start the
climb, the attacks started coming. George controlled things for a bit, but then we just started riding tempo to try and maintain control. I rode on the
front for a while, and guys still were attacking.
Garzelli (Mercatone Uno) attacked, and went up to
three or four guys who were just sitting in front of
us. I kept it steady, but every time I looked up,
Garzelli was pulling as hard as he could to keep the
group away. We still had 15km to climb, but every
time I saw the group, he was on the front making
hell for me.

With eight kilometers to go, Tyler and Kevin
took over. They set tempo to the top and in doing
so, they dropped Olano. Olano was suffering big
time. After I pulled off, I set myself a steady tempo,
because I knew I had to try and make it over as
close to the leaders as possible. Well, when I
reached the top, Olano was just in front of me. Like
I said, he was having a bad day. Christian—who
again had good climbing legs—was with me in the
Olano group.

Kevin told me that while he was riding tempo
on the Tourmalet, Virenque came up to him and
asked him what his problem was. Kevin told him he
didn't have a problem, what was *his* problem?
Virenque looked at Kevin and asked him if he was
going *à bloc*. That means all-out, or very hard.
Kevin looked at Virenque and told him, "No. Are
you going *à bloc*?" As he said that, Kevin clicked up
a few gears and rode away. It was funny and
Virenque was pissed....

VIRENQUE

Christian and I caught up to the
first group just in time to start the
last and final climb. We rode tempo
and, as usual, guys started attacking.
It seems like it is always the jerks
that attack and get nowhere.... In
the middle of the climb, Escartin
attacked. He attacked hard on the
steepest part of the climb. Right
away, Lance went with him, along
with Zülle. Just behind, I saw
Virenque start to go, trying to bridge the small gap.
Well, he didn't make it. He went for 200 meters
and then blew. The whole time Virenque was trying
to chase, Kevin was sitting behind, chuckling to
himself. On the climb, Virenque kept looking
around; it must have been driving him crazy that
Kevin was there.

Meanwhile, going over the top were three of
the favorites: Lance, Zülle and Escartin. In the back
were Dufaux, Virenque and Olano. The chase was
on. The front guys, in their group of 12, were riding
well together; and the rear group of 40 couldn't
close the gap. I was in the third group with
Christian, a few Rabobanks, a couple of Festinas
and a couple of ONCEs. Also in our group was
Garzelli—which pissed me, since that guy made

today living hell for me, and here he was way off the back. I did everything to make his ride to the finish as uncomfortable as possible. I just don't like that guy anymore.

Today, Escartin pretty much secured his place on the podium. Virenque, Dufaux and Olano are now over four minutes back. Escartin should be able to hold on to that kind of lead in the time trial with relatively little problem. And since Lance still has six minutes over second place, I think he should be able to hold on to that lead, too. If he doesn't, I personally will beat him up!!

I suffered big time today, much more than yesterday. After doing so many efforts yesterday, I was paying the price a bit today. I think the same thing happened with Dufaux, Virenque and Olano. Today, after riding tempo at my limit, I then just dug deep and suffered, trying to keep contact with a group over the climbs. I was pedaling as hard as I could, but it didn't seem like I was going anywhere. My legs have worn down and I'm lucky there are only flat days left. The one thing we flatlanders are looking forward to tomorrow is that we will now have six guys riding on the front. No more saving Tyler and Kevin for the mountains. The mountains are over, and now everyone can share in the work....

I'm sick of riding in the wind; it seems like since day one, we have been on the front. If I really push it, maybe I can get Lance to take a few turns in the paceline....

You can tell that a lot of us are tired—tired of the race, tired of working, tired of four weeks on the road, and tired of the Tour. Our tempers are short; sarcasm isn't funny; and small mistakes seem like huge problems. I'm sure, though, that with just a few more days left in the Tour, things will start relaxing a bit, as we start to celebrate and enjoy the team's accomplishment.

the feed zone.

By now, the Elli trio was two minutes ahead, and that gap grew to almost five minutes before about 4km from the top of the Soulor, where Escartin unleashed a blazing attack on the left of the Postal Service tempo train. Armstrong immediately came around on the right to catch the Spanish climber, but the only others to join them were Zülle and Belli. Virenque didn't have the strength to go across the gap, nor did Dufaux, despite a long, long pull by one of the Swiss rider's Saeco teammates, Commesso.

By the Soulor crest, and now 3:05 behind the three leaders, the Escartin quartet had swept up earlier chasers Arrieta of Banesto, Contreras of Kelme, and 1998 mountains competition winner Christophe Rinero of Cofidis. And by the bleak, cloud-blanketed Aubisque summit, 61km from the finish, the Escartin-Armstrong-Zülle express had passed another of the earlier chase groups (Roland Meier, Serrano, Garcia and Vinokourov), and begun the final long descent of this 1999 Tour, 1:25 behind the front trio.

Another 2:50 back came the group with Virenque and Dufaux—their hopes of shooting for the podium in Paris looking ever more distant. Their fate was finally sealed when, after taking back Contreras, Belli, Serrano, Arrieta, Vinokouroov and Meier into their ranks, the Escartin three joined forces with the Elli trio with 36km to go.

Escartin, Armstrong, Zülle and Contreras were doing nearly all the work at the front, with the dynamic Escartin being particularly fired up, knowing that he was almost guaranteeing himself a spot on the Tour podium for the first time.

On reaching the streets of Pau, with a 5km loop remaining, the gap between the 12 leaders and the 42-man chase group was 2:30. The attackers had won; now it was time to contest the stage victory. The three "Goliaths"—Armstrong, Zülle and Escartin—seemed to agree that the "Davids" could fight it out…which they did. Six went on ahead, and in what was probably the slowest finishing sprint of the Tour, a real David (Etxebarria)—the St. Flour stage winner—just hung on to win again, ahead of a weary Carlos (Contreras) and a once-again unfortunate Alberto (Elli).

As for that guy named Lance, he again defended his lead in the mountains with panache. After the stage, he had to utilize different skills in choosing to face the press and address the questions on his integrity posed by the article in *Le Monde*. In concluding his remarks, answering what he called the "desperate" journalists who hinted that he wasn't a clean rider, Armstrong said, "What they wanted was for me to crack on the bike, and I wasn't going to crack for them."

STAGE 17

Mourenx–Bordeaux • July 22

Sprinting 101

HOW COME ERIK ZABEL MESSED UP AGAIN? In the first massed sprint finish since he pulled his feet from the pedals in Thionville, losing to Cipollini, Zabel seemed to have everything going his way on this 17th stage. First, there was no Cipollini to worry about. Second, the finish into Bordeaux—where Zabel had won in 1995 and '97—was one that seemed to suit the German's strengths. And third, he was the only sprinter still with a complete team at his disposal.

Indeed, Zabel's Telekom teammates worked perfectly together, to help quench a 140km-long breakaway with 14km left, and then lead their star sprinter with a long paceline through the streets of Bordeaux, on a complicated run-in to the wine city's historic heart.

Another bonus for Zabel was the crash less than 1500 meters from the line that eliminated his closest rival in the points classification, O'Grady. But even during the first week, Zabel seemed to come up short in every sprint. Was it the pressure of being the Telekom team leader for the Tour? Or had he simply lost the speed that netted him six stage wins in his first three Tours? Or maybe focusing on winning a fourth consecutive green jersey had sapped the energy he needed to win a stage? In this respect, Zabel's case resembled that of the 1980s' sprint king, Sean Kelly. The Irishman didn't win any stages in three of the four years that saw him take the green jersey.

Even so, Zabel and his team should have done better in Bordeaux. Each Telekom rider took Zabel closer and closer to the line before peeling off, until the last one pulled over with about 200 meters to sprint. It seemed to be an ideal leadout, but the Telekoms clearly hadn't reckoned on the head wind that was blowing off the nearby Garonne—which saw the German sprinter "die" with about 30 meters still to go.

In contrast, Steels simply followed Zabel's wheel all the way through the final kilometer, and came flying past in the final 50 meters to win his third stage of the race. McEwen was another who came past the Telekom sprinter before the line, while Hincapie, still hoping for a breakthrough, jumped at the right time, but didn't have the speed to match Steels's charge, and crossed in fourth.

Perhaps Zabel would get it right in Paris....

STAGE 18
Jonzac–Futuroscope • July 23

French leave

NOT SINCE 1926—WHEN THE 17 STAGE WINS WERE SHARED by Belgians, Dutch, Italians and a Luxembourger—have the French gone through a whole Tour de France without winning a stage. It's not as if the home riders didn't have a chance this year. Although they lack a top time trialist or sprinter at the moment (neophyte sprinter Jimmy Casper has the speed, but not the experience), there are plenty of French riders who had a chance for stage wins at this Tour. Heulot nearly snagged one with his brave breakaway on the stage to Alpe d'Huez...Simon came close, with his second place behind Etxebarria at St. Flour...and then there was this stage into Futuroscope.

There were five Frenchmen in the 13-strong winning break that formed over the day's only categorized climb, at Pamproux, 56km from the finish: Casino's Frédéric Bessy, who started the break after emerging from an earlier attack; La Française des Jeux's Jean-Cyril Robin, who joined Bessy after sprinting for KoM points with Piccoli;

Cofidis's Claude Lamour; BigMat's Thierry Bourgignon, the Tour's oldest rider; and the ambitious Simon of Crédit Agricole, still riding on a cloud after winning the French national pro championship in late June.

Since the break formed, the 13 riders had been fighting crosswinds blowing across Poitou's fields of wheat, corn, vines and sunflowers. That wind kept the group working hard together, to stay clear of a peloton that was tired from earlier chases; and but for the ONCE team, which was still fighting Banesto for the overall team prize, no other teams wanted to make another hard chase.

And so the race for the stage win was between the 13 riders in front. Two teams had two riders in the break: Casino and Banesto. Casino's Bessy had little chance of success, as he had been out front for most of the stage. Then there was his Kazakh teammate Vinokourov, the best-known rider in the break, who would probably wait for the sprint to make up for his losing the stage into St. Etienne, in which he attacked too soon.

As for the two Banesto riders, Garcia Acosta and Solaun were riding for the team prize because no ONCE men were in the break. So instead of going for the stage win, the two Spaniards were riding hard to make as much time as possible on the pack (the eventual three-minute gap, times two, gave them a handy six-minute

Easy street

I've gotten second on this stage before, but I guarantee you that won't happen this year. The good thing about today is that we have six guys riding on the front, instead of our usual three or four. There is no need to save anyone for the mountains, now that they are behind us.

Pascal is sitting second from *lanterne rouge* right now. Lanterne rouge is the name given to the last rider in the overall. Jay Sweet (BigMat) held that position for roughly the whole Tour, until he was eliminated two days ago when he finished outside the time limit. Actually, this was the second time for him to finish outside the time limit, but the commissaires felt sorry for him and kept him in the race. If anything, he should get the award for most competitive. He never gave up, even when he would get dropped over the first climb. For a couple of days, he rode over 100km on his own and would finish only four minutes behind the gruppetto. *That's* determination.

For once, finally, we didn't have to work today. I couldn't believe it. I didn't know what to do with myself. I saw guys in the race whom I hadn't seen in three weeks. But even though I was off of the front, it was not an easy day. The start had some big rollers, and over the top of each one was a lactic-acid burner. When your legs are trying to decide how they feel, these rollers drive home the point: tired. As I had hoped, the sprinter teams were doing their job controlling things. A few breaks would go up the road, and right away Mapei would chase them down. Eventually, eight guys got away and built up a lead of eight minutes pretty quickly. The first team to start chasing was Polti. Virenque was scared of losing his G.C. position to Stephan Heulot as the first French rider. I loved it…. Later, the sprinter teams started helping to try and bring the break back for a field sprint. At one time there must have been 20 guys riding on the front. Needless to say, it was a very fast day.

At the finish, Steels won easily over Zabel, who had the full train leading into the finish. I think Zabel must be getting desperate by now….

George said that today was the best day of the Tour for him. He didn't have to work; he got to sit on the wheels all day; and it was over quickly. I think the best day of the Tour will be the day after the Tour finishes.

Speaking of the day after the Tour finishes,

L'Équipe, the French sports newspaper, says that they traditionally follow the winner of the Tour for one day after it finishes. I have a feeling that tradition will be broken this year. Like Lance wants a bunch of journalists who have been breathing down his back for three weeks to be with him the day after the Tour finishes. Forget about it!

George and Lance have some criteriums lined up for after the Tour. The first criterium is Monday night, and then they have one every other day after that. There is no rest for the weary.

Yesterday, Olano had his climbing bike with the small wheels out again. It didn't do him any good. With the small wheel, he rides a 56 front chainring to make up for the difference. It's a shame that Olano is on the ONCE team this year. He is the weakest link on their team. The guys were always waiting for him and trying to help him to stay in the first group. Without Olano, I'm sure they would have had three or four guys everyday in the first group….

There are only two teams with full squads left in the race: Telekom and Lotto. There are lots of teams with fewer riders, but Saeco and Lampre each have only three riders left.

Each night, Julian, our head mechanic, brings Lance's bike in the hotel room with him. He sleeps with the bike just in case something might happen outside. You never know if someone might steal the cars or trucks or whatever. It has happened before.

Yesterday was a hard day in the mountains. At the bottom of the climb, it would be sunny; then, as we climbed the mountain, we would enter into the clouds. But as we approached the top of the climb, the clouds would disappear and the sun would come back out. The coolest sight was after going over the top of the Tourmalet and looking down and seeing a ceiling of white clouds. It took about 5 kilometers of descending before we entered the clouds, or fog. Once we were in the fog, we were not able to descend fast, because we couldn't see 10 feet in front of us. At the bottom of the climb, it would become sunny again. The mountains provide lots of variations in temperature and weather…and yesterday was no exception.

gain, probably enough to take the $35,000 team prize in Paris).

The critical point in the run-in to Futuroscope came with 4.5km to go, just where the course turned right, and changed the strong crosswind into more of a tail wind to the finish. It was immediately after this turn that Mondini of Cantina Tollo—a member of several breaks between the Alps and Pyrénées—made a very smart attack. "I knew that Bessy was on my wheel, and I knew that he was tired, so I accelerated," said the Italian. "It turned out to be a good move."

Indeed it did. Once clear, he used the power from his 6-foot 3-inch, 178-pound frame to open a 100-meter gap that no one seemingly wanted to close. In the end, Robin went away from the others on the slightly uphill finish, but the former Postal Service rider was too late to catch the delighted Mondini. The French had lost again.

STAGE 19
Futuroscope TT • July 24

Exclamation mark!

IF THERE WERE ANY DOUBTS ABOUT ARMSTRONG'S WORTHINESS to join the likes of Induráin, Hinault, Merckx and Anquetil on the winners' list at the Tour de France, then his victory in this final time trial ended them. In fact, those five-

Danger, spectators!

First off, I want you to know that the amount of people watching the race every day is incredible. There are rows and rows of people lining the course. Some are nice, some are freaks, some are fans of cyclists, and maybe some are not. On the mountain day, Christophe Rinero almost got into a fight with a spectator. He was climbing up the mountain and this guy started chanting, "Rinero without EPO, Rinero in the back." Rinero took a right turn to the side of the road to chase the guy down. Christophe was not happy, and I guarantee you that if he weren't racing, he would have chased the guy down the hill…. Another bad incident happened yesterday: Someone sprayed pepper spray into the peloton near the finish in Bordeaux. Five or six riders got dropped immediately, because they couldn't breathe, had watery eyes and were vomiting. I don't know, but I think the UCI should have given these guys the same time as the peloton.

Some people are fans and some are not. We are always surrounded by people at the start and at the finish. There are no gates, no walls and no barriers keeping you away from us. This is what appeals to the people and makes cycling that much more special.

This morning the Vampires came again. This time only Lance got tested. I think they were testing the top riders on the G.C., so that meant only one or two from each team.

Today's race was fast again, the same as yesterday. It must be deceiving when you see the average speed for a race. We go slow the first hour, so that kills our average. I'll tell you that yesterday and today, every time I looked down at my speedometer it was reading 50 kph. We are not having any easy days on this Tour.

The first break that got away contained 20 riders. There was no ONCE, Banesto or Mapei. This was perfect for us. Actually, anything that went away was okay for us. Every time there was a break, the closest guy to Lance was usually 50 minutes.

Because of the team G.C., Banesto and ONCE were chasing a lot of the breaks back. Finally, after four major breaks and after 130km, the final break went away. There was a Banesto in there this time, but again no ONCE. They rode on the front the whole last part of the race, trying to keep their six-minute lead on team G.C. The whole team rode, except Olano and Peron.

At the finish, Mondini (Cantina Tollo) won by jumping away with about 2 kilometers to go—again denying a French rider a win in this year's Tour.

Our morning meeting was very simple; in fact, it was so simple we had it over the walkie-talkies from one camping car to the other. Our one job was to keep Lance in the front and out of trouble. The meeting was over in five minutes. About 40 minutes after we had the meeting, Christian looked up and asked us if we were going to have a meeting this morning. We all started laughing. He had been listening to music with his headphones on, so he hadn't heard anything. We told him Johan said he had to attack from the gun, serious.

The time trial is tomorrow. Lance's lead is pretty safe; and each day we tend to relax a little more and realize we pulled it off—or Lance pulled it off. We are all excited about riding on to the Champs with the yellow jersey on our wheels…. Actually, one year, LeMond with the yellow jersey attacked the peloton and came on to the Champs 30 seconds ahead of the pack. The crowd went wild. Bernard Hinault once won on the Champs wearing the yellow jersey—how cool is that?! After the TT, it might be possible that Lance will have more than a seven-minute lead on the second-placed rider. With that much time he could probably get lapped and *still* keep the jersey. Don't worry, we won't let that happen….

time winners were the only previous riders to sweep a single Tour's time trials. Whether Armstrong will add four more *Tour* wins is, of course, a whole other question. But his performance at Futuroscope showed that the American has the power, talent and character to match the top winners of the past.

With a six-minute-plus lead, Armstrong had no need to take another stage, but "soft-pedaling" is not an expression in the tough Texan's vocabulary. "It would have been easy for me today to not have the motivation, or to do an effort of 90 percent; but I wanted to prove that the *maillot jaune* was the strongest man in the race," he later said.

Wanting to achieve such a goal was a daunting task, particularly with an opponent as determined and talented as Zülle. The 30-year-old Swiss—probably the most consistently successful time trialist of the 1990s—was second in the prologue and second at Metz. What's more, the Futuroscope course favored Zülle's abilities far more than Armstrong's. Like Induráin, the Swiss rider has the build of the prototypical time trialist: long, muscular legs; deep chest; and aerodynamic position.

Armstrong doesn't have the perfect build, and is still learning to pace himself for the full distance of these longer time trials, even if he has greatly improved his style—legs turning straight as pistons, at a consistent cadence of around 108 rpm. At Metz, the American had demonstrated a lack of pacing by gaining 18 seconds on Zülle in the opening 10km—and conceding 15 seconds to the Swiss in the final 5km. Interestingly, the final 5km were the flattest and straightest part of the Metz course, and ridden into a head wind.

There was also plenty of wind at Futuroscope, on an afternoon of warm sunshine, on a course that attracted huge crowds. The clockwise circuit was basically flat, but it had many short, out-of-the-saddle uphills, snaking back roads, and small towns where blind corners demanded total concentration.

Armstrong would have to work harder than he did at Metz to find his focus. In that earlier time trial, he had ridden the complete course three times, he had been focusing on the stage for the whole opening week, and there were no distractions. Here, he had managed to ride only the opening 42km of the 57km course; and, a day from the Tour's finish, not only was he the center of media focus as the *maillot jaune*, but he was also being sought out by the many friends and family members who had arrived for this climax of the Tour.

One special arrival was his mother, Linda Walling, who clutched a small U.S. flag as she sat in a prime viewing position—the front seat passenger of the Tour sports director, Jean-François Pescheux. She had been present in Oslo when Armstrong won the 1993 world's—his rainbow jersey has a prominent place in her Texas home—and now she was going to watch him defend the yellow jersey of the Tour.

With the main contenders starting at three-minute intervals, Armstrong began three minutes after Escartin, and six minutes behind Zülle. So the American would know at each time check where he stood. The first split came after 13.5km of mainly crosswind riding, on a rolling road between fields of just-harvested wheat and still-growing corn. Zülle went through in a time of 16:15, matching the fastest-to-then time by Olano. The 135-pound Escartin, finding it hard to hold a straight line in the strong side wind, was expectedly slower (16:43)…but then Armstrong came through like a missile in 15:59. It was a start as impressive as the one he made in Metz.

The next section of the course was the hardest, in that it was mostly into the wind, and included many tight turns in the villages of Vendouevre-du-Poitou, Ouzilly and Lencloitre. Out of town, the course followed a narrow, twisting back road until Lencloitre, then emerged onto a wider highway for a few kilometers. Armstrong was also fastest on this 14.5km section, in 19:35—five seconds faster than Zülle—while Olano (20:35) and Escartin (21:01) were both fading fast. In fact, moving into contention here was Hamilton, whose 20:03 split was the third best.

The talented Hamilton, recovered from his crashes earlier in the Tour and seeing how fast he could go at the end of a three-week race, said he had trouble keeping a good line because of the conditions. "It was hard for a little guy like me in that wind," he later said.

Meanwhile, Zülle was fully into his stride and looking stronger, as his Banesto team director Eusebio Unzue kept up a non-stop, amplified barrage of encouragement: "*Ven-ga, ven-ga, ven-ga....*" And on the third section of cross- and tail winds, between the 28km and 42km points, Zülle passed a struggling Dufaux for three minutes. He covered this 14km section in 15:24, which proved 23 seconds faster than Hamilton...and just three seconds slower than Armstrong—who blasted by Escartin at the 20km-to-go marker.

Armstrong's lead by now was 24 seconds on Zülle—who continued his upward progression over the final 15km, the part that Armstrong had only looked over in a car. Hamilton, too, was finishing strongly, and, despite almost falling on a turn near the finish, he covered this final part in 17:29. This compared with a challenging 17:09 by Zülle, while Armstrong, who also misjudged one of the late turns, had his weakest leg, with 17:22. "I was just tired," the race leader said, "I was just trying to get to the finish."

It was a brave final flourish by the Postal leader, and was enough to win him the stage by just nine seconds from Zülle, with Hamilton an excellent third, only 1:35 back. Zülle's consolation was moving up to second overall over an exhausted Escartin—who battled to the end, losing four minutes to his Swiss rival. In turn, Hamilton climbed from 16th to 13th overall.

The other main changes involved Virenque, who dropped from fifth to eighth, and Spanish champion Casero—who took fourth on the stage (two seconds slower than third-placed Hamilton) and moved into fifth on G.C. But those final modifications were just a footnote to what was probably Armstrong's toughest stage win. It may not have been quite as spectacular as Le Puy du Fou, Metz or Sestriere, but his fourth stage win of the Tour left a very proud Mom still clutching that flag. She would now be able to wave it even *more* vigorously in Paris.

STAGE 20
Arpajon–Paris [Champs-Elysées] • July 25

Changing fortunes

SO ZABEL DIDN'T MAKE IT. His Telekom team again gave a perfect leadout for the pocket German sprinter, who looked resplendent in his all-green uniform, riding an all-green bicycle. But resplendent or not, the first man to win four consecutive points titles went through another Tour without a stage win. In contrast, an until-now under-achieving Robbie McEwen finally won a Tour stage after three years of try-ing—and in so doing, unwittingly saved the Tour for Rabobank, a team that had just confirmed it would not be re-signing the 26-year-old Aussie sprinter.

The difference between Zabel and McEwen on the Champs-Elysées was a matter of motivation. The German had already clinched the green jersey, and he seemed to lose focus in the final 50 meters of this with-the-wind sprint. He *did* have that great leadout, but again seemed to launch his from-the-front sprint a little too early. In contrast, McEwen tagged Zabel and Steels—who sat up after being passed by the Aussie—and then made his charge on the outside, to put his wheel ahead of Zabel with about 30 meters remaining. The result was suddenly clear, because, as McEwen noted, "When you get to the front, you get that extra rush of adrenaline."

In the post-stage press conference, McEwen complimented his Rabobank teammates: "Today, they rode like they should ride; that's what you should expect from a professional team." But he didn't change his views expressed in Bordeaux a few days earlier that "our guys were beaten before they started."

FRANKIE'S DIARY @ July 24 @ Futuroscope

Ciao

Today is my last article. There are a few reasons for this. One is that the hotel we stay at in Paris in now was built in 1970 or something, and getting on-line is impossible. Two is that after the race we usual-ly have to change and get ready to go out pretty quickly. Three is that I have not seen my wife for about seven weeks, and I don't think it would go over too well if I opened my computer to write an article. Four is that the writing bug in me has dwindled considerably. I hope I've made it interesting for you and that you've learned more about the insides of the Tour. The results don't always tell the whole story....

Today was a relatively simple, straightforward 57km time trial. It was one big loop with not too many turns, but it was very, very windy. It seemed like there was a crosswind the entire day. At least, I never felt a tail wind; then again, I'm a bit under the weather. I came down with a cold two days ago and I'm suffering. I became too worn down after the last two mountain days, and my body caved in. I can't complain, though, because we are at the end of the Tour. It's bet-ter to be sick now than earlier in the weeks.

Today I could feel the pain in my lungs, while trying to ride; it's not a good feeling. Lance was on fire again. He had an all-yellow skinsuit for the TT, but it turned out not to fit him right. He also had a yellow TT helmet, but since he wasn't wearing the all-yellow skinsuit, he threw that to the side also. I don't think it mattered what he wore—he still would have won.

Tyler also had an incredible ride. His determina-tion in the TTs is hard to match. He finished a fantastic third place. There's been a very noticeable increase in the number of American flags that are out on the road waving us on. Today, there were lots of Americans lin-ing the course. As for the French, they definitely know how to make it a comfortable day out at the bike race.

I saw many portable picnic tables, couches, lounge chairs, and even mattresses. It's as though they bring their mini-home to the race. Umbrellas, coolers, tables, chairs, portable TVs, everything to make the hours pass as comfortably as possible.

After today, whatever the G.C. results are, they will stay the same. It's a tradition on the last day that we don't really race until the final circuits. Granted,

GEORGE HINACPIE AND FRANKIE ANDREU

we don't always go slow either. One year, the Italians had to catch a flight out after the race, so they went to the front and rode tempo all day. It was horrible, the whole day we were single file and didn't get to relax at all. I hope this year will be like the old ways.

Tomorrow morning we take the TGV (high-speed train) to the start city for the last day. Normally, the first three teams on G.C. get first-class cars, while everyone else is in the back. Since tomorrow is the last day, we will be celebrating a bit. Look for us wearing something special on the Champs. I thought of the idea, Lance approved it, and Pearl Izumi put it into action [yellow socks and yellow gloves]. Pearl had one day to get it done, so I give them the thumbs up.

After the Champs, we are having a big party with the team and all the sponsors. The last couple of nights, we have been trying to build up our toler-

ance for alcohol. The first night I had one beer and was as loose-tongued as you get. The second night we were working on the wine, George made it to five glasses, when he decided he had hit his threshold. At the party, I'm sure we'll have a mixture of beer and wine, which will probably be a disaster for all of us. At this point, I don't think anyone cares.

Now that the Tour is over, Lance will be busy doing some criteriums in the Netherlnds and Germany. He'll also be busy doing a lot of television and press stuff in America next week. But for the rest of us, it's back to bike racing like it used to be. In two weeks I have the San Sebastian World Cup race, then the Tour of Denmark, Hamburg World Cup, and maybe the Tour of Holland. But while the season may be only half over, since we did so well at the Tour, it doesn't really matter what happens the rest of the year—in my opinion.

I do need to give a "thanks" to Bikesport, my local bike shop at home in Dearborn, Michigan. I've mentioned before how important our staff is to the success of the team. On the road, our mechanics keep everything working; and when I'm at home, it's Bikesport that keeps me on the road. I just want them to know that their help makes all the difference in the world.

It's hard to believe I've been writing every day for three weeks. At the start, it's easy; but as the last week approaches, it becomes more difficult. This probably became obvious in how I wrote and the length of the entries. Every year after the Tour you think to yourself, "Never again—it's too hard"; and it's the same feeling with these articles. But like I said before, I hope you enjoyed the columns and learned something about racing in the Tour.

Ciao,
Frankie

McEwen's comments and Rabobank team boss Jan Raas's earlier criticism of his Aussie sprinter cemented the parting of the ways between the two men. But with a win in Paris now in his *palmarès*, McEwen should not have too hard a job finding a new team for 2000.

Workin' 9 to 5

I've ridden eight Tours and never once did I think I would one day be on the winning team of the Tour de France. I would watch how Banesto's riders, working year after year, somehow managed to stay in the front when everyone else was dead. I saw Telekom chase and chase countless breaks day after day, trying to defend the yellow jersey. After each stage, I would think that their teams would not be able to do the same thing the next day. Each day, as I lay in bed completely shattered from the stage, I tried to understand how the Banestos and Telekoms were able to ride on the front from start to finish. I didn't think what they did was possible. The Tour was hard enough without having to work each day. The courses, the speed, the riders, the length—everything added up to surviving the Tour, not to attacking it....

Well, this year all that changed, with the arrival of Lance Armstrong at the Tour. Sure, Lance had done the Tour before, but each year before this one was for either learning or trying for a stage win. This year, those ideas were not options. Lance was only interested in winning—not one day, but the whole thing.

The carnival began at the prologue. Lance had talked about how he was going to win the prologue, and as I sat there watching him cross the line, I realized that he won easily. At that point I also realized the size of the project that lay in front of us. Winning the Tour not only takes a strong team and a very strong leader, but also a lot of luck.

From day one, Lance set out to prove his point that he was in France to win the Tour. The team rode on the front from day one to drive this point home—to our competitors, and also to ourselves. Some of the hardest days we experienced were when Lance was not in the jersey.

One chase we did that changed the outcome of the race was after the water causeway. Some might have seen it as taking advantage of a situation—but this is a bike race. Some may say we—meaning the teams that rode on the front—broke an unwritten code of conduct: not to attack when riders crash. The fact is that the causeway was a major obstacle of the race, and everyone knew it. Everyone knew you had to be in the front—or risk the consequences of being in the back. You could compare it to the first section of cobbles at Paris-Roubaix. Everyone knows you have to be in front to avoid something bad happening. Nine times out of 10 somebody crashes or flats—it's inevitable. Are we supposed to wait? I don't think so. And the causeway falls under this sort of circumstance.... There were also a couple other times where the entire team went to the front to chase down groups that we felt were dangerous. We were racing that first week not because we had the jersey, or for the jersey, but for the final victory in Paris.

The whole team deserves credit for a great Tour. One rider who got thrown into the deep end this year was Christian Vande Velde. Christian, riding his first Tour, had to defend the yellow jersey with the rest of us for three weeks. This is not something you would want when riding your first Tour. We babied him a little in the first week, but after that it was sink or swim because of the circumstances. Well, Christian actually got better as the days passed. By the end, he was floating like a buoy, instead of sinking like an anchor.

Both Kevin Livingston and Tyler Hamilton were the team's life support system in the mountains. Their strength rattled everyone's cages when they realized it was more than Lance that they were up against. The other contenders had to defeat three guys in the mountains to break into the yellow jersey—something they failed to do.

Early on, we lost Jonathan Vaughters, who could have made a world of hurt disappear for us flatlanders on the team. As it was, the team tried to make climbers out of us non-climbers as long as possible on the mountain stages. I can remember going flat-out uphill, when Kevin would roll up alongside of me and ask if everything was okay. At the same time, Kevin was telling me how he would be going all out and Lance would roll up alongside of him and tell him that it was time to start putting the hurt to these guys. At this point there were only maybe seven guys in the front group with them. I guess the suffering is all relative by how far up the mountain you are.

One of the most used-up guys on the team would have to have been Pascal Deramé. During the whole Tour, Pascal only got one day off from riding on the front, and that was only because I told him to stay off the front. When not riding tempo on the front, Pascal's job was riding in the wind for Lance. All day and every day during the first week, Pascal kept Lance out of harm's way, in the front, and rested. For that first week, Pascal was Lance's chauffeur and we were the police escorts keeping the area secure.

Then there was Peter Meinert-Nielsen, George Hincapie, Christian and myself, who logged many, many, many kilometers riding on the front.

As embarrassing as it sounds, I now know the shape of each of these guys' behinds like the back of my own hand. Peter, who rode four days longer than he should have, finally retired with a swollen knee the size of a softball. We may have had a bunch of Volkswagens setting tempo on the front of the group, but it was nice knowing we had our Ferrari waiting in the back with a full tank of gas. Lance was our Ferrari, and since he repeatedly proved he was the strongest, he deserved to win the Tour.

As each day in the Tour passed, the kilometers seemed longer, we grew more tired, the pressure and stress of the race increased (especially for Lance), and our motivation continued to increase (especially for Lance). We experienced three weeks of anxiety and glory, while each day we accomplished the unthinkable. We kept the yellow jersey for 14 days, won four stages, and arrived in Paris with Lance in tow in yellow. It was a dream come true for our team—and for many Americans.

STAGE 15: St. Gaudens—Piau-Engaly. July 20.
1. Escartin, 173km in 5:19:49 (32.456 kph); 2. Zülle, at 2:01; 3. Virenque, s.t.; **4. Armstrong, at 2:10**; 5. Van de Wouwer, at 2:27; 6. Casero, s.t.; 7. Nardello, at 2:45; 8. Dufaux, s.t.; 9. Francisco Garcia (Sp), Vitalicio Seguros, at 3:39; 10. Belli, at 4:00; 11. Beltran, at 5:03; 12. Elli, at 6:07; 13. Roland Meier (Swi), Cofidis, at 6:26; **14. Hamilton**; 15. Lelli, both s.t.; 16. Francisco Mancebo (Sp), Banesto, at 6:40; 17. Etxebarria, at 7:01; 18. Olano; 19. Peron, both s.t.; 20. Gonzalez Galdeano, at 8:09.
Others: 23. Tonkov, at 11:16; 24. Moreau, s.t.; **43. Livingston, at 21:36**; 44. Guerini, at 22:03; **51. Andreu, at 25:08**; **74. Hincapie, at 36:48**; **103. Vande Velde, s.t.**
Eliminated: Jay Sweet (Aus), BigMat-Auber 93; Damien Nazon (F), La Française des Jeux.
DNS: Dierckxsens; Mario Scirea (I), Saeco-Cannondale; Giuseppe Calcaterra (I), Saeco-Cannondale.
DNF: Hamburger; Stéphane Barthe (F), Casino; Didier Rous (F), Festina; Francesco Secchiari (I), Saeco-Cannondale.
Overall: 1. Armstrong, 2910.8km in 72:45:27; 2. Escartin, at 6:19; 3. Zülle, at 7:26; 4. Dufaux, at 8:36; 5. Virenque, at 9:46.

STAGE 16: Lannemezan—Pau. July 21.
1. Etxebarria, 192km in 5:17:07 (36.327 kph); 2. Contreras; 3. Elli; 4. Vinokourov; 5. Arrieta, all s.t.; 6. Marcos Serrano (Sp), ONCE-Deutsche Bank, at 0:05; 7. Belli, at 0:21; 8. Tonkov; 9. Garcia; 10. Zülle; **11. Armstrong**; 12. Escartin, all s.t.; 13. Bessy, at 2:13; 14. Simon; 15. Piccoli; 16. Lanfranchi; 17. Casero; 18. Laurent Madouas (F), Festina; 19. Lelli; 20. Nardello, all s.t.
Others: 25. Olano, at 2:13; 26. Dufaux; 34. Virenque; **37. Hamilton**; **45. Livingston**; 48. Guerini, all s.t; 56. Moreau, at 13:05; **65. Vande Velde**; **66. Andreu, both s.t.**; **112. Hincapie, at 26:20.**
DNS: Beltran.
Overall: 1. Armstrong, 3102.8km in 78:02:53; 2. Escartin, at 6:15; 3. Zülle, at 7:28; 4. Dufaux, at 10:30; 5. Virenque, at 11:40.

STAGE 17: Mourenx—Bordeaux July 22.
1. Steels, 199km in 4:22:29 (45.488 kph); 2. McEwen; 3. Zabel; **4. Hincapie**; 5. Martinello; 6. Michaelsen; 7. Pascal Chanteur (F), Casino; 8. Mondini; 9. Capelle; 10. Vinokourov, all s.t..
Others: 34. Escartin; 36. Olano; 41. Zülle; **42. Andreu**; 44. Dufaux; **51. Armstrong**; 55. Virenque; **59. Vande Velde**; **60. Hamilton**; **69. Livingston, all s.t.**
DNS: Tonkov.
Overall: 1. Armstrong, 3301.8km in 82:25:30; 2. Escartin, at 6:15; 3. Zülle, at 7:28; 4. Dufaux, at 10:30; 5. Virenque, at 11:40.

STAGE 18: Jonzac—Futuroscope. July 23.
1. Mondini, 184.5km in 4:17:43 (42.954 kph); 2. Jean-Cyril Robin (F), La Française des Jeux, at 0:03; 3. Vinokourov; 4. Piccoli; 5. Claude Lamour (F), Cofidis; 6. Simon; 7. Garzelli; 8. Jörg Jäksche (G) Telekom; 9. Elio Aggiano (I), Vitalicio Seguros 10. Thierry Bourgignon (F), Big-Mat-Auber 93, all s.t.
Others: 30. Livingston, at 3:07; 31. Armstrong; 33. Dufaux; 34. Zülle; 35. Escartin; **41. Hamilton**; 43. Olano; **44. Hincapie**; 51. Virenque; **84. Vande Velde**; **116. Andreu, all s.t.**
Overall: 1. Armstrong, 3486.3km in 86:46:20; 2. Escartin, at 6:15; 3. Zülle, at 7:28; 4. Dufaux, at 10:30; 5. Virenque, at 11:40.

STAGE 19: Futuroscope TT. July 24.
1. Armstrong, 57km in 1:08:17 (50.085 kph); 2. Zülle, 1:08:26; **3. Hamilton, 1:09:52**; 4. Casero, 1:09:54; 5. Verbrugghe, 1:10:20; 6. Olano, 1:10:35; 6. Belli, 1:10:49; 7. Gonzalez Galdeano, 1:10:45; 8. Voigt, 1:11:02; 9. O'Grady, 1:11:04; 10. Peron, 1:11:10.
Others: 16. Vande Velde, 1:11:58; 22. Escartin, 1:12:28; 23. Dufaux, 1:12:30; **27. Livingston, 1:13:09**; 38. Virenque, 1:14:05; 52. Guerini, 1:14:52; 53. Garzelli, 1:14:53; **59. Hincapie, 1:15:24**; **93. Andreu, 1:16:55**;
Overall: 1. Armstrong, 3543.3km in 87:54:37; 2. Zülle, at 7:37; 3. Escartin, at 10:25 4. Dufaux, at 14:43; 5. Casero, at 15:11.

STAGE 20: Arpajon—Paris (Champs-Elysées). July 25.
1. McEwen, 143.5km in 3:37:39 (39.558 kph); 2. Zabel; 3. Martinello; 4. O'Grady; 5. Carlos Da Cruz (F), BigMat-Auber 93; 6. Michaelsen; 7. Commesso; 9. Steels; 10. Wesemann, all s.t..
Others: 23. Hincapie; 35. Casero; 49. Olano; 55. Virenque; 63. Zülle; 68. Escartin; 75. Dufaux; **86. Armstrong**; **88. Hamilton**; **89. Vande Velde**; **90. Livingston**; **127. Andreu, all s.t.**

86th TOUR DE FRANCE. July 3-25.
Final overall
1. Armstrong, 3686.8km in 91:32:16 (40.273 kph); 2. Zülle, at 7:37; 3. Escartin, at 10:26; 4. Dufaux, at 14:43; 5. Casero, at 15:11; 6. Olano, at 16:47; 7. Nardello, at 17:02; 8. Virenque, at 17:28; 9. Belli, at 17:37; 10. Peron, at 23:10; 11. Van de Wouwer, at 23:32; 12. Etxebarria, at 26:41; **13. Hamilton, at 26:53**; 14. Heulot, at 27:58; 15. R, Meier, at 28:44; 16. Salmon, at 28:59; 17. Elli, at 33:39; 18. Lanfranchi, at 34:14; 19. Contreras, at 34:53; 20. Totschnig, at 37:10; 21. Mario Aerts (B), Lotto-Mobistar, at 39:21; 22. Guerini, at 39:29; 23. Gianni Faresin (I), Mapei-Quick Step, at 40:28; 24. Gonzalez Galdeano, at 43:39; 25. Marcos Serrano (Sp), ONCE-Deutsche Bank, at 45:03; 26. Francisco Garcia (Sp), Vitalicio Seguros, at 45:31; 27. Christophe Moreau (F), Festina, at 45.34; 28. Francisco Mancebo (Sp), Banesto, at 50:31; 29. Luis Perez Rodriguez (Sp), ONCE-Deutsche Bank, at 52:53; 30. Simon, at 53.21; 31. Armin Meier (Swi), Saeco-Cannondale, at 1:00:10; 32. Garzelli, at 1:00:45; 33. Javier Pascual Rodriguez (Sp), Kelme-Costa Blanca, at 1:01:20; 34. Massimiliano Lelli (I), Cofidis, at 1:01:27; 35. Vinokourov, at 1:02:23; **36. Livingston, at 1:06:10**; 37. José Castelblanco (Col), Kelme-Costa Blanca, at 1:08:05; 38. Commesso, at 1:09:15; 39. César Solaun (Sp), Banesto, at 1:10:01; 40. Udo

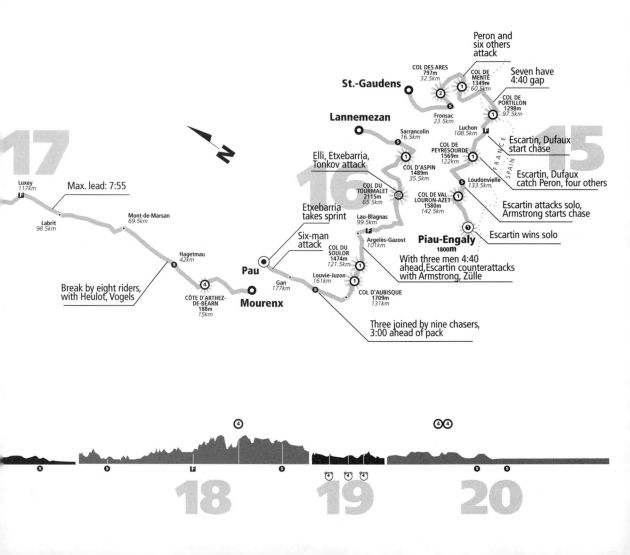

Peron and six others attack

COL DES ARES
797m
32.5km

COL DE MENTE
1349m
60.5km

Seven have 4:40 gap

St.-Gaudens

COL DE PORTILLON
1298m
97.5km

Fronsac
23.5km

Luchon
108.5km

Lannemezan

Sarrancolin
16.5km

Escartin, Dufaux start chase

COL DE PEYRESOURDE
1569m
122km

Elli, Etxebarria, Tonkov attack

COL D'ASPIN
1489m
35.5km

17

Escartin, Dufaux catch Peron, four others

Luxey
117km

Max. lead: 7:55

16

COL DU TOURMALET
2115m
65.5km

Loudonvielle
133.5km

15

Labrit
98.5km

Mont-de-Marsan
69.5km

Lau-Blagnas
99.5km

COL DE VAL LOURON-AZET
1580m
142.5km

Escartin attacks solo, Armstrong starts chase

Hagetmau
42km

Etxebarria takes sprint

Argelès-Gazost
101km

Piau-Engaly
1800m

Escartin wins solo

Break by eight riders, with Heulot, Vogels

Six-man attack

Pau

COL DU SOULOR
1474m
121.5km

With three men 4:40 ahead, Escartin counterattacks with Armstrong, Zülle

CÔTE D'ARTHEZ-DE-BÉARN
188m
15km

Gan
177km

Louvie-Juzon
161km

Mourenx

COL D'AUBISQUE
1709m
131km

Three joined by nine chasers, 3:00 ahead of pack

18   19   20

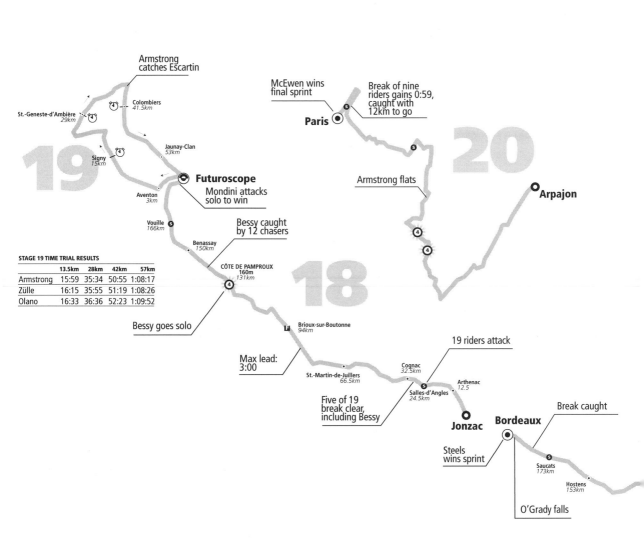

Armstrong catches Escartin

St.-Geneste-d'Ambière
29km

Colombiers
41.5km

Jaunay-Clan
53km

Signy
15km

Aventon
3km

Vouille
166km

19

Futuroscope
Mondini attacks solo to win

Bessy caught by 12 chasers

Benassay
150km

CÔTE DE PAMPROUX
160m
131km

18

Bessy goes solo

Brioux-sur-Boutonne
94km

Max lead: 3:00

St.-Martin-de-Juillers
66.5km

Five of 19 break clear, including Bessy

Cognac
32.5km

Salles-d'Angles
24.5km

Arthenac
12.5

19 riders attack

Jonzac

Steels wins sprint

Bordeaux

O'Grady falls

Break caught

Saucats
173km

Hostens
153km

McEwen wins final sprint

Break of nine riders gains 0:59, caught with 12km to go

Paris

20

Armstrong flats

Arpajon

STAGE 19 TIME TRIAL RESULTS				
	13.5km	28km	42km	57km
Armstrong	15:59	35:34	50:55	1:08:17
Zülle	16:15	35:55	51:19	1:08:26
Olano	16:33	36:36	52:23	1:09:52

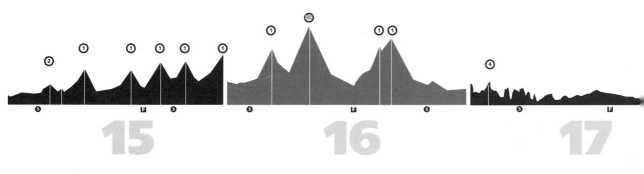

15

16

17

Bölts (G), Telekom, at 1:11:51; 41. Steve De Wolf (B), Cofidis, at 1:11:54; 42. Frédéric Bessy (F), Casino, at 1:15:26; 43. Miguel Peña (Sp), Banesto, at 1:19:26; 44. Laurent Madouas (F), Festina, at 1:20:42; 45. Geert Verheyen (B), Lotto-Mobistar, at1:23:24; 46. José Luis Arrieta (Sp), Banesto, at 1:24:29; 47. Francisco Cerezo (Sp), Vitalicio Seguros, at 1:26:50; 48. Bourguignon, at 1:27:43; 49. Manuel Fernandez Gines (Sp), Mapei-Quick Step, at 1:30:20; 50. Mariano Piccoli (I), Lampre-Daikin, at 1:31:21; 51. Lylian Lebreton (F), BigMat-Auber 93, at 1:32:51; 52. Robin (F), at 1:33:14; 53. Marco Fincato (I), Mercatone Uno-Bianchi, at 1:36:57; 54. Jon Odriozola (Sp), Banesto, at 1:41:55; 55. Marco Serpellini (I), Lampre-Daikin, at 1:42:04; 56. Michael Boogerd (Nl), Rabobank, at 1:42:22; 57. Fabian Jeker (Swi), Festina, at 1:42:25; 58. Rafael Diaz Justo (Sp) ONCE-Deutsche Bank, at 1:43:36; 59. José Gomez (Sp), Kelme-Costa Blanca, at 1:45:50; 60. Voigt, at 1:47:47; 61. Santos Gonzalez (Sp), ONCE-Deutsche Bank, at 1:48:21; 62. Dmitri Konyshev (Rus), Mercatone Uno-Bianchi, at 1:49:10; 63. Peter Farazijn (B), Cofidis, at 1:55:01; 64. Hernan Buenahora (Col), Vitalicio Seguros, at 1:55:33; **65. Andreu, at 1:59:01;** 66. Stefano Cattai (I), Team Polti, at 1:59:49; 67. Christophe Oriol (F), Casino, at 2:01:06; 68. Vicente Garcia-Acosta (Sp), Banesto, at 2:01:46; 69. Fabrice Gougot (F), Casino, at 2:02:05; 70. Christophe Mengin (F), La Française des Jeux, at 2:04:03; 71. Rik Verbrugghe (B), Lotto-Mobistar, at 2:04:31; 72. Marc Lotz (Nl), Rabobank, at 2:08:08; 73. Steffen Wesemann (G), Telekom, at 2:09:22; 74. Stéphane Goubert (F). Team Polti, at 2:10:58; 75. José Rebollo (Sp), ONCE-Deutsche Bank, at 2:12:57; 76. Prudencio Induráin (Sp), Vitalicio Seguros. at 2:14:15; 77. Laurent Brochard (F), Festina, at 2:14:42; **78. Hincapie, at 2:16:35;** 79. Christophe Rinero (F), Cofidis, at 2:16:35; 80. Jörg Jäksche (G), Telekom, at 2:16:44; 81. Gianpaolo Mondini (I), Cantina Tollo-Alexia, at 2:17:34; 82. Gilles Maignan (F), Casino. at 2:18:02; 83. Cédric Vasseur (F) Crédit Agricole, at 2:18:23; 84. Maarten Den Bakker (Nl) Rabobank, at 2:19:03; **85. Vande Velde, at 2:23:58;** 86. Javier Ochoa (Sp), Kelme-Costa Blanca, at 2:24:14; 87. Riccardo Forconi (I), Mercatone Uno-Bianchi, at 2:25:02; 88. Laurent Lefèvre (F) Festina, at 2:25:08; 89. Zabel, at 2:26:01; 90. Dominique Rault (F) BigMat-Auber 93, at 2:27:17; 91. Pascal Chanteur (F), Casino, at 2:28:00; 92. Aggiano, at 2:28:33; 93. Alexei Sivakov (Rus) BigMat-Auber 93, at 2:29:40; 94. O'Grady, at 2:30:07; 95. Massimo Giunti (I), Cantina Tollo-Alexia, at 2:30:25; 96. Thierry Gouvenou (F), BigMat-Auber 93, at 2:32:11; 97. Patrick Jonker (Aus), Rabobank, at 2:32:20; 98. David Navas (Sp), Banesto, at 2:33:31; 99. Fabio Sacchi (I), Team Polti, at 2:33:39; 100. Laurent Desbiens (F), Cofidis, at 2:34:01; 101. José Vidal (Sp), Kelme-Costa Blanca, at 2:34:22; 102. Jaime Hernandez (Sp), Festina, at 2:36:04; 103. Davide Bramati (I), Mapei-Quick Step, at 2:36:15; 104. Steels, at 2:36:28; 105. Anthony Morin (F) La Française des Jeux, at 2:36:37; 106. Frédéric Guesdon (F) La Française des Jeux. at 2:37:27; 107. Erik Dekker (Nl),

Rabobank, at 2:38:05; 108. Fabien De Waele (B), Lotto-Mobistar, at 2:39:21; 109. Beat Zberg (Swi), Rabobank, at 2:39:29; 110. Kai Hundertmarck (G), Telekom, at 2:39:32; 111. Ludovic Auger (F), BigMat-Auber 93, at 2:39:38; 112. Peter Wuyts (B), Lotto-Mobistar, at 2:39:50; 113. Marco Pinotti (I), Lampre-Daikin, at 2:40:00; 114. Silvio Martinello (I), Team Polti, at 2:43:14; 115. Christophe Capelle (F), BigMat-Auber 93. at 2:45:17; 116. Lars Michaelsen (Dk), La Française des Jeux , at 2:46:20; 117. Claude Lamour (F), Cofidis, at 2:46:26; 118. Rolf Huser (Swi), Festina, at 2:47:27; 119. Chris Boardman (GB), Crédit Agricole, at 2:47:48; 120. Mirco Crepaldi (I), Polti, at 2:49:14; 121. Henk Vogels (Aus). Crédit Agricole, at 2:49:17; 122. Robbie McEwen (Aus), Rabobank, at 2:49:23; 123. Sébastien Hinault (F), Crédit Agricole, at 2:51:03; 124. Sergio Barbero (I), Mercatone Uno-Bianchi, at 2:51:09; 125. Gabriele Colombo (I), Cantina Tollo-Alexia, at 2:51:43; 126. Carlos Da Cruz (F) BigMat-Auber 93. at 2:51:48; 127. Rossano Brasi (I), Polti, at 2:52:01; 128. Thierry Marichal (B), Lotto-Mobistar, at 2:54:06; 129. José De Los Angeles (Sp), Kelme-Costa Blanca, at 2:54:40; 130. Sébastien Demarbaix (B), Lotto-Mobistar, at 2:58:32; 131. Marcus Ljungqvist (S), Cantina Tollo-Alexia, at 3:00:09; 132. Anthony Langella (F), Crédit Agricole, at 3:02:20; 133. Bart Leysen (B), Mapei-Quick Step, at 3:03:11; 134. Massimiliano Napolitano (I), Mercatone Uno-Bianchi, at 3:05:09; 135. Pedro Horillo (Sp), Vitalicio Seguros, at 3:05:31; 136. Jan Schaffrath (G), Telekom, at 3:05:41; 137. Luca Mazzanti (I), Cantina Tollo-Alexia, at 3:06:28; 138. Alessandro Baronti (I), Cantina Tollo-Alexia, at 3:07:07; 139. Thierry Loder (F), Cofidis, at 3:11:55; 140. Pascal Deramé (F), U.S. Postal Service, at 3:14:19; 141. Jacky Durand (F), Lotto-Mobistar, at 3:19:09.

Points: 1. Zabel, 323pts; 2. O'Grady, 275; 3. Capelle, 196; 4. Steels, 188; 5. Simon, 186; 6. McEwen, 166; **7. Hincapie, 166**; 8. Mondini, 141; 9. Moreau, 140; 10. Martinello, 130.

King of the Mountains: 1. Virenque, 279pts; 2. Elli, 226; 3. Piccoli, 205; 4. Escartin, 194; **5. Armstrong, 193**; 6. Zülle, 152; 7. Arrieta, 141; 8. Dufaux, 141; 9. Peron, 138; 10. Van de Wouwer, 117.

Teams: 1. Banesto (Sp), 275:05:21; 2. ONCE-Deutsche Bank (Sp), at 8:16; 3. Festina (F), at 16:13; 4. Kelme-Costa Blanca (Sp), at 23:48; 5. Mapei-Quick Step (I), at 24:13; 6. Telekom (G), at 41:00; 7. Vitalicio Seguros (Sp), at 42:44; **8. U.S. Postal Service (USA), at 57:13**; 9. Cofidis (F), at 58:02; 10. Lotto-Mobistar (B), at 1:09:02.

Young riders: 1. Salmon, 92:01:15; 2. Aerts, at 10:22; 3. Garcia, at 16:32; 4. Mancebo, at 21:32; 5. Perez Rodriguez, at 23:54.

Most aggressive: 1. Durand, 61pts; 2. Heulot, 55; 3. Gouvenou, 51; 4. Morin, 46; 5. Simon, 42.

PART THREE

Reflections

Interviews with Tour winner Armstrong

PART I
July 24, 1999

THE LEADER OF THE TOUR DE FRANCE got to travel first class in 1999. He was whisked off a moutaintop by helicopter to his hotel, was given a personal camper van to change into clean clothes at stage finishes, and, on the morning of the Tour's final stage, was given the controls of one of France's 300-kph TGV express trains, during the transfer from Futuroscope to Arpajon.

After his session on the high-tech train's "flight deck," Lance Armstrong was as excited as a small boy who had just ridden a bicycle for the first time. All in all, he was having fun being the Tour leader, but not in an egotistical way. He may have been winning the world's biggest bike race because of his immense personal strength; but someone who has stared death in the face and come back—thanks to the vision, dedication and skill of a crack medical team—knows that teamwork is the only way to go.

In the TGV's first-class lounge, Armstrong was surrounded by the people who had help make it possible. Notably, there was the U.S. Postal Service directeur sportif Johan Bruyneel, who, Armstrong said, "is the one who presented the idea (of winning the Tour), and believed in it, the boss, from the beginning. His passion…his goals were contagious.

"Not only did he have the vision at the beginning, but the performance of the team speaks for itself. And the whole team, everybody raised their level. He's very organized."

While Bruyneel—a former top-10 Tour finisher and stage winner—had the vision and the organization skills, Armstrong provided the inspiration. It was the Texan's personality and leadership that not only focused everyone before the Tour on coming to their peak, both physically and mentally, but also inspired the Postal team to new heights during the race.

A typical Postal attitude was expressed by Kevin Livingston, who trains with Armstrong throughout the year. In 1998, he was Bobby Julich's first lieutenant at Cofidis; this year, he performed an even more impressive task for Armstrong. Unwilling to take praise, Livingston said, "That's the team, and feeding off each other, being in the lead.… It really does (make a difference) mentally. We rode at the front for three weeks. I never sat in the middle of the group for long, and if I did, I was nervous, because I wanted to be in the front, whether there's a crosswind or—I don't care if I get dropped; I want to be up there, I want to be playing a role with everybody."

With such team dedication in mind, Armstrong was asked if there was a moment that stood out emotionally more than any other, in terms of the team's togetherness. He replied, "No. This team, from the very beginning, was close.… There was not one fight, never one disagreement. Nobody ever raised their voice. The chemistry of the team (was ideal), with the variety of personalities—with a young kid like Christian (Vande Velde), with an older guy like Frankie (Andreu), with a quiet guy like George (Hincapie), with a crazy guy like Kevin (Livingston).…"

The other members of the squad to finish the Tour were Tyler Hamilton, who finished 13th overall despite two bad crashes (on stage 2 and stage 9); and Frenchman Pascal Deramé, who worked as hard as anyone, on the flats and in the mountains. The two teammates who did not finish were Jonathan Vaughters, who, had he not crashed out on stage 2's Passage du Gois, would have considerably helped ease the work load on Livingston and Hamilton in the mountains; and Danish veteran Peter Meinert-Nielsen, who played a big part in the team's first-week tempo sessions, before a knee injury forced him to abandon on stage 13.

So seven were still together on the TGV, as they headed toward Paris on July 25, with the end of their shared journey in sight. Armstrong, wearing small sunglasses that helped him focus his thoughts as much as combat the glare from press photographers' flashes, spoke with passion, pride and persuasiveness about the Tour...his Tour.

✯   ✯   ✯   ✯   ✯

"IT WAS A FANTASTIC THREE WEEKS," HE ENTHUSED. "I think the most emotional time, and the most surprising time, was the prologue. We all knew we were riding good, and *I* felt good. But to win and to take the (yellow) jersey, that was an emotional high. To put it in perspective, it was the only moment I cried in the three weeks. I think that says a lot."

His emotion was heightened because the prologue victory brought confirmation that all the hard work of the previous six months had been exactly on target. Following coach Chris Carmichael's counsel, Armstrong had focused on developing his power and his climbing ability. In May, there were the long training rides he made in the Alps, Pyrénées and Massif Central, covering all the Tour mountain stages. And every month, he did a time-trial test up the Col de la Madone, near his European home, in Nice.

At an interview earlier in the Tour, Armstrong revealed that in his last test up the 12km Madone climb, immediately before the Tour, he broke the unofficial hill record, riding it in 30:47, compared with the 31:30 of former Giro and Vuelta winner Tony Rominger. What's more, Armstrong's power output for that half-hour effort was 490 watts—right up there with Miguel Induráin.

Perhaps, then, it was not such a surprise that the Postal rider emulated Induráin's 1993 victory in the Tour prologue at Le Puy du Fou. But what few people knew is that Armstrong achieved his win *despite* being in pain from a scary crash 24 hours earlier.

It happened as Armstrong was riding a fast practice lap of the prologue course, with teammate Hincapie just behind him. Armstrong wanted to be at full speed when he reached the course's critical climb, right after a downhill right turn. There was a line of cars before the turn, but the Postal leader saw that the hill itself was clear and so he was riding hard, when a car—the Telekom No. 3 team car, driven by Frans Van Looy—pulled out from the line just at the moment Armstrong looked down to check his gearing.

"I was probably doing 55 k an hour," he recalled, "George was behind me, and (he shouted), '*Lance*!' As soon as I looked up, it was too late. When I saw him [Van Looy]—I had about half a second when he was turning into me—I thought, 'This is unbelievable.' I just smacked the side of the car, and went flying over the handlebars. I caught his mirror on my right ribs. It looked really *bad*. But because I had speed, when I hit the ground, I just slid. I really had no road rash, no cuts. I had discoloration, I had a little bruise on my ribs....

"I was sore for days. The next day, I was really sore all over.... I think when you have a moment like that, you automatically tense up so quickly and so intensely.... Everything with my arms and my back was *so* sore."

Sore or not, Armstrong won the prologue the next day, and then went through the Tour's remaining 3680km with never a hint of another crash. "I credit the team for that," Armstrong said, "because they always kept me out of trouble.... If it was windy, or if it was in a city where it was dangerous, they were always there." In fact, he said, he never saw one crash; and the only fallen rider he saw was Julich, in the Metz time trial.

That stage was the Tour's second turning point, with Julich being forced to abandon and Armstrong winning his second stage to claim back the yellow jersey from sprinter Jaan Kirsipuu of Casino. But while this win gave the American a two-minute margin over his main competition, he knew that the Tour was far from won. He knew that his biggest test—the Alps—lay ahead.

"Yes, there were a lot of questions before: 'Can he climb? Will he be dropped in the high mountains?'" Armstrong acknowledged. He made his reply on the stage over the Galibier to Sestriere—where he won again. "It was good to answer those questions," Armstrong continued. "I achieved that purpose there. And then to take extra time was also good...."

He perhaps understated his phenomenal victory at Sestriere, as that stage in left him with a seven-minute lead over eventual runner-up Alex Zülle of Banesto. Armstrong's teammates Livingston and Hamilton played a big part in helping their leader prepare for that stage-winning coup—his final attack being reminiscent of the pre-cancer Armstrong, on climbs like the Ben-Ahin and Mur de Huy in his 1996 Flèche Wallonne victory, and his winning attacks in various Tours DuPont on the Beech Mountain and Mountain Lake climbs.

Armstrong wasn't called upon to make another violent effort until the spectacular Pyrenean stage to Piau-Engaly, when Fernando Escartin of Kelme-Costa Blanca made his impressive solo attack on the Val Louron-Azet ascent. With the Spaniard's lead approaching three minutes, Armstrong knew that he needed to do something to take control of the situation.

"Kevin and Tyler had pulled the whole way," Armstrong recalled, "and the only people that were left were really (Richard) Virenque and (Laurent) Dufaux and Zülle, and they didn't seem to be going after Escartin. So I didn't want it to be four, and then five (minutes)...you never know with things like that. So I wanted to keep the gap in check...."

This explains the race leader's first attack of that stage; but what about the other one, at the foot of the final climb to Piau-Engaly? About 10km from the summit, Armstrong went hard, dropped all the other contenders, and appeared to be on his way to closing the gap on Escartin. Why did he make the move when he did?

"Johan thought it was a good time to go, because the others again were not really riding. So he just said, 'Go now.' To him [Bruyneel], I looked like I was feeling good. But I went too early. I suffered...."

That was probably the only time in the race that the instant radio communication between Bruyneel and Armstrong was counter-productive. Left to his own devices, the American would probably have waited until he was feeling better before making the move. As it was, Zülle and Virenque caught back, and then left him behind in the final half-kilometer.

Armstrong put down his slight setback to a combination of hunger knock "and the other attack on that other climb. That was a hard attack. On a day like that, especially in the third week, you only have a couple of those and they really take it out of you. That day, I was still feeling the attacks from Sestriere. Those efforts.... You have to be careful with those efforts, though I gained a lot of experience in that sense: Now I know that if I feel good like that, and I'm gonna make attacks like that, I have to be very careful when and where I do that...."

☆   ☆   ☆   ☆   ☆

FATIGUED FROM RIDING SO HARD ON THE STAGE, Armstrong didn't need the incident that followed the finish at Piau-Engaly: A French TV reporter ran after the *maillot jaune* to show him the now-infamous *Le Monde* article, which claimed that Armstrong had tested positive for corticoids. "I was so tired, I had no idea what he was taking about," Armstrong recalled, "but I didn't care. I was tired, at the end of the day. I was really, really tired...."

That moment and the ensuing 24 hours, said an emotional Armstrong, marked his psychological low point of the Tour.

"He called me a liar," stated the Texan, who was at a loss for words until he added, "What can I do? I think we all know what they were trying to do. It's complete rubbish. It's desperate, sensational, vulture journalism...." Armstrong did not say anything to the media about the claims in *Le Monde* until a press conference the next day in Pau. "I had nothing to hide, so...I wanted to get through that day, and I wanted to get to the finish, and then explain myself," he said. "I knew if I got into Pau that *once again* I would appear...and they can ask as many questions as they want. I would have done it every day."

What Armstrong explained was that the trace of corticoids in his urine sample the day after the prologue came from a topical skin cream. When did he use the cream?

"I've had these saddle sores since the first training camp in the Pyrénées, because it was raining every day, and we were training so much," Armstrong said. "At the start of the Tour—it actually got a little bit better during the Tour—I had, not a *saddle* sore, but just a scar-tissue cyst underneath here. It was large. It was killing me. So I used it [the cream] sporadically the whole time. And it's gotten smaller. But I've never really sat on the bike comfortably this Tour, because you can't go in there and really do anything for it. You can't really drain it, or cut it open in the middle of the race."

The Pau press conference came at the end of another difficult mountain stage, over the Tourmalet, Soulor and Aubisque climbs. On his bike, Armstrong acted like the true *patron* of the Tour, matching Escartin's attacks, and then working hard in the eventual 12-man break—even though he had no need.

When asked why he was so active in the break, Armstrong replied, "He [Escartin] asked me to work. He's a good friend of mine, and I respect him a lot. He asked if I would work and help out, and I knew he wanted to get away from Dufaux and Virenque. And so.... "Obviously, I have the complete right to sit on and do nothing; but if you're the *maillot jaune*, I think you have a responsibility to show yourself, and show your strength, and to be involved."

Then, toward the end of that stage, the American chatted with Zülle. What did the Swiss say? "He said he was nearly dropped when Escartin was going (hard) on the Soulor.... Yeah, he was going very hard. And I was.... The last kilometer of the Soulor was the most I suffered at any time."

Armstrong then explained why it was so hard: "You'll notice that on all the climbs, I sat down the whole time and spun a small gear. That's all we did in training this year, always sat down, always *souplesse*, always high cadence. And when I need to stand up and go big gear, I can. So on the Soulor I stood up the whole time, pushed a big gear [39x19 and 39x17].... The Soulor is pretty steep at the end."

☆ ☆ ☆ ☆ ☆

WITH HIS STRENGTH IN THE MOUNTAINS, LEADERSHIP OF HIS TEAM, magnanimity with his rivals, and a no-nonsense approach to the media, Armstrong emerged from the Tour enormously popular with the crowds. But most of all, of course, he was a hero because he had fought back from a terrible cancer to conquer the Tour de France.

When he was lying in a hospital bed in Indianapolis, undergoing one of those intensive bouts of chemotherapy, did he ever think about riding again? "I didn't think about racing...but with the chemo, the anti-nausea drugs, it's so *hard* to think. I had a difficult time reading...watching TV...listening, speaking.... No, I never thought about it. I was just a little scared...a lot scared at times...and I just wanted to get better."

Armstrong then remembered, during his periods at home between the chemotherapy sessions, how hard it was even to ride a bike, let alone think about training. "Maybe I did too much sometimes," he said. Then he remembered one particular ride with his friend and fellow Austin resident, Livingston: "I had to get off and lie in a yard, I was so.... After 30 minutes (riding), I was just wasted...completely exhausted...almost like deadish. I shouldn't have been there.... They were scared. Kevin was ready to get a car. But...I rode home, just needed a little rest."

Just over two years later, this man the media dubbed the "miracle man" was standing atop the Tour de France podium, after one of the most dominating performances in the race's storied history. As Armstrong stood there in Paris, his head bared, his hand on his heart, listening to the stirring sound of a military band playing *The Star Spangled Banner*, his almost-gaunt face reflected pride in his team, joy for his mother Linda and wife Kristin...and, most of all, the pain and suffering he had fought through to reach this ultimate achievement in his sport.

Armstrong himself summed up his contrasting emotions as the TGV train neared the end of its journey. "It's beyond belief," he said. "It's just a win, win, win, win, win—for everybody. It's a win for me, it's a win for you, it's a win for cancer, it's a win for my team, it's a win for cycling in America, it's a win for the Tour de France, it's a win for humanity. And I don't take credit for any of it.

"I take credit for 5 percent of it, if that. I give all my credit to my doctors, to my team, to Johan, to the sponsors, to my family.... Hey, I really didn't do that much. I trained hard, but without those other folks, there's no way.... You can't win the Tour without a team, and I couldn't win the Tour without Kristin always being supportive, and Johan having the belief, and the sponsors being supportive, and the doctors saving my life. It's been fantastic. This win's for them."

✮   ✮   ✮   ✮   ✮

ARMSTONG'S MODESTY IS A CHARACTERISTIC THAT HAS BLOSSOMED since he was diagnosed with cancer. When he was younger, he was much more extrovert. For instance, at the 1993 world championships in Oslo, Norway, he celebrated his victory all the way along the finish straight, punching the air, blowing kisses to the crowd, repeatedly thrusting his arms into the air, and whooping with joy. In contrast, when he crossed the line in Sestriere to take this Tour's first mountain stage, he simply raised his arms once and barely cracked a smile. He now likes his celebrations to be more private.

Asked about the plans being made to greet him on his return home to Austin, Texas, in early August, he said, "I don't like the big attention. I prefer for it to be kind of quiet, but I understand. Austin has been fantastic, and they've all been following it...watching the coverage and having a good time."

But he *was* looking forward to the celebrations in Paris at the end of this final day at the Tour. "Today will be special for us, yeah," said Armstrong, referring to himself and his team. "The Champs-Elysées...and to have all my family there, and all my friends...Kristin's family, my Mom. Crazy...."

Friends and family rank high on the Tour champion's list of priorities, and they will continue to play a big part in his future plans. "I want to race as long as my family is comfortable, and Kristin's comfortable," he said. 'I'll race as long as I am at a high level, as long as its *fun.*

"And, can I win the Tour de France again? I don't know. I have no idea. Every year's different, and next year the course will be different, and the riders will be different, but I'm not old...."

Armstrong then returned to an earlier remark about his being the same age as the Spanish star Miguel Induráin when he won the first of his five consecutive Tours de France. He asked, "Is it true that Induráin, when he won his first Tour, that he was 27?"

"Yes" was the answer, "27, 28, 29, 30, 31—five years. And he retired when he was 32."

"Hmmm," Armstrong contemplated. "Well, we'll see...."

PART II

August 15, 1999

Even when sitting across a pine dining table demolishing a bowl of wheat flakes, Lance Armstrong has an intensity in his blue-grey eyes that makes you want to believe in miracles. He openly says that his recovery from cancer was a miracle, and you believe him. Asked if he is aware of that when he's racing, the cropped-haired Texan says, "I'm always aware of what I've been through—a hard time trial, a hard part of a race—always. When I say always, on a daily basis…. And I'm so involved in the community that I still have dear friends that are living that life; and the foundation is such a big part of my life…."

The honesty of Armstrong also compels him to add: "You know, if I chose to put it all behind me. To never have a charity, to never talk to patients, never deal with patients, never work with patients, then I might not think about it."

He then retells a story about a recent invitation he had to go on a golfing trip with the chairman of the Lance Armstrong Foundation, Geoff Garvey. "He said it was October 1st, 2nd and 3rd. I said, good, I'd love to go. Let me just run it past Kristin. I didn't even think about it. Then she looked at the calendar…. You know, October 2nd is the most monumental day in my life. It didn't even register. And when she saw in a second that it was the anniversary [of his cancer diagnosis]. She said of course you can't go golfing then. So I called back Garvey…."

"So I think the potential for me to forget about it all is there. But I don't want to forget about it."

Armstrong is remembering these things in a relaxed, hour-long interview that has a late start. Arriving 15 minutes early for the appointment didn't make any difference. On answering the tap on the front door, dressed in a loose, plain grey T-shirt and baggy shorts, Armstrong said, "You caught me off-guard. I'm on a phone interview with *Interview* magazine. Can you come back at 9:30?"

"No problem."

After all, it's a peaceful Monday morning in Vail Village. A Rocky Mountain high. There's just a hint of autumn in the calm, clear air, which accentuates the closeness of pine-covered Vail Mountain's summer-green ski slopes. A bright sun pierces a cloud-dappled sky, casting deep shadows on Gore Creek that flows swiftly between kitschy Bavarian-style inns and tony Rodeo Drive-style boutiques. The scene is so perfect that just below the Armstrongs' fourth-floor condominium, a city employee removes the dead blooms from a flower bed with a pair of scissors. It's as if the whole town is being manicured.

Certainly, for Lance and Kristin Armstrong, this is the perfect place to wind down, after the post-Tour de France whirligig they've been living through. They seem at home in their borrowed condo. Armstrong's road and mountain bikes lean against a wall, next to a window overlooking the village square. A detailed map of the area sits on the table, with some trails marked on it that morning by an earlier visitor, local off-road guru Mike Kloser.

The Armstrongs have even brought along their tiny furball of a dog named Boone, who jumps up and down and yelps when the journalist arrives back at 9:30. "Pick him up," asks Armstrong, who's still on the phone with the writer from *Interview*, coaching her through the ins and outs of the Tour de France. Eventually, he's free.

"How long has it been since the Tour's over?" Armstrong asks, wearily stifling a yawn, "A month?"

Then, when he's reminded that the Tour finished just three weeks ago, he sits up alertly and exclaims, "Shit … noooo, it's been longer than that!"

No, it's just that all he has done in the previous 22 days makes it seem like a lot, lot longer.

Take the day of talk shows he endured on national TV. Was he terrified of facing those cameras all day long? "No," Armstrong answers, already scooping the last drops of milk from the cereal bowl. "The *Today Show,* and things like that, I'd done in the past. There's nothing to be terrified about. You just get up there and answer the questions…just answer them honestly. Letterman was a little nerve-wracking, 'cause you never know where that's gonna go. I'd never done anything like Letterman or Leno…. Letterman was really nice. He's a cool guy."

As he pushes the bowl to one side and focuses on two slices of toast he's just made, Armstrong says, "All this stuff has happened so fast, and we've just been going from place to place to place, I don't have a lot of time to get nervous before these things. I don't know…."

He takes a swig of thick orange juice before saying, "The White House was interesting because I'm not…."

Then, under his breath, he says, "*How* shall I say this?"

A long moment passes before he gathers his thoughts and continues: "I mean, I'm not….

I don't agree with a lot of the stuff Bill Clinton's done. But it was interesting to meet him and to be around him and feel what he's like, his air. You can see that he's very charismatic and a really smart guy. And its great to meet the President. Come on, it's good for everybody.

"Interesting to be there.... So much news has been made about these rooms in the last 18 months.... And you meet Betty Currie...Buddy the dog. Weird things like that.

"Clinton was into it, though. He was really excited. We gave him a bike, a helmet, a (yellow) jersey...."

Whether in Washington, Austin, Vail or New York, Armstrong remarked about the number of people who had watched him on TV at the Tour de France. "I've noticed a difference," he said, comparing his present "fame" with how he was regarded before his Tour win. "It's not like I'm a Sean Connery walking around. But you can see people have paid attention. It's pretty neat. And they've all been respectful...really nice.

"Even in New York City—that was my first time back in the United States—I didn't know people had paid attention. Just random people. A big fire truck drives by with four or five New York City firefighters inside when I'm standing outside the hotel, and the next thing you know all five guys are hanging outside the fire truck going crazy: 'Lance, you're the man!' And I'm like, wait a minute, who are they talking to? They're talking to a different Lance...."

Like those New Yorkers, Armstrong has a seemingly permanent high energy level. After finishing his toast, he sits back and starts to drum the table with his fingers. Asked whether he will attend the upcoming Interbike trade show in Las Vegas, he says, "I won't go to the show very much...it's just too exhausting," adding that he will make just one public appearance, "just for Giro. The other (sponsors) are doing receptions and parties."

"I'll be playing a lot of golf, though," he adds with a laugh. "I'm bringing my mountain bike and my golf clubs."

But to Vail, he has brought only his bikes. "I didn't want to bring my clubs, because I knew I wouldn't ride my bike then," he explains.

And he knows he has to ride the bike to prepare himself for his two appearances for the Trek-Volkswagen mountain-bike team: Vermont's Mount Snow, coming up in four days, followed a week later by Colorado's Mercury Tour at Steamboat Springs. This is the third day into Armstrong's Vail sojourn, and he already has been busy. His four-hour road ride on Saturday included the 11,000-foot Fremont Pass; and yesterday, after being informed that there was a mountain-bike race in nearby Winter Park, he decided to show up.

How did it feel riding a mountain bike for the first time in seven months? "The altitude was hard," he says. "And any descent—even if it's straightforward for these guys—was hard for me. Yesterday's course was supposed to be not real difficult, with a lot of pedaling, a lot of fire roads. But they had so much rain, and they changed the course a little bit that it ended up being really rooty, and rocky, and slippery."

Armstrong's wife Kristin, momentarily massaging his neck, says, "He finished covered in mud. His face was all black, except for his smile. He looked so cute." She doesn't say that her husband tried to jump across a knee-deep creek on his bike, with the inevitable consequences.

Smiling again, the Tour de France champion continues, "My mechanic for the mountain-bike team, Scott Daubert—who was the one who told me about it Saturday night—said, 'You'll like it. It's easy. It's one of my favorite courses, and it's fast. It's great for you.' So I said, 'Okay, great, I'll do it.' And I got out there, and I thought if *he* thinks this is easy…. He called me after the race, and said, 'Oh man, I'm so sorry. They changed the course.' Everybody there thought it was a lot like Mount Snow—the roots and the slipperiness."

Doing a tough off-road race wasn't in Armstrong's original plans: "I didn't want to do anything hard for the first four days getting here, because I thought that would be detrimental. I knew the race would be hard, but I thought it would be better for me if I had a local race under my belt for Mount Snow. Instead of going to Mount Snow and not having done a race since Park City (in 1998)—I would have been soooo nervous. So now having done this, and especially being able to ride at the front [he finished second to Jimi Killen] and do the technical stuff easier than I thought I would, I'll feel a lot more comfortable at Mount Snow."

The conversation turns to Europe, and to Armstrong's statement after enduring a media grilling at the Tour on "doping" allegations that he was not going to live in France anymore. Is that true? "No, we're going to stay in France for now. Primarily because we're just having the baby, and to go back would be too hard. But the first day there's any problems—whether it's the tax man or the CRS (police) invading our privacy—we're leaving the very next day, baby or no baby, the whole family. Leaving. It's not worth it. Kristin couldn't live some place knowing they just come and break down your door, invade your privacy like that. The French are an envious breed…and that's unsettling.

"I mean, our neighbors, and everybody in Nice is great. The mayor's nice, and supportive. But you never know. And that's unsettling. When we're in Austin, I *know* that we have our peace and privacy. That's our right. But in Nice, we don't have that.

"No, we're gonna stay there. We love our house; the training's fantastic there; and I don't know where we would go if we left. Everyone's there. Kevin's there, Frankie's there.

It's got everything—airport, weather, training, teammates, great house, great neighbors. We have our haunts, favorite restaurants…they're all nice. It's a real community there. We'd feel funny leaving. So we're staying for now."

Living and training in Nice was certainly a contribution to Armstrong's successful 1999 Tour de France. Asked if the Tour will again be his focus in 2000, he replies, "We'll do just what we did this year. Once they announce the course, then we'll have a better idea about how we'll prepare. But we'll do the same thing—do all the training camps, go and see the time-trial courses, completely go out of our way to learn it… robably run into some guys out there now (that they know what I did this year).

"That was a big advantage…having ridden these courses start to finish. Everybody knows the climbs. They see the profiles…. But to go there and actually start in a place and finish in the finish places, is different."

In his reconnaissance trips this year, did he go hard on a finish such as Sestriere, where he would win the stage a couple of months later?

"No, rode easy. The problem with that stage was that the Galibier was closed at the top. So I rode by bike up the Galibier and turned around and came back down…. And the next day we drove to Briançon, and did Montgenèvre and Sestriere, and just went easy because it was the day after the Galibier. And it was snowing at Sestriere. It was dumping snow…a blizzard. Two degrees…..

"Both camps, we had bad weather. Not one day was nice. The first camp in the Pyrénées, the first day we were going to ride to Piau-Engelay, and it was raining…cold. Johan (Bruyneel) said, 'No, you can't get out in this. We'll just drive.' We started to drive part of the course, and I said, 'Stop the car. Let me out. This is ridiculous.' So I rode the rest of the way. He couldn't believe it, thought I was crazy.

"But it's great when you have a car, with spare clothes. I wasn't cold once. And we'll do all that again."

Still tapping his fingers on the table, Armstrong details his upcoming program. "I'm not really going to stop training (this year), riding both my road bike and mountain bike in the off-season. Do less riding in October, but November, December, I have to train. I can't stop."

Is he afraid of putting on weight? "I don't know about that. I already put on weight since the Tour. Because I like to eat. Weight's important. I was heavy at the beginning of (the 1999) season. I put on 10 pounds at least in the winter. Maybe more. But if that happens, you have to start training earlier.

"When you do these camps in May, you have to be so serious then. Two months is not a lot of time. I can safely lose 2 kilos (4.4 pounds) a month. Even then, that would be hard.

You'd be hungry, and you've got to train a lot. It's better not to get in that position. It's easy to say that now, but we'll see in January."

Armstrong said in 1996, before he was diagnosed with cancer, that he knew that he would have to lose weight if he were going to challenge at the Tour. His subsequent bouts of chemotherapy caused him to lose muscle depth, particularly in his upper body; but that wasn't the only reason for his slimmed-down, on-the-edge body we all saw at the Tour de France. Knowing he put on about 12 pounds last winter, was it really hard to take off the weight?

"Yeah. You just have to go and be in a deficit. You're hungry...."

How does he cope with that?

"You realize it's what you have to do. You think about the alternative. If you satisfy your hunger with a big snack or a candy bar, it's not going to do you any good in July. I was more serious about my diet this year than ever before. That was one of the biggest differences. I weighed food, yeah, ask Kristin. That's the only way you can get an exact measurement. You have to weigh the cereal, your pasta, your bread, everything. Absolutely. Got a little digital scale."

He turns to his wife and says, "Hey, Keek? Weighing the food?"

"Those were serious times," she agrees. "Have to add up everything (you eat), then calculate all your output to make sure. I mean, he was like a mathematician with the calculator every day. It was crazy, but it worked."

Armstrong then explains, "I also shifted around my training. I would leave later, ride through lunch, only eat twice a day. I'd eat a satisfying breakfast, so I'd be full and could go training an hour or so later, and just go for six or seven hours. If I left at 11, I'd get back at 5 or 6. Maybe, sometimes, I'd have a little smoothie afterwards, a protein thing, but then you can almost go straight into dinner. And then you go to bed early because you're tired from training.

"This was in May and June; at all the camps I did that. At both camps I lost weight, because there was so much riding. Gained form, and lost weight."

Another element of Armstrong's success was converting from a big-gear to a low-gear climber. "You know, that SRM really helped a lot," he says, pointing to the power meter computer fixed to the bars of his road bike, "because it has cadence on it. In the past I never knew what 80 rpm or 100 rpm were. I had no idea. I had the gear, had the heart rate, and had the speed, and went with what was comfortable. To have a constant indication of what your rpm is, is totally different. There are times when you're doing a climb and you think I'm really spinning, and you look down and you're doing 75 rpm.

And you're not (spinning). That's a big gear. That helped a lot."

So what rpm was he aiming at for the climbs?

"At least 90. But that depends how steep the climb is. When you start to ride better, you can ride faster and spin a higher gear. Like in a lot of the time trials I was doing over 100."

Working out is also on Kristin Armstrong's mind at this point. She comes across to kiss her husband good-bye and asks, "What time are you going to work?" She's referring to a long mountain-bike training ride he has planned. He says that the ride will start at 11. He'll be back at 3. As his wife heads out, Armstrong asks, "Can you put some more toast on there? I'm hungry."

He'll soon be removing two slices from the toaster, spreading them with cream cheese, and then making a circular pattern with the honey squirter. He's not weighing his food at this point, but knows that he'll soon burn up those calories—and he'll skip lunch.

He continues with his exposé on his climbing style. "We had two-way radio transmission even at the training camps this year. Johan would say, 'High gear, in the saddle.' In the past, I would always stand up, climb out of the saddle. This year, in the saddle. At training camp, every climb, in the saddle, regardless. If it meant I went slow, or if it meant I suffered more, if it meant I get dropped by the other guys, doesn't matter. Just stay on the saddle."

Armstrong warms to a subject whenever he gets talking about it. And so the conversation continues. When it comes time to get ready for his ride, he still wants to talk. He says that in late September, he's going fishing with Oakley's Mike Parnell to Canada, probably Vancouver Island. "It's good to get away," he says. "They catch some big fish up there, apparently. You can fish inland in the rivers and streams, fly fishing for salmon, or you can fish out in the ocean for big fish., halibut or whatever. I'm not a fanatical fisherman, but...."

"Then October, we're having the baby, and October, November, December, I'll try to relax."

The pressure of being a Tour winner is something new. Armstrong is now one of the big fish. He seems to be coping with it well. He enjoys his life, enjoys his cycling. And as he shakes the hand of the journalist on his way out, those intense eyes have the look of a man who knows where he's going. Now it's time for a bike ride....

Lance Armstrong
and the cancer patients

COLLEEN CAN LIGHT UP A ROOM like a torch, and her conversation on this cool March day kindles with warmth and hope like the Olympic flame. The topics bouncing back and forth between the six people standing rather comfortably in this nearly closet-sized room have a foundation in unabashed sincerity. This scene could be anywhere—at the park, a local coffee shop or someone's kitchen. The electrical charge in the air feels like the pulse of endearing friendships that have survived the ages. It's nothing short of uplifting. It's real. It's life.

The conversation swings from Colleen's work in public relations for a large computer software company, to Rick's trip up from the Silicon Valley, to Larry's studies at the local community college, to Lance's typical-Texas-diet that always has, and always will, include a couple more Shiner Bocks than one might expect. Sometimes the topic slams head-on into the tie that binds this eclectic group.

This is no coffee shop, it is Oregon Health Services University where Dr. Craig Nichols presides as the resident urological cancer expert. The small room is a bright sanitary white examining room. Colleen sits on the edge of the examination table. She pulls off her baseball cap to show her hair is thinning, but certainly not surrendering to her chemotherapy treatments, which are only half completed. Rick's enthusiasm for surviving the past year since his treatments ended pours from his heart with a revelation that the experience has changed him forever, for the good. He's more aggressive in life, his horizons have expanded and, the ups and downs carry powerful motivating emotion. Colleen's husband chuckles. "She's already aggressive enough," he says. The other rather aggressive personality in the room simply smiles and listens, very comfortable as he watches the spotlight land elsewhere. Lance Armstrong's survival clock now reads 2 years 6 months—halfway to the magical five-year mark that stands as the unofficial stay of execution. Cancer has changed Armstrong in a different way. His aggressiveness hasn't waned. His perspective has waxed.

THE CLOCK MOVES SWIFTLY TOWARD 10:30 A.M. Armstrong hasn't put anything in his stomach this morning except for the 32 ounces of a barium mixture that lit up his insides for a CT Scan an hour earlier. This is one of two biannual exams for Armstrong, when Dr. Nichols checks on progress with a barrage of tests—blood work, CT Scan, chest X-rays and a physical. But the tests make up only a fraction of Armstrong's visit. There is always someone new to meet or some old acquaintance to catch up with. It's all part of Armstrong's new family, and he fits right in like a strong-willed older brother who knows when to speak up and when to listen.

"With cancer you immediately become part of this huge new family," Armstrong says. "It's immediate. Suddenly there are all these new people, new friends, new advisers—a whole new family. It's really something special."

Armstrong says that the impromptu meeting in Dr. Nichols's office isn't standard fare, but it does represent the kind of relationships cancer survivors forge. Armstrong met Rick a while back, but Colleen and Larry were introduced to him that morning. The same scenario occurred a few minutes earlier with the nephew of a famous rock 'n' roll star, whose presence created a bigger clamor than Armstrong's. They hadn't met before. It didn't matter. The connection was immediate.

"You won't find a couple of survivors sitting around talking about the weather and box scores," Armstrong says, "unless they've been sitting around talking for a long, long time."

Dr. Nichols finally breaks up the chat session. Colleen needs to start her treatments. Rick needs to head home. Larry's ready for a checkup. And Armstrong needs something to eat.

WITH A CUP OF COFFEE, SCONE AND CINNAMON ROLL IN HAND, Armstrong heads across the OSHU complex that is nestled on a hillside overlooking Portland. Most of the green hills were covered with blackberries back in 1978 when Nichols graduated from medical school here. Nichols forged his powerful reputation most recently at Indiana University, where he treated Armstrong. But Nichols got a chance to come home, so Armstrong followed Nichols for his checkups. Armstrong believes Nichols saved his life. It's obvious in their interaction.

Armstrong pauses in the lobby of the Mark O. Hatfield research center to take a cellular phone call, and then tells the story of Rick. Like a lot of the members of Armstrong's new family, he met Rick through e-mail. Rick was diagnosed with testicular cancer. He was two days away from surgery to remove both testes. He was looking for support.

"I'm no doctor, but having both testes removed sounded radical to me," Armstrong says, "so I told him to contact Dr. Nichols."

Rick celebrated his one-year anniversary with both his testes intact, and cancer on the run.

ARMSTRONG IS NO DOCTOR, BUT HIS KNOWLEDGE OF CANCER RUNS DEEP. As he sits in the office earlier that morning drinking his barium solution, which tastes like watered-down fruit punch-flavored cough medicine, Armstrong and Nichols chat like two cancer-fighting colleagues, not patient-doctor. Armstrong asks about the treatment of fellow cyclist Ernie Lechuga, who was diagnosed in November. As soon as Armstrong got word of the young Southern Californian's fate, his foundation got involved. That involvement saved the day for Lechuga. Armstrong and Nichols hope it saves more than that.

Nichols is the key man in Armstrong's foundation. He has brought on experts from around the world. The foundation has lofty goals. It awarded $300,000 in research grants before its one-year anniversary. Just like his cycling career, Armstrong shoots for the moon. He refuses to be only a figurehead. And that means weekly teleconference calls. Armstrong can't sit back and let others run the show. It's not his nature.

"Never has been," Armstrong says as he thinks back to his strong-willed childhood, "never will be."

STILL, THE MAN WHO HAS SEEMINGLY DEFEATED PAIN AND AGONY time and again on his bicycle to achieve scintillating results can become peloton fodder in the presence of his greatest enemy. Dressed in a hospital gown, Armstrong lies alone on the table at the mouth of the CT Scanner. His arms stretch over his head, so as not to obscure the view of his innards. His feet squirm nervously. The lights go dim. Technicians leave the room. Armstrong is one-on-one with his fate.

"A lot of things race through your mind," says Armstrong, who loses the aura of all-American world champion in his gown and becomes just another patient fighting for life. "You can't help but have doubt pop into you mind. You wonder why there's a long pause, or why are they talking in the other room. Last time I was here, the technician came back in (after seeing the X-rays) and asked, 'When do your treatments start?' I told him he'd have to ask my doctor about that…. There are still some scar tissues that show up. They don't know that, though. It helps to know what's going on, that's why I ask a lot of questions. I can read my chest X-ray as well as any doctor. Same for blood work results. I think you have to know."

BACK IN THE OFFICE, NICHOLS POPS ARMSTRONG'S X-RAYS into the hanging light displays. Armstrong moves in for a closer look. "Looks good, very good," says Nichols. Then he points to areas here, and there, and there again, where blots the size of golf balls appeared in X-rays during Armstrong's battle. "They were everywhere," Armstrong says.

Blessed with a clean bill of health, Armstrong can get on with his professional life. His goals are hefty for 1999. As he prepares for an assault on the Tour de France, Armstrong will shoulder a burden that most riders won't. Each night, Armstrong will log onto the Internet and check his e-mail. He gets 40-50 messages a week through his address at his foundation's Web site, http://www.LAF.com. There are always messages to respond to, and he responds quickly and, always, from the heart.

"It's just something that I do now," Armstrong says. "With my cycling, my wife, the foundation—my life is just crazy now. Crazy."

Armstrong understands that crazy can be a relative term.

"Sometimes all I need to do is send a little note of encouragement," Armstrong says. "But sometimes…the other night I had to send a note to the family of a kid who didn't make it. What do you say? I wrote just three or four lines, but it's really hard to know what to say. But I don't mind that challenge. I really don't. And it's not a distraction at all. I'd go crazy now if all I did was train and eat and sleep. I just love it."

ARMSTRONG JUMPS IN THE CAR AND HEADS TO NIKE HEADQUARTERS, where he a couple of meetings about cycling shoes await. Then another dinner. Then a red-eye home to see his wife Kristin. Cancer hasn't slowed Armstrong down, on or off the bike. And when he combines the two, they deliver a staggering blow like one of his patented attacks on Philadelphia's Manayunk Wall. Folks like Colleen, Rick and Larry follow

Armstrong's escapades through a clipping service. His actions fuel their fight. "My friend told me after I'm done with treatments I should consider a career in bicycle racing," says the rock-star nephew, drawing a laugh from Armstrong. The idea that his accomplishments motivate fellow cancer patients is uplifting, but now Armstrong aims his periscope at another audience.

"The message about cancer is changing," Armstrong says. "It used to be that message came from family and friends of someone who lost the battle. But that message has a new face now. It is the face of survivors. We are telling the story now. And that makes it more meaningful."

$$\star \quad \star \quad \star \quad \star \quad \star$$

Ann Arbor, Michigan
July 1999

THE MORNING LIGHT SNEAKS past the curtains and casts an angelic light across the perfect, hairless head settled comfortably on a pillow, its infant-like features emphasizing the peaceful sleep of Jim and Pam Nieters's baby. Anders Nieters is not really a baby, though, and his room shares the homey features that decorate many a 14-year-old's private digs. His carbon-fiber Giant CFR Three stands close to his bed, locked into its wind trainer awaiting its next adventure, just below the University of Michigan cap that has a couple of autographs and numbers scribbled across it. Above Anders's bed hang the most valuable treasures: a pink Giro d'Italia leader's jersey with the distinctive Saeco emblem across the front and the signature of Ivan Gotti jumping out from the bright background, right next to the U.S. Postal Service jersey with Frankie Andreu's John Hancock visible from across the room.

Anders's sleep is sound—sound enough that Jim carries on a conversation just a few feet away. He can't speak in whispers because of the roar of the air filtration device the size of a typical water heater that sits just a few feet from Anders's bed, cleaning the air of any wandering germs. The sound, more than anything, breaks the normalcy of the scene, and tends to focus attention on the intravenous tree that towers next to the bed, with a few plastic tubes draping down and disappearing under the sheet where Anders is tucked into a fetal position.

Anders is not in his home. He hasn't been for much of the past four months. Anders is at Mott Children's Hospital in Ann Arbor, Michigan, which has been his home away from home almost exclusively since St. Patrick's Day. It was just before noon on March 17 that results of some blood work came back and finally, conclusively, isolated the cause of Anders's malaise. The swollen glands that started a cause for concern three weeks earlier, the neck ache that was followed by periods of loss of coordination that was followed by the sores in his mouth, were not mononucleosis as suspected. No, Anders was diagnosed with AML leukemia, a form of leukemia that strikes just 20 percent of leukemia cases and is much tougher to treat than the other forms. Two hours later, Anders, Jim and Pam were in a room at Mott, absorbing the impact of cancer full force.

Halfway across the world on that day, recovery was the challenge for Lance Armstrong. Not his recovery from testicular cancer, although a day doesn't pass that it doesn't cross Armstrong's mind. No, Armstrong had just finished the eight-day Paris-Nice bicycle race, taking it on as nothing more than a training ride. He was recuperating from a number of spring mishaps that could have undermined his unrelenting focus on the Tour de France. But time would prove that the miscues were nothing more than a bump in the road.

Physicists say that time isn't the linear entity most folks on the street believe it is. Whether or not you embrace that theory makes no difference. Linear or not, there is one truth about time: For mere human beings, it represents opportunity. Time is something everyone has. Some, pessimists say, have more time than others. The optimists know that any amount is plenty.

Fast-forwarding ahead to this sultry Sunday, July 25, 1999, Anders and Armstrong are again separated by thousands of miles. They did share the same space once. That was two years ago when Armstrong appeared at the Ann Arbor Festival of racing. That was the day Anders decided to take up bicycle racing and joined the Ann Arbor Velo Club. When Armstrong learned of Anders's illness through teammate Andreu, Armstrong offered a morale-boosting e-mail. But on this day, as Armstrong prepares for his final ride in the 1999 Tour de France, Anders prepares for his own, very different kind of day.

Four months have passed since March 17. On July 1, as Armstrong made final preparations for the Tour, Anders had a bone-marrow transplant, getting a donation from his 11-year-old sister Ingrid. Five days later, as Armstrong took a breather from the pressure of the *maillot jaune* by passing it on to Jaan Kirsipuu, Anders celebrated his 14th birthday in the hospital's isolation ward. And, as Armstrong fended off his final Tour challenges in the Pyrénées, Anders battled an infected gall bladder. But today is Armstrong's moment of triumph, a moment borne from his insatiable desire to prove to people around the world who have been touched by cancer—people like Anders, Jim and Pam—that there is no such thing as an irrevocable death sentence.

In the piercing glare of Anders's deep blue eyes, as he studies and sizes up a new acquaintance, one can sense that he understands that truth. He admits that since the day his father told him that life-altering news he has been waiting for a watershed of sorts. "I just figured that sooner or later it would really hit me," Anders says, his words chosen carefully after serious contemplation that belies a 14-year-old. "That I would feel disbelief, or something like that. But that just hasn't happened."

Instead, Anders has endured with an inspiring level of patience and strength. Jim talks one minute about the incredible pain tolerances of world-class athletes like Armstrong, and the next minute about Anders not whining, not screaming—not even flinching—as doctors frantically dug into his arm with needles in a desperate attempt to get a blood sample, during one of the more frightening moments of his battle. Pam, her voice quivering and tears flowing, can't hide the waterfall of emotion welled up inside, as she calls her son's demeanor stoic. Jim points out that the question he has never heard from Anders is: Why?

Anders says in private that he views the world differently than he did five months ago. The hours upon hours spent in his hospital bed provide plenty of time for thought. But on the three or four occasions that he says he has felt sorry for himself, he decided to look ahead and move on. He sees the younger kids in the hospital ward display an unwavering zest for life. And he knows there's always someone out there who has it worse than he does. He doesn't feel 14 anymore. "I've grown up a lot," Anders says.

The day's shining moment arrives at 5 p.m. Eastern Daylight Time. Anders has avoided the temptation to send his laptop to a cycling Web site, to learn what went on in the final stage in Paris. He has saved it for the television broadcast. Jim couldn't wait; he checked the Internet hours ago. Anders sits up in his bed as the show begins, with Pam sitting on the bed in front of him, and Jim in a chair slightly off to the side. Six eyes are glued to the screen, until Armstrong delivers a candid interview about his fight with cancer. Then, Anders begins to rock front to back and spends more time watching his father's reaction than reacting on his own. Armstrong admits everyone is frightened when the cancer verdict is delivered. Armstrong admits he thought he was going to die. The intensity of Anders's rocking increases. Could he be facing that moment he has been waiting for? Or, could he just be thinking about Pam, which he admits he does from time to time? "It's really hard when I know it's hard on my Mom," he says.

Three silent minds watch the show, while a fourth eavesdrops on them, wondering just why he was invited into this incredibly private world. Then he remembers: "If there is any way to help someone diagnose leukemia sooner, maybe for one dentist to make a connection between mouth sores and the disease, that would be wonderful," Jim says. "Time means everything."

After minutes of silent thought, Anders takes the tube from his side and suctions mucus from his mouth, as he must do about every five minutes. He has thought long and hard about any message he wants to deliver, given this unique forum. "The most important thing is knowing that other people care," Anders says, his eyes intensifying in a search for acknowledgment. "That really means a lot. That helps more than anything."

Armstrong cares, Anders—and thanks to him, thousands of others do, too. Pleasant dreams, Anders. See you on the road. Soon.

Anders's left the hospital before the end of July. His prognosis was good.

Festina fallout
Skepticism reigns after '98

EW OF THOSE WHO SAW LANCE Armstrong raise his hat to reveal the two large horseshoe-shaped scars on his bald pate at the Korbel Night of Champions in December 1996 could have ever imagined that the 27-year-old Texan would be here in Paris, atop the podium of the Tour de France. But it has happened. It is by any definition one of the—if not *the*—greatest comeback stories in sport. The only problem is that this comeback appears right on the heels of one of the biggest drug scandals in sport...and both took place at the Tour.

In the run-up to 1999, race director Jean-Marie Leblanc proclaimed this year's event a Tour of Redemption, a chance for cycling to show that the sport and the Tour had transcended last year's troubles. As for Armstrong, from the outset he didn't care to discuss the issue of doping. He was here to race and didn't care about those "who are here for a drug story." But it was clear that anyone who did well at this Tour would be put under a microscope. And from day one, that was Armstrong.

At Le Puy du Fou, writers, radio reporters and TV crews returned to the Tour with memories of Willy Voet, Festina and the Tour of '98 still etched in their minds. There remained an air of skepticism and, frankly, who could blame them?

Jean-Michel Rouet, for the past 10 years a cycling editor at *L'Équipe,* said there were years' worth of reasons, years' worth of lies, years' worth of gushing prose about the heroics of now-questionable past champions....

"The big fallout from last year," Rouet said, "is that everything has now changed. We now know that *everyone* in the sport can f—k us. You have to be very clever and ask questions all the time and do it now more than ever."

"Last year," another writer observed, "we had the French police hand us our scandals on a silver platter—news conferences every night, expulsions—it was almost too easy. This year, people are here looking for a story...and maybe willing to *make* a story."

The effect that the scandalous 1998 Tour de France had on the coverage of the 1999 Tour de France quickly became apparent. On the morning of the prologue word spread that two or three riders had exceeded the Union Cycliste Internationale's maximum allowable hematocrit level of 50 percent. At least one Internet report offered that three riders had been ejected from the race. Well, the UCI had, indeed, tested each of the Tour's 180 riders on the morning of the prologue, and later that day it issued a report saying all had passed. However, queries revealed that some riders had come to the Tour with medical certificates confirming their naturally high hematocrit levels.

"Bullshit," uttered one reporter upon learning of the riders' dispensation. But the one cyclist whose name was known, the U.S. Postal Service's Jonathan Vaughters, openly discussed the three-month process required before receiving his medical certificate. The story faded. The drug issue lapsed...for two days.

Then *L'Équipe* revealed that the UCI's newly introduced test for corticoids had uncovered one positive among the four riders tested at the end of the Tour's first stage. As one of the four, Armstrong found himself fielding questions. On the morning of stage 4, Armstrong, no longer in the yellow jersey, was in a heated discussion with two writers—one Spanish, one French—as he rode toward the start.

"Yes, it is your job to print the truth, but it isn't your job to print speculation; and that's what this is … just speculation," Armstrong argued.

The UCI later issued a statement noting that one rider *had* exceeded the level, but also had medical certification. The announcement was again greeted with skepticism, largely because of a UCI policy designed to "protect riders' confidentiality," which has created a situation in which medical certificates are not produced or discussed until there is an alleged positive drug test. The background buzz of drug speculation continued.

But it wasn't until Sestriere that the tone of the Tour truly changed. Armstrong grabbed control of the race, attacking in the final climb of a mountainous 213.5km stage that crossed the Galibier and finished in the Italian ski village.

Un Tour a deux vitesses—a Tour of two speeds—became a recurrent theme in the pages of many newspapers. It posed a simple question of fairness, but did so based on the assumption that *anyone* who raced well at the Tour simply had to be involved in doping—especially one who, just two years earlier, was dealing with the aftereffects of chemotherapy.

In St. Gaudens, Armstrong held a press conference—a rest day tradition for the yellow jersey—in which the U.S. Postal rider fielded questions, many of which again focused on the issue of drugs. One reporter asked when Armstrong had last taken medication. His answer, a very specific "December 13, 1996...chemotherapy."

That same day, Belgian rider Ludo Dierckxsens was pulled from the race by his team, after it was revealed that the Lampre-Daikin rider had used Synactin, a banned injectable corticoid. Dierckxsens had been tested five days earlier, following his stage 11 win into St. Etienne. It was during that test that the 34-year-old Belgian national champion informed UCI medical authorities that he had used the drug to correct a knee problem. But the drug is banned, with or without a doctor's prescription. And while Dierckxsens's doping controls came back negative, the acknowledgment of the drug's use itself required that the rider be considered positive from that point on.

On that rest day, too, UCI medical officials appeared with an experimental test for the detection of perfluorocarbures—PFCs—chemicals designed to aid emergency patients who may not have immediate access to transfusable blood. PFCs act to transport oxygen to the muscles, and do so without raising hematocrit level. Dangerous, but effective. Are some riders willing to risk it? "Maybe, but I can't believe they would," said UCI medical chief Dr. Leon Schattenberg. "It's too dangerous."

While PFCs break down quickly, there are traceable residuals left in the body for weeks. The UCI and French Cycling Federation coordinated on the introduction of new urine and breathalyzer tests, the results of which may not be available until weeks after the Tour, Schattenberg told *VeloNews*.

On July 19, the Web site of the French newspaper *Le Monde* ran an article citing laboratory sources as saying that samples from several riders—including those from Armstrong—had shown traces of corticoids. The levels were below those required to show positive on the new test, but the suggestion was there. Armstrong again was under fire.

As riders gathered in Lannemezan the next morning, Armstrong stayed in his team van, speaking with five-time Tour winner Eddy Merckx and waiting until the last minute to sign in and ride the Tour's final mountain stage. That day, the UCI issued a statement, a communiqué noting that Armstrong's sample had indeed shown minute

Attacking the silence

The man who should know says Christophe Bassons was and is a clean rider. In his memoirs, Festina's infamous soigneur Willy Voet wrote that the young rider steadfastly refused to participate in the team's organized doping program. He held his ground as others went along, but he also held his tongue....

Things have changed, at least for Christophe Bassons. This year, as a member of La Française des Jeux, the 25-year-old winner of a stage at the '99 Dauphiné Libéré vocally campaigned against doping in cycling, hoping to urge his fellow riders to join him in what he believed may be an increasingly loud call to clean up the sport he loves.

Bassons even found support from some in the peloton earlier in the year. But as the season progressed toward the Tour de France *Monsieur Propre*—as his former Festina teammates called him—became more vocal and found himself increasingly isolated.

Writing a daily Tour diary for the newspaper *Aujourd'hui,* Bassons made it clear that despite a year of police actions, court investigations and public pronouncements by cycling officials, he believed the sport was far from clean and that drug use still often determines the outcome of a race. Far from accepting that this was the "Tour of Redemption"—as Leblanc labeled this year's race—Bassons, though never portraying himself as the *only* clean rider in the peloton, did publicly question whether anyone could win a Tour stage in this environment without using drugs themselves.

That claim led to an exchange between Bassons and Armstrong on the stage to Sestriere. Bassons wrote in his column that the Postal Service rider—who at that point had already won two stages of the Tour—approached him and suggested that if he were unhappy with the direction of the sport, he should leave. Armstrong characterized the conversation differently.

"I went to him...as he puts down all the racers when he declares he's the only clean rider in the peloton. That's completely false," Armstrong recalled. "Then he says that no one can win a stage without EPO. That's bullshit. So I said to him, 'Christophe, I sup-port what you're saying...but there are right ways and wrong ways of going about it. You're doing it the wrong way. It's bad for you, bad for your team, and bad for your sponsor. You're just going to isolate yourself. The best thing you can do is be quiet.' And he replied, 'I don't have to be a cyclist. I can be a doctor...a lawyer...whatever.' So I said, 'Go and do it then.' That's all I said. I didn't tell him to go home....

"You don't bite the hand that feeds you. If he continues like that, he's gonna be a part of the annihilation of the sport...not its resurrection. Nobody supports him...."

No one *did* support him...or so it appeared to Bassons. While Bassons's column on Armstrong generated a quick and largely positive response from the media, Bassons found himself further isolated from other riders, even members of his own team. On the morning of the Stage 12 departure from Saint Galmier, the *Aujourd'hui* column was noticeably absent that day and soon after the race began, it was announced that Bassons had pulled out of the Tour the night before and was on his way home.

"I cracked. I have spent 13 very difficult days on the Tour. I have waited for someone to break the silence but it hasn't happened," Bassons later said. "The evening of my abandonment, my employer [Marc Madiot] asked me not to speak anymore about doping to the journalists on the Tour...that would have been worse."

Bassons went home and contemplated his future. Unconfirmed reports suggested that Madiot would like to dump Bassons from the squad, but the team's sponsor is adamant about keeping him on board. Either way, Bassons is likely to ignore Armstrong's advice that "The best thing you can do is be quiet."

"There are two problems in cycling: the first is doping, the other is the silence," Bassons reflected. "Unless you deal with the second, you can not succeed with the first."

Right or wrong, at least one voice out there will be attacking the silence.

levels of corticoids, the result of Armstrong's use of the topical ointment Cemalyt in the treatment of a saddle sore.

Again dogged by drug reports, Armstrong held a news conference soon after the peloton's arrival in Pau. One reporter offered an easy question, asking what sort of message Armstrong might have for others with cancer.

"You know, sometimes they say that stress causes cancer," the Tour leader replied. "So my first message is, 'Don't come to the Tour de France and wear the yellow jersey.'"

Another journalist, this one from *Le Monde,* reminded the yellow-jersey holder that he had denied using any medication since 1996. "You swore that you were not using medications. How do you reconcile that?" he asked.

"So Mister *Le Monde,* are you calling me a liar or are you calling me a doper?" Armstrong shot back. "First off, I didn't *swear* to anything. I was asked if I was given an exception by the UCI to take banned substances. Of course not. I was asked if I have a prescription to take anything. This is where perhaps the confusion comes in. When I think of taking something, I think of pills, inhalers, injection…. Quite honestly—it might be a mistake—I didn't consider skin cream to be *taking something,* but I congratulate you on stirring up a lot of controversy."

Armstrong later noted that "the first thing some of these people want—some of the journalists, some of the people who are grabbing for straws—is for me to crack on the bike. And I wasn't going to crack."

He didn't crack. Armstrong rode on to Paris, and the issue—for the time being—took a back seat.

That news conference, in some ways, represented something of a turning point. The issue had been trivialized: Suggestions of doping, of use of performance-enhancing substances, had been reduced to questions of skin cream and a saddle sore.

Schattenberg said he was "flabbergasted" by the Armstrong case. "It's hysterical right now," he told *VeloNews.* "We have journalists who speak of the ethics of sport and of fair play…and not many of them are willing to meet that standard themselves. Where are their ethics?"

It may indeed have been an issue of an over-eager press, but French Cycling Federation president Daniel Baal didn't think that was the entire problem. Baal, also a UCI vice president, suggested that the problem lay squarely on the shoulders of the sport's governing body and its policy of shielding information—riders' hematocrit levels, the names of riders given exemptions, the identities of those holding medical certificates.

"Complete openness, total transparency will do the most to dispel the current climate," Baal said the following day. "It would have avoided the Armstrong problem."

So the issue of doping remains and will dog anyone who achieves success in this sport—until convincing proof is shown that drugs don't still play a role in cycling. Had it not been Armstrong in the spotlight, who else? Alex Zülle? The man who came in second in this year's Tour de France, was at the center of the Festina scandal of 1998. Fernando Escartin? The third-placed rider's Kelme team pulled out of last year's Tour in protest of police tactics being used to uncover the use of drugs. Richard Virenque?

Un Tour a deux vitesses? A fair question that will probably not be answered until everything is placed and kept out in the open. Until then, true champions won't get their due, largely because of the lingering fear that too many cheats and pretenders in the past had not earned *their* due honestly.

Armstrong's winning bikes and components

I t wasn't all that long ago when the Americans were a rarity at the Tour de France. Oh to be certain, American riders were, too, once rare—indeed, not seen at the Tour until the early 1980s, first winning the Tour in 1986—but American bikes didn't make their presence known until 1997. There were, of course, American bicycles used in the Tour before that—the custom-made Huffys of the 7-Eleven team, the disguised Litespeeds of the Motorola and Festina teams, a few Serottas here and there....

But 1997 marked the year when two full-blown U.S. production bicycles made their simultaneous appearances at the world's greatest bike race. That year, the Italian Saeco squad signed on Connecticut-based Cannondale as its bike supplier and cosponsor, and the American U.S. Postal Service cycling team riders showed up astride their all-carbon OCLVs, made by Trek of Waterloo, Wisconsin.

In the first two years, the Saeco squad proved a wise and successful investment for Cannondale. Super sprinter Mario "the Lion King" Cipollini sprinted and won on a series of custom, large-tubed aluminum rigs. The marketing types at Cannondale seized on the opportunity, supplying SuperMario with bikes painted to match the leader's and points jerseys he'd accumulated at that year's Giro d'Italia and Tour de France. Each bike was a rush-ordered, custom-spec-ed special Cannondale built to Cipollini's exact specifications. The Italian star repaid the sponsorship and the bikes many times over, most notably after a 1997 stage win when the tall, handsome sprinter looked into a television camera, smiled and said, "Cannondale, is best bike, eh?" The impact in Europe was almost immediate. Demand for Cannondales grew to such a degree that by year's end, every major European manufacturer had embraced the large-diameter aluminum tube as a frame material of choice.

For Trek and the Postal team, the start wasn't quite as flashy, but the ultimate result in racing terms—and possibly commercial terms—was greater. Early on, the team had only modest successes, making the bikes less noticeable. But technologically, the OCLV probably represented a more significant advance than did its welded aluminum counterpart. And by 1999, the OCLV Trek accomplished something that no other American bike at the Tour had achieved: It was a Trek that the yellow jersey wearer rode down the Avenue des Champs-Elysées. It was a stock production bicycle—a 58cm version of the Trek 5500—that Lance Armstrong rode during each of the road stages of the 1999 Tour de France.

Not only was Trek the first American bike to win the Tour, it was also the first stock production bike in recent memory to do so. Traditionally, riders on modern pro teams have been supplied with custom bikes, built to their exact specifications. Trek, however, employs a technology that limits the company's ability to produce unusually sized models, so fitting the bike revolves around adjustments in stem and seatpost, noted Postal mechanic Geoff Brown.

Trek guards its OCLV—Optimum Compaction Low Void—carbon technology jealously, producing the frames in a separate and locked facility that requires special clearance to enter. The frame material consists of a combination of carbon fiber and a temperature-sensitive epoxy. The material is layered in opposing directions, with heavier reinforcements placed in high-stress areas.

Armstrong's frame weighed in at 2.4 kilograms, the bike itself around 17 pounds, light enough so as not to require radical changes as the Tour moved into the mountains. Beyond a set of aluminum cogs used for the mountain stages, the bike stayed pretty much the same throughout the Tour: a stock 58cm Trek OCLV, 12cm Cinelli stem, 175mm Shimano Dura-Ace cranks. It is the bike he rode to an impressive stage win at Sestriere. It is also a bike that pretty much anyone with $3600 in their pocket can walk into a shop and ride home.

While Trek can claim a big victory on the road stages, Armstrong did opt for another American company's bike during the Tour's three time trials.

For riders of a technical bent—and there always have been plenty of those—the time trial affords the opportunity to shave a few seconds here or there by choosing the correct gears, the proper frame, and finding just the right position on the bike. But as has been the case in recent years, the Tour prologue no longer affords bike companies or designers the opportunity to try out radical new ideas or make a last-minute introduction of some outlandish time-trial design. The materials commission of the Union Cycliste Internationale has made sure of that. The fare will be even more conservative in years to come as strict design criteria would come into effect in January 2000.

Clearly, the motor makes the difference, especially in the so-called race of truth, but at Le Puy du Fou, Metz and Futuroscope, the Armstrong engine relied on a custom-built titanium Blade time-trial bike, actually built in Tennessee by Litespeed. The custom frame alone would retail for around $6000, according to Litespeed.

Equipped with the same 175mm cranks he used on the road—"He doesn't like to mess with fit once he has it right," noted Brown—Armstrong had his time-trial bike set up with a gear combination of 54-46, an 11-21 freewheel at Futuroscope, and 55-46 and 11-23 at the Metz and prologue time trials.

The mislabeling didn't seem to bother Armstrong's main bike sponsor, which doesn't even sell a time-trial-specific bike. Said Trek's marketing director Dick Moran, "He's wearing yellow. I won't complain about anything. He can ride anything he wants. I'm just happy he likes the road bike as much as he does."

Though framebuilders often get most of the credit, the components on a bike are big, big business as well. The competition between component companies has historically been intense...except at the Tour. The French race has, for some strange reason, been almost the exclusive stomping ground of Italy's Campagnolo. Marco Pantani, Jan Ullrich, Bjarne Riis, Miguel Induráin and Greg LeMond all used Campagnolo components in their race toward the podium in Paris. Indeed, the last time any company other than Campagnolo took the yellow jersey, was when LeMond powered his way to an eight-second victory in the 1989 Tour. He was then riding on Mavic components.

But one company had never won a Tour de France. Though Shimano had been on the bikes of professional racers for 25 years and made appearances at every Tour since the Dura-Ace group was first introduced, none of its riders managed to take yellow in Paris. There were world championships, there were classics and World Cup wins, there were wins at the Giro d'Italia, but never at the Tour de France. It was enough to make the most superstitious a bit worried....

But in 1999, the "curse" was lifted. Armstrong and the Postals didn't even seem to notice that they weren't supposed to be winning this race as they pressed toward Paris. Nothing—not even a silly old coincidence—would stop 'em.

While the Postal team universally approved of their Trek bikes, the team had a few problems with the Trek-made Rolf Vector Pro wheels they brought to the Tour. The Rolfs, initially designed by engineer Rolf Dietrich, employed a unique paired spoking pattern that offered greater strength and rigidity than did standard-laced wheels. But a pair of crashes during the decisive stage to St. Nazaire uncovered a potentially serious problem in the way some of the wheels had been manufactured.

Tyler Hamilton had what Postal team officials described as a "particularly violent" crash early in the stage. Not only had Hamilton's fork broken, but his tubular Rolf wheel had broken in such a way as to expose a dangerous and jagged edge, which could have caused serious injury to any rider who hit it.

Postal's head mechanic Julien DeVries—previously Eddy Merckx's and LeMond's personal wrench—decided that the risk was too great and the team stopped using the tubular version of the Rolf. Christian Vande Velde, who, like the Casino team of Jaan Kirsipuu, rode the clincher version of the wheel continued to do so for the duration of the Tour. The remaining members of the squad switched to the wheels offered by another team sponsor, Mavic.

By the Tour's first rest day in the alpine village of Le Grand Bornand, Moran and Dietrich joined up with the team and arranged for the delivery of new wheels. Dietrich pointed to a production flaw in the rims' welded seam, which contributed to the problem. "We have it solved," he said.

But many of the Postals, including Armstrong, had been using Mavic's new Ksyrium road wheels, based on a radical new design.

Weighing in at about 700 grams for a front tubular and 900 for a rear, the wheel was designed to replace Mavic's popular Helium road wheel. The all-black Ksyrium SSC features 18 bladed aluminum spokes in the front and 20 in the rear. The "Zicral" alloy spokes, the company claimed, offered about 10 percent more strength than a steel spoke of equal weight.

Perhaps the wheel's most unique feature was the method used to "drill" the rim. Rather than employing a mechanical drill to pierce both horizontal walls of the rim, Mavic used a super-heated bit to create a melted "chimney" on only the inner wall. That chimney was then threaded to accept an over-sized splined nipple.

The outer surface—the one with which the tire or tube comes in contact—would, therefore, remain entirely smooth, allowing clincher users to even avoid using rim tape. The technology could also represent a necessary step in the eventual development of a tubeless road tire.

The absence of rim tape and metal eyelets used to reinforce drilled holes gave the wheel better acceleration because of the lower weight at the outer portion of the wheel. Interestingly, the rear wheel employed a somewhat counter-intuitive spoking pattern in that the drive-side was laced radially with a cross-two on the non-drive side.

The wheel immediately attracted attention. Several teams requested additional supplies and Armstrong relied almost exclusively on the wheel throughout the Tour. Indeed, Mavic became keenly aware of the potential boost its wheel had gotten and the evening before the final stage to Paris, Mavic's Yves Hezard presented DeVries with a special yellow-anodized pair of Ksyriums for Armstrong's bike.

And at the start of the next day's stage, Armstrong's bike was ready: its Trek OCLV frame in its standard red-white-and-blue glory, its Dura-Ace group ready to shed its 25 years of bad luck at the Tour, and a bright, bright yellow pair of Ksyrium wheels. The bike was ready. The wheels were ready...but on the road to Paris, Armstrong suffered the *only* flat tire he had encountered in the entire Tour...no problem, but there was only a bright red Helium atop the support car for the switch. The best laid plans....

A tale of two people

Lance Armstrong's victory in the 1999 Tour de France has special meaning for me. It's a sense of accomplishment for two people who I have met. One has had a great impact on my life, while the other offers inspiration for the future. One has conquered the dreaded disease of cancer, the other fought a valiant battle but lost.

Lance's achievements have been widely chronicled over the past month. The other person lived in relative obscurity.

These two people could not be more different. Lance is a product of the 1970s and '80s. Raised by his mother in Austin, Texas, he came to national prominence as a triathlete and has proven himself as one of the world's premier bike racers. Triathlons, road races, and now mountain bike races—along the way, he beats cancer. Is there anything this man can't do? I congratulate Lance on being superhuman and a true role model.

The other person is a product of the 1940s, growing up in Japan during World War II. He, too, was a driven man; always challenging what could not be achieved. Always questioning the status quo (wanting to crash his car to see if the airbag really worked). So patriotic, he was about to lie about his age so that he could join the U.S. Navy (lucky for us, his father caught on before he enlisted). He, too, was an aspiring athlete, as he was one step away from a professional baseball contract (once again, his father intervened, convincing him to work in the family business, instead)—his idol was Ted Williams. Instead of baseball, he earned a college degree in mechanical engineering and then joined the workforce as Japan was emerging from the ruins of a war.

You may have heard of this man's accomplishments. He was a true fan of bicycle racing. He founded the Shimano Cycle racing team—one of Japan's premier amateur road racing teams—as a tool to develop the world's best bicycle components. This man was running "Shimano Skunk Development," before it even existed! He was the driving force behind the development of the original Dura-Ace, Shimano's first road racing components; the original Deore XT, the world's first mountain-bike components; the Shimano Index System; Hyperglide; Shimano Pedaling Dynamics; and Shimano Total Integration shifters. This man is my late uncle, Keizo Shimano.

Keizo was doing cartwheels in his office when Freddy Maertens won the first world championships by a Dura-Ace-equipped rider. He flew to Italy when Andy Hampsten won the Giro. I know he is smiling as Lance rides into Paris. Lance is the first Shimano-equipped rider to win the Tour de France. After 25 years, Keizo's goal has been achieved. Unfortunately, Keizo could not witness this great feat, as the disease that Lance defeated was too great for Keizo to overcome.

Congratulations, Lance, on your victory, and thank you for the inspiration.

—*Kozo Shimano*

EDITOR'S NOTE: KOZO SHIMANO IS THE VICE PRESIDENT OF SHIMANO'S BICYCLE COMPONENT DIVISION, STILL THE LARGEST PART OF A COMPANY STARTED IN 1921.